Modern Hebrew Literature Made into Films

Lev Hakak

University Press of America,® Inc.
Lanham · New York · Oxford

Copyright © 2001 by
University Press of America,® Inc.
4720 Boston Way
Lanham, Maryland 20706

12 Hid's Copse Rd.
Cumnor Hill, Oxford OX2 9JJ

Library of Congress Cataloging-in-Publication Data

Hakak, Lev.
Modern Hebrew literature made into films / Lev Hakak.
p.   cm
Includes bibliographical references.
1. Motion pictures and literature—Israel.
2. Israeli fiction—Film and video adaptations. I. Title.
PN1995.3 .H26 2001   791.43'6—dc21   2001027958 CIP

ISBN 0-7618-1984-3 (cloth : alk. paper)

CONTENTS

ACKNOWLEDGMENTS

I wish to thank the University of California, Los Angeles, for supporting the preparation of the manuscript. I thank Mrs. Susan Chapman for her style editing. I thank Mr. David G. Hirsch, Jewish and Middle East Bibliographer and Dr. Eliezer Chammou, Middle East Librarian, both at Charles E. Young Research Library, University of California, Los Angeles. I thank Mrs. Zvia Margalit of the Tel-Aviv Cinematheque and Genazim Institute of the Hebrew Writers Association in Israel for their assistance.

Chapter 1

A Brief History of Modern
Hebrew Literature

Hebrew Literature and Jewish literature are not synonymous. Jews produced Jewish literature in various languages. The Hebrew language was spoken from 1200 BC to 200 AD but, from about 200 until the late 19th century, it did not serve as a general form of oral communication. Nevertheless, from biblical times onward, it never stopped being a literary medium, mostly for religious writing. But even in the Bible one finds narrative writing and what can be considered secular poetry and prose — although it was subsumed into the holy canon and given a religious construction — notably Song of Solomon, perhaps Proverbs. In the Middle Ages, the renaissance of Hebrew spread from Palestine westward in the years 800-1300. Most Hebrew writing was religious and legal, but one finds examples of secular narrative and poetry. The years 900-1200 were *The Golden Age* in Spain; during this time, poets of high literary accomplishment appeared. They wrote secular and religious Hebrew poetry and created in other Hebrew fields — including philosophy, grammar, Biblical commentary and philology.

In its pre-Israeli period (500-1880), Hebrew literature wandered from one territory to another, and it existed in a literary symbiosis with other Jewish literatures and with non-Jewish literature (Even-Zohar, 1973, pp. 427-431). The center of Hebrew cultural activity was first in Israel, then in Spain It moved to Italy and Holland, then to Germany, to Austria (Galicia), then to Poland, Lithuania and Ukraine, and then on to Israel (Halkin, 1958, pp 2-3).

From the beginning of Modern Hebrew literature until the 1930s, the authors who wrote in Hebrew did so by their own choice, for idealistic reasons. They usually knew Yiddish and a European language, but decided to write in Hebrew despite the fact that it was not their mother tongue; it was not spoken in their place. Sometimes there was opposition to using Hebrew for secular literature. It had a limited circle of readers, and it could not bring them recognition among non-Jewish readers. The modern Hebrew writer had a plethora of written Hebrew works to draw from — the Bible, Talmud, Midrash, prayer books, medieval prose and poetry, Hassidic prose and more — sometimes the high literary achievements in these works (especially the Bible) discouraged the modern Hebrew writer.

There are various opinions as to when Modern Hebrew literature began and what is the best periodization for it. Secularism identifies the modern period as its basic characteristic. Some think that it began at the end of the 17th century when the authority of the Jewish community was interrupted (see Halkin, 1970, pp. 29-32). Others think that it began during the later half of the 18th century, with the German Jewish Enlightenment (see Klausner, Vol. 1, pp. 1-11; Kurzweil, pp. 1-146; Shapira, pp. 47-580). Yet, according to another view, (Lachover, Vol. 1, p.4, pp. 14-44) Modern Hebrew literature began with Moses Hayyim Luzzatto (1707-1746), who was the spiritual successor of the Italian-Hebrew humanists of the 16th and 17th centuries. Luzzatto was also influenced by the secular ideas of modern non-Jewish literature, and his plays represent "new spirit."

Often the periodization of Modern Hebrew literature (for example Silberschlag, 1972) is divided into the periods of Modern Hebrew literature in European (1781-1921), Palestinian (1905-1948) and Israel periods.

The European period includes the beginning of the Enlightenment (*haskala*, hereinafter Enlightenment) literature in Germany, Galicia and then Russia (1781-1881); and then Modern Hebrew literature in Russia and Poland (1881-1920).

The first center of Modern Hebrew literature was in **Germany** (1781-1830) where intellectual Jews were exposed to European Enlightenment, to Italian and Dutch Hebrew cultures. Enlightened Jews professed that the beliefs and practices of the Jews must be consistent with reason.

The Enlightenment movement advocated the westernization of Jewish life, enlightenment of the Jewish people, removing the barriers between the Jews and other nations and attaining civil rights for the Jews. Jewish social, economic and religious backwardness were the deterrent to Jewish emancipation. Enlightenment could provide the Jews with access to gentile society, support their political rights and make them productive. Enlightenment literature strove to promote educational, civil and humanitarian goals. It was didactic literature; its objective was to educate the reader in moral, social and aesthetic senses. The enlightenment literature revitalized Hebrew literature and the esteem of the Hebrew language. The Hebrew language was chosen because it was the language of the educated Jews, and it also had the respect of being the language of the Bible.

The leader of the German Jewish enlightenment was Moses Mendelssohn, who wrote literary and philosophical works. A Hebrew monthly magazine (*ha-Me'assef*), a pioneering periodical in which the leading figures of the enlightenment movement published, was published in Germany in 1783. Naftali Hirz Wessley was the leading Hebrew author of the German period. In his epic, *Poems of Splendor*, he preached enlightenment; he also promoted modern educational methods and general studies. During the German enlightenment there were other authors who published Hebrew epic poems but not notable narrative prose. At that stage, there were also Hebrew authors in other countries.

The German orientation of German Jews led to the dislodgment of Hebrew as the language of the enlightened Jews there, and the center of Hebrew literature moved to Polish **Galicia** (1820-1860), where two periodicals serving Galician enlightened Jews were founded (*Bickered ha-'Item*, 1820-1831; *Kermes Hemmed*, 1833-1856). Galician enlightenment emphasized Jewish studies written in Hebrew and historical research with romanticism. Galician Hebrew authors promoted Hebrew prose-satire. In 1819 and 1838, the satirist Josef Perl published two satires about the Hasidic movement. Hasidism captured the heart of many Galician Jews at that time, and Perl attacked, from the point of view of an enlightened Jew, what seemed to him to be Hasidic superstitions and ignorance. Isaac Erter (1845) satirized various characters, including Hasidim, and enlightened physician, Nachman Krochmal, wrote philosophical works; he also outlined a scheme for Jewish history. There were also Galician poets, such as Meir Letteris and Samuel David Luzzatto, who produced lyrical poetry. Luzzatto also wrote essays and philological work.

The center of enlightenment moved to **Russia** (1840-1881), where major Hebrew writers appeared. Abraham Mapu is the first Modern

Hebrew novelist, and the first Hebrew novel is his romantic idyll *Ahavat Ziyyon (The Love of Zion,* 1853*)*. In his later work, Mapu attacked the social evils of his time. He promoted the enlightened Jew and fought against some orthodox concepts. He published historical novels (1853, 1865), promoting enlightenment ideas, and attempted to depict contemporary Jewish life in a social novel (1857-1864). Adam Haccohen Levensohn was a poet whose poetry had a moral, didactic goal. His son, Mikha Yosef Levensohn, published (in 1851) a volume of lyrical poetry about love, nature, biblical themes and impending death (he had tuberculosis). The poetry, short stories and journalism made Yehuda Leib Gordon the central author of the Russian Jewish enlightenment. He wrote romantic poems on biblical themes (from 1871). He fought injustice in Jewish life caused by Jewish tradition. He questioned rabbinical and biblical views, urged for earthly Jewish life, rejected excessive spiritualism and legalism in Jewish life, and demanded new status for the oppressed Jewish women. The Hebrew novel also evolved with the works of Perez Smolenskin and Reuben Asher Braudes, who published novels promoting the views and ideology of the Jewish enlightenment.

The Modern Period (1881-1917) of the European period is marked by literary refinement. Under European influence, Hebrew critics pleaded for realistic descriptions of Jewish life in order to achieve social changes. Political events and pogroms (in the 1880s) disillusioned many enlightened Jews, and the sarcastic criticism in which the enlightenment treated the old way of Jewish life became more balanced and soft. However, the new Jewish nationalism, too, did not neglect the desire for national Jewish modernization. In Russia, Ahad Ha'am (Asher Ginzberg), the father of the Modern Hebrew essay, and the most influential figure in Hebrew literature at his time, presented a nationalistic ideology in his essays. He wrote secularly spirited articles about major Jewish national issues and published a high standard Hebrew periodical (*Hashilloah)*. He viewed the Jewish people as a unique nation standing above all other nations in its moral genius. The Zionist movement was a revisiting of national ideas. Jewish intellectuals had to educate and prepare the Jewish people for national renewal: Jewish settlement in Palestine will create a spiritual center for the Jewish nation; it will preserve the Jewish people. Mendele Mokher Sefarim's (Shalom Abramovich) Hebrew literary works reflect the new style. With realism and artistic writing, he changed the high biblical enlightenment style (1865) of his early works to a sophisticated but simpler prose style (1909), which became a milestone in Modern

Hebrew literature and a model for his disciples. Mendele treated Jewish East European life hardheartedly and satirically, but also, at times, with understanding. His stories about Jewish ghetto life attracted a relatively wide circle of readers.

In Poland, there developed a neo-romantic center of Hebrew literature, with David Frishman, Y.L. Perez and Mikha Yosef Berdichvski, stressing literary forms, style and aesthetic achievements more than ideas, but with some attacks on the realism of Russian Jewish writers. Frishman wanted to bring European literary inclinations to Hebrew literature and, in his stories, he presented a collision between beauty and Jewish life instead of the repetitively protested against collision between reason and Jewish tradition. In the 1880s and 1890s, Perez ''s short romantic stories about Jewish life in East European little town and his positive, romantic, sentimental, Hasidic tales were popular. Berdichevski questioned traditional Judaism, viewed Judaism as stagnant, and described the rebellion of the individual against tradition.

In the late 19th century, the readers of Hebrew books increased among East European Jews, who were exposed to the notion of speaking Hebrew, to nationalism and to Zionism. The pinnacle of the European period is the literary works of the Russian-born Hayyim Nahman Bialik and Shaul Chernihovski. Bialik's spectacular command of Jewish traditional resources deepened his literary style and enriched his imagery. He used various genres in his work. He is considered the national poet because he wrote nationalistic poems (1892-1917) about major national issues, disapproving of the deterioration of the Jewish people in exile and urging them to go for a new fate. He also wrote lyrical poetry, natural and passionate love poetry and short stories. Various important poets, such as Ya'acov Cahan, Ya'acov Fikhman and Ya'acov Steinberg belonged to Bialik's school. Shaul Chernihovski wrote about nature, beauty and love as well as about Jewish themes. He was committed to the goals of European culture. In his poems, he utilized European poetic genre-ballads, Idylls and sonnets. As to content, he raged against the suppression of life, power, beauty, freedom and passion of Jewish tradition. He related to historical and biblical events in the life of the Jews from his point of view and brilliantly amalgamated them into his own poetic views and expressions. He immigrated to Israel in 1931 and, unlike Bialik, continued to write extensively in Israel, too, and gave beautiful expression to his loyal love for Israel. Zalman Shne'or was also of Bialik's generation. He described massacres of Jews, expressed disillusionment in mankind, and viewed the future of European civilization with pessimism (1915). He also wrote erotic poetry. Uri Nissan Gnessin published meditative stories with interior monologues and psychological insight.

Hebrew literature accompanied the movements of *Enlightenment, Hibbat Zion* ("love of Zion") and *Zionism* and accepted their ideas. After the Enlightenment literature, Modern Hebrew literature was produced, first mainly by Eastern European Jewish authors, many of whom immigrated to Israel, and then by authors who mainly produced in Israel. In the 1880s, several Hebrew writers moved to the land of Israel, among them Eliezer Ben-Yehuda, who revived the Hebrew language, was a lexicographer; and the father of modern Hebrew Palestinian journalism, and Moshe Smilansi, who was the first Hebrew author to publish fiction about the Arabs.

The Palestinian Period (1905-1948) is subdivided into the **Ottoman time** (1905-1917) and the Mandate time (1920-1948). At the early Palestinian period, more and more major writers went to Palestine (few did not stay there); for example, in the years 1907-1914, Uri Nissan Gnessin, David Shimoni, S.Y. Agnon, Y.H. Brener, Rahel, Devora Baron and Ya'acov Steinberg went to Palestine. While Hebrew authors in Europe were influenced by the literature of the country where they were educated, in Israel they were exposed to influences from world literature brought by authors who immigrated to Israel from various countries. The vocabulary of spoken Hebrew in Palestine grew, and its use introduced new elasticity. Brener in his psychological, pessimistic prose in Russia and Palestine often depicted neurotic, intellectual Jewish characters without foreseeable solutions.

Most of the writers in Palestine, before 1939, immigrated to Israel, and their views expressed gloom. Sometimes the desire to present reality in its fullness collided with their identifying with Zionist ideology. The Zionist solution and immigration to Israel do not resolve the problems of the suffering individual (Agnon, Brener). There was also a literary debate between those who wanted "literature for literature," evaluated solely on the basis of its aesthetic achievements, and those who wanted literature to express and guide the public.

More and more Hebrew writers came to Palestine during the **Mandate Period (1917-1918).** There were several reasons for Palestine's (Israel beginning 1948) becoming the center of Hebrew literature: the Russian revolutions of 1905 and 1917 and the 1881 pogroms Russia resulted in Jewish emigration from Russia to America and to western Europe. The anti-Zionist Soviet policy inflicted destruction on the Russian center of Hebrew literature. After World War I and the Russian Revolution, there was a prohibition on Hebrew publications, and Hebrew authors were imprisoned. The status of Jews declined in other Eastern European countries. The rise of Yiddish in Europe and America decreased the number of Hebrew readers. In the late 1930s and during the Holocaust, the Nazis exterminated Hebrew culture from Europe. All this, and the Jewish assimilation, disrupted Hebrew cultural activity in Eastern Europe. For a few years some of the Hebrew writers founded a center in Berlin; others immigrated to New York, but the majority of Hebrew writers immigrated to Palestine, where an "Ere Israel Genre" developed and a Hebrew Writers Association was organized. The population in Israel increased, and it depended more and more on the Hebrew language. After World War I, Hebrew literature in Israel began being central to Hebrew literature and, toward the late 1930s, it became exclusive, with the exception of peripheral literature in America. The younger writers in Israel were pioneers with socialist ideas and a dream of a new society.

The move of the center of Hebrew literature to Israel, where Hebrew was a spoken language, quickly generated several changes, among them — the increase in the participation of the Sephardim and women in Modern Hebrew literature, the acceptance of the Sephardi accentuation and an increase in accurate quality of translation from world literature to Hebrew. Also, authors who began writing in Diaspora in a foreign language and moved to Israel shifted to Hebrew (Sadan, 1962).

In poetry (see Burnshaw) the younger poets wanted to break away from the classical poetic structures.

The most prominent writer of this generation was Shmuel Yosef Agnon, a prolific novelist and short story writer who, in 1966, won the Nobel Prize for Literature. Like Bialik in poetry, he was a man of unquestionable genius. In his modernistic, realistic and surrealistic work, he made a significant contribution to the renewal of Hebrew. He related to the psychological, philosophical, religious and social dilemmas of his time and recaptured the traditional lives of former generations. In his psychological, symbolic, surrealistic and existential stories, Agnon wrote about the Jewish emotional experience in Austria, Germany, Galicia and Palestine. In his pietistic fiction, as well as in his modern love stories, he described the existential tragedies of modern life.

Other leading prose writers of the Mandate period were Hayyim Hazaz, Yehuda Burla, Yiz hak Shami, Asher Barash and Devora Baron. Hazaz began publishing in the 1920s; he wrote realistic stories in a literary style, describing Jewish life in Ukraine, the pioneers' life in Palestine and their milieu and Yemenite Jews in Israel and Yemen. Burla was one of the early modern Sephardi writers. He wrote novels and short stories about the life of the Sephardi Jews in the Near East and in Jerusalem. In his short stories and novellas, Shami used Arabic and Yiddish idioms; he depicted life in Palestine, Jewish life in Syria, Bedouin life and he portrayed Arab characters' temperament and rules of honor without romanticizing them or criticizing them as an outsider. Gershon Shofman is known for his artistic brilliance in his phenomenally concise, psychological, analytical, lyrical sketches and short stories depicting individual, Jewish, Israeli and human life in general. Baron described the suffering of Jews in the *shtetl*; she was one of the first women who wrote Hebrew prose.

The leading poets of the Palestinian period were Avraham Shlonski, Nathan Alterman, Uri Z vi Greenberg and Leah Goldberg. Shlonski challenged the collective-nationalistic, rational poetry of Bialik's school; he supported modernism, and advocated individualistic poetry with the use of spoken Hebrew. Shlonski expressed with rich images and melodious language the ennui, horror, alienation and grief of the suffering Jew; the Jewish pioneer with his dreams and hardships in Palestine; the good qualities of agricultural life there and the refuge one finds in love. Alterman was a leading "imagist" poet, with surprising expressionist metaphors, using poetic symmetrical repetition and schemes of stanzas, lines and rhymes. He wrote love poems of romantic agony, ballads about love and death and portrayed repetitively a figure of the dead-alive lover who haunts his living woman, protects her but also waits to be unified again with her. Alterman published poetry with striking images and systematic symmetry of rhymes, lines and stanzas. He described the poet as a wandering troubadour without any materialistic possessions or commitments, the city with its ennui, loneliness, hostility and attractions, love that brings people close then makes them distanced and longing. He also wrote light popular satirical poetry. Goldberg wrote symbolic poems with universal themes and simplicity of forms and language, using traditional verse forms. She did not write ideological poems but rather poems about love, nature, death, beauty, family and the age stages of a man's life. Greenberg wrote in a rich, passionate, expressive, mystic style like a stormy prophet, warning the Jews of their fate in order to prevent the repetition of Jewish tragedies. He rejected European civilization for luring the Jews and leading them to their massacre.

The State of Israel Period began with the creation of the State of Israel (1948). After the Palestinian emigrant writers, it was the time for Israeli literature. There were Israeli authors who gained recognition earlier (see the chapter about Yizhar's *Hirbet Hiz'ah*). Based on the territorial criterion that views "Israeli literature" as literature that belongs to a place (land of Israel), to the population in that place, its language and culture, there are those who claim that "Israeli" Hebrew literature began around 1880. As mentioned above, in the 1880s, several Hebrew writers moved to the land of Israel, among them Eliezer Ben-Yehuda and Moshe Smilansi.

The older writers related to the land of Israel as the land of their Zionist dreams, but also nostalgically remembered the Eastern European landscape. Hebrew was not their mother tongue; they were familiar with rabbinic and medieval Hebrew literature. But their Hebrew was learned, and they were influenced by European literature. In Israel, the geographic scope of the landscapes they described in their literary work included both European landscapes and the Israeli landscape. Most of the writers of the State of Israel Period were secular, Palestinian born, or came to the land in their childhood. They brought new themes and new styles to Hebrew literature. And they used less learned but lively and flexible Hebrew, a language that often was their mother tongue, with neologisms and allusions to the Bible, to other sources of ancient Jewish literature and to Modern Hebrew literature. They also drew upon spoken Hebrew. They related realistically to the landscape of Palestine into which they were born. For them, it was not an idealized, distant land of Zionist fulfillment. They had more education in Modern Hebrew literature and in the Bible than in rabbinical literature, and were closer to West European, English and American literature than to Eastern European literature. The declaration of Hebrew as the official language of the State of Israel was a driving force for Hebrew literature. Poetry and prose prospered, and then drama followed suit.

The writers who began writing in the 1940s often wrote about what came after the Holocaust, such as Holocaust survivors, the years of the struggle for the establishment of the State of Israel, the War of Independence, the founding of the State of Israel and the life in it. S. Yizhar,

Yitzhak Ben-Ner, Yoram Kaniuk, A.B. Yehoshua and Amos Oz, whose literary works are discussed in this book, are all Israeli-born. Hebrew was their mother tongue; it was the language they spoke daily. Yiddish did not have any significant impact on their style, if any.

The Palestinian writers' generation supported the Zionist-Socialist ideology. These writers produced literature that promoted this ideology and stressed the collective and its needs rather than the introspective individual. But, in the literary works of the State of Israel period, the Zionist-Socialist ideology of the previous generation was questioned. Some young authors of this period served in the Palmah (the crack army unit of the War of Independence). The Palmah soldiers were only three percent of the Israeli force in the War of Independence, but their place in the national memory is far greater. Some claim (see Z ahor) that this was so because it was the wish of the political system, but others claim that it is because the Palmah had an impressive number of fighters who had literary talent, among them Nathan Shaham, Yehuda Amihai, Hayyim Guri, Matti Meged, Hillel, Hayyim Hefer and Dan Ben-Amoz. The young authors, in the early phase of their works, supported the Socialist-Zionist ideology and emphasized the significance of the collective more than those of the individual. Israeli-born authors wrote realistic prose about the Israeli War of Independence, the kibbutz and the underground movements. S. Yizhar, Moshe Shamir, Aharon Meged, Nathan Shaham and Hanokh Bartov are some of the well-known authors of that period. Shamir published realistic novels, historical novels and short stories. He described the warriors of the 1948 War of Independence. Meged is a prolific author of novels, short stories, plays and essays whose themes reflect the constant changes in Israel. Nathan Shaham, a dramatist and a prose writer, wrote about individuals who face events and powers beyond their control, the extent of duty and the importance of the emotional experience. The common Bartov published novels, short stories and plays about Israeli identity in Israel, a country without a clear identity.

The younger writers faced a crisis of ideology, which is reflected in the literary works discussed in this book. In the 1950s, they expressed their feelings that the heaven-on-earth dream was not fulfilled by Israel's harsh existence. Wars, economic and social problems, materialism and egoism were unexpectedly unresolved by the creation of the State of Israel. Israeli literature of the late 1950s gave individualistic expression to the alienation of modern secular man; it portrayed lonely individuals who became disillusioned with ideology and utopian hopes.

In the early Israeli period, leading poets, such as Hayyim Guri and Amir Gilboa', gave poetic expression to Zionist ideology, the Holocaust and the alienation of modern man. Yehuda Amichai is the leading poet of the later phase of poetry in Israel; he employs spoken Hebrew; irony; humor; original, precise metaphoric language; poetic schemes; and free verse. Many of his poems are about love with its tenderness, pain and joy. In Israel, poetry is relatively well read and there are distinguished poets such as Dan Pagis and David Avidan (both dead), Nathan Zach and Dalia Rabikovitch, to mention a few.

Israeli literature is less concerned with ideological, nationalistic issues even when it is about Israelis, and it expresses more and more the problems of the individual. New poets and writers come to the scene every year. The literary productivity in Israel is very high and praiseworthy. Some additional authors of Israeli prose will be mentioned here: Benjamin Tammuz, David Shahar, Nissim Aloni, Aharon Apelfeld, Yehoshua Kenaz, Amalia Kahana-Carmon, Ruth Almog and Yaakov Shabtai.

In his novels and short stories, Benjamin Tammuz wrote about the causes and results of human conduct. In his various styles — including poetic-lyrical and satiric-didactic — he wrote about the establishment of Israel, love, tensions between traditional Judaism and being an Israeli, Jews and Arabs, art and reality. Shahar wrote short stories, novels and an epic novel series. Many of his stories take place in Jerusalem, where the sacred and profane collide. Aloni is best known as a dramatist, his characters are alienated and lonely. The approaching Holocaust, fleeing and living in concealment during the Holocaust and social and spiritual destruction are expressed in the prose of Aharon Appelfeld. In his novels, Kenaz presents various Hebrew styles of immigrants; he describes various aspects of Israeli life such as the Israeli army life in the 1950s, and writes about universal conditions such as the torment waiting for us at the end. In her stories, novels and novellas Kahana-Carmon often focuses on the human state of death-in-life. In her novels and short stories, Ruth Almog explores the cultural, social and historical intricacy of Israeli society and its individuals. Yaakov Shabtai is influential in his stream-of-consciousness style and in his use of vernacular language. He published novels, plays and short stories, and he wrote about Israelis disillusioned about their pioneer-Zionist dreams and about the children of these pioneers.

Modern Hebrew literature is minor literature if the criterion is the (relatively small) number of its readers, but it is major literature if it is judged by its quality. It is influenced and enriched by various literatures. The number of Israeli authors who are highly accomplished is relatively high compared to Israel's small population (about 5 million).

The following additional names of Israeli authors (some are deceased) are mentioned with the recognition that many not less important names of authors were omitted. In prose, Haim Be'er, Ehud Ben-Ezer, Pinhas Sadeh, Yitshak Orpaz, Shulamit Hareven, Yehudit Hendel, David Grossman, Orly Castel-Bloom, Batya Gur, Yehudit Katzir, Savyon Librecht, Ronit Matalon, Meir Shalev, Etgar Keret, Hanoch Levin (a dramatist), Yehoshua Sobol (playwright). In poetry, Zelda, Hayyim Guri, Aharon Shabtai, Yair Hurvitz, Yona Wallakh, Meir Wieseltier. Sepahrdi Jews also produced writers such as Amnon Shamosh, Shimon Ballas, Eli Amir, Sami Michael, Nir Shohet, Aharon Almog, Shlomo Kalu, Lev Hakak, Yitshak Gormezano Goren, Uziel Hazan, Dan Benaya Seri, Dorit Rabbinian, Ronit Matalon and Albert Suissa. And poets such as Aharon Almog, Erez Biton, Shlomo Zamir, Moshe Sartel, Lev Hakak, Zvi Hakak, Shlomo Avayo, Amira Hes, Yoav Hayik, Sheli Elkayam, Yosi Ozair, Z ippi Shahrur, Roni Somek, Sami Bekhor Shitrit.

Gershon Shaked presents Israeli prose in his five volumes history of *Hebrew Narrative Fiction 188-1980* (see Shaked, *Ha-Sipporet*). Silberschlag's work (see Silberschlag) may guide the English reader until 1970. For a quick reference, the English reader may use the *Hebrew Writers: A General Directory*, published in 1993 by the Institute for the Translation of Hebrew Literature(Shaked, Editor, *Hebrew Writers*). This Directory is periodically updated on the website http://www.ithl.org.-il//mainpage.html. The reader will find far more details about the authors and their works than he finds here and, on the above-mentioned site, he can find updated information about the translations of the works of each author. The above-mentioned publications were in front of me while I wrote this chapter.

In this book, the stories "Winter Games" by Yitzhak Ben-Ner, *Hirbet Hiz'ah* by S. Yizhar and *Himmo, King of Jerusalem* by Yoram Kaniuk are about the pre-state period in Israeli history. *Three Days and a Child* by A.B. Yehoshua, *My Michael* by Amos Oz, *The Lover* by A.B. Yehoshua and *Black Box* by Amos Oz all take place in the State of Israel. "Winter Games" is a story of Yemenite man, a member of a Jewish underground movement in Palestine during the Mandatory regime. He sacrificed his life for his people, but died in a decayed Jewish village without proper help. In his lyrical prose of *Hirbet Hiz'ah*, Yizhar explores the spirit of the sensitive individual soldier in the unified group during the War of Independence. In Kaniuk's *Himmo King of Jerusalem*, the deformed, moving character of Himmo illustrates the consequences of the War of Independence. The war and the warriors are not glorified, and there are no winners in war. Where war claims its toll, Eros is unattainable. In *Three Days and a Child* (1968), Yehoshua describes the new Israeli who tried living an idealistic life in a group and also tried individualistic life in pursuit of personal goals, but remained restless, lonely and aimless. The victory in the War of Independence and the establishment of the State of Israel did not put to rest the forlornness, bewilderment, estrangement, turmoil, lack of fulfillment and longing of the individual who could not find answers to his needs in group-oriented solutions. In *My Michael* (1968), Oz draws a picture of the meaningless and distorted lifestyle of the Israeli upper-middle class of the 1950s. A. B. Yehoshua 's *The Lover* presents the story of Zionism and the population in the land of Israel over a period beginning in 1881, focusing on a few months before and after the October 1973 Yom Kippur War. Yehoshua portrays the social disintegration of the Israelis and their distance from the Zionist dream. Oz's *Black Box* begins with the story of the old settlers in Palestine in 1930 and ends in 1976; about a year before the Labor party in Israel was defeated in the elections for the first time. This defeat was a result of the vote of Sephardi and Near Eastern Jews, who felt for a long time like underdogs in Israel. The novel presents hard realities about Israel's doomed future.

Some notes about Hebrew literature will be briefly presented here. In 1962, The Institute for Translation of Hebrew Literature was founded; it was financed by the Israeli Foreign Ministry and The Ministry of Education. In addition, in Israel there are few independent agencies for translation. Some writers use foreign agencies or agents to represent them. A regular Hebrew book in translation appears in one edition or in two editions; each one comprises 3,000 to 5,000 copies. Between January and October of 1998, for example, 125 translated Hebrew books in various languages appeared, including children's books (32) and, at the same time, the translation rights for 100 books were sold.

In the last decade, Israeli authors succeeded more than in the past at selling their books in translation. The success is reported in Italy, Germany, India and China, Spain, Greece and Holland. There are, of course, exceptions. *Minotaur* by Tammuz (see above) appeared in seven editions in Italy alone, and 30,000 copies were sold. David Grossman, A.B. Yehoshua and Yaakov Shabtai are popular in Italy. Shabtai received exceptionally laudatory criticism in Holland and in Germany and, in each country, 20,000 copies of his book were sold. Meir Shalev's *In his House in the Wilderness* sold well in Holland in a hard cover.

As of the end of 1998, Efraim Kishon, with his humorous style, was translated into many languages. There were 301 translations of his books into various languages; Amos Oz - 272; S.Y. Agnon - 118; A.B. Yehoshua - 90; Aharon Appelfeld - 79; David Grossman - 79; Yoram Kaniuk - 77; Yehuda Amihai - 74; Uri Orlev - 69. The above numbers reflect the number of books that appeared in translation in various languages per each author. The original Hebrew book is only one, which was translated into various languages, and each book of translation is included in the above numbers.

BIBLIOGRAPHY

Alter, Robert, edited. *Modern Hebrew Literature.* Introduction, pp. 1-12. Behrman House, Inc., 1975.

Burnshaw, Stanley, Carmi, T., and Spicehandler, Ezra, editors. *The Modern Hebrew Poem Itself.* Schocken Books, New York, 1966, pp. 197-210.

Even-Zohar, Itamar. "Israeli Hebrew Literature: A Historical Model." *Ha-sifrut,* Vol. IV, No. 3, Jul 1973, pp. 427-440, English.

Halkin, Shimon. Mavo la-Sipporet ha-'Ivrit. Mif'al ha-Shikhpul, Hebrew University, 1958, pp. 2-3.

_____. Simon. *Modern Hebrew Literature, from the Enlightenment to the Birth of the State of Israel: Trends and Values,* new ed., New York, Schocken Books, 1970.

"Hebrew Literature." In *Encyclopedia Britanica.*1998, pp. 483-486.

Sadan, Dov. *'Al Sifrutenu: Massat Mavo.* Reuven Mas, 1950, in pp. 53-60. Reprinted in *Avnei Bedek,* Hakkibutz Hammeuchad, 1962, pp. 9-66, in pp. 51-58.

Shaked, Gershon. Vol. 1: *Ha-Sipporet ha-'Ivrit 1880-1970.* Hakibbutz Hameuchad and Keter Publishing Houses Ltd., 1977.

_____. Vol. 2: *Ha-Sipporet ha-'Ivrit 1880-1980, Ba'arez u-va-Tefuza,* Hakibbutz Hammeuchad and Keter Publsihing Houses Ltd., 1983.

_____. Vol. 3: *Ha-Sipporet ha-'Ivrit 1880-1980*: *ha-Moderna ben Shete Milhamot — Mavo Le-Dorot Ba'arez* , Hakibbutz Hameuchad and Keter Publishing Houses Ltd., 1988.

_____. Vol. 4: *Ha-Sipporet ha-'Ivrit 1880-1970*: *Be-Havlei Doram.* Hakibbutz Hameuchad and Keter Publishing House Ltd., 1993.

_____. Vol. 5: *Beharbei Eshnabbim bi-Khnisot Zedadiyot.* Hakkibbutz Hameuchad and Keter Publishing House, 1998.

Silberschlag, Eisig. *Modern Hebrew Literature, From Renaissance to Renaissance, Hebrew literature from 1492-1970.* Vol.1, New York, Ktav, 1973.

_____Vol. 2: *Hebrew Literature in the Land of Israel,* (1870-1970). New York, Ktav, 1977.

_____. (S.Ei.). "Hebrew Literature, Modern." In *Encyclopedia Judaica*, Keter Publishing House, 1972, Vol. 8, pp. 175-214.

Zahor, Ze'ev. "Yefei ha-Belorit ve-ha-To'ar: Ekh Zakha ha-Palmah le-Yokra?" *Yediot Aharonot*, May 5, 2000, p. 25.

Y.D. "'Ivrit, Sifrut." *Ha-Iznsiklopedia ha-'Ivrit*, Vol, pp. 670-719.

Chapter 2

THE ISRAELI CINEMA: A BRIEF SURVEY

GENERAL OBSERVATION

The first period of pre-State Israeli film began in 1899 and lasted through 1917. Still pictures and motion pictures (slides, phonographs and kinematograph) displayed the positive achievements and success of the Zionist movement in Palestine in order to support its propaganda and increase the number of its Jewish supporters. The genre of Zionist propaganda films promoted new Jewish culture, farming, love of the Jewish nation and its land. These films perceived the significance of the individual only in his being part of a group that implements national goals, the presentation of Israel as the place of redemption for the Jewish people, and contributing to Jewish national consciousness and national renascence. However, Zionist film influenced filmmaking before and after the establishment of the State of Israel in 1948.

"The first movie of Palestine" was made in 1911; it provided a visual image of Jewish life in Palestine where Zionism was implemented. Ya'acov Ben-Dov is considered "the Father of the Israeli Film." He immigrated to Israel in 1908 and made many documentary movies (Gross, 1991, p. 30) in an effort to preserve Jewish renascence in the homeland. Few movies were filmed in Palestine in 1911 through 1917, and those were collections of pictorial illustrations of the success of Zionism in Israel, showing that the return to the homeland was possible and successful. Individuals produced the movies as a private initiative, and the filmmakers were Zionists who accepted the directives of the Zionist establishment and needed its support. The commitment of the moviemakers to the promotion of Zionism set back their artistic accomplishments (Halachmi, 1995, pp. 11-46) and elicited criticism.

The concept of "the Israeli catch in the art" related to the artist's dilemma: Should he only sing the praise of the Jewish settlements in Palestine and idealize it, or should he depict a true and realistic portrayal of life — including its painful and problematic aspects, which could damage its image but also catalyze the problems' solutions? Should a moviemaker present a selective reality as representative "evidence" of Jewish life in Palestine and conceal the bitter truth about its problems in order to support the Zionist movement?

It was not until 1932 that two plot-driven movies were produced in Palestine — both of which strove for artistic success and were free of Zionist sponsorship: *Va-Yehi Bimei and'Oded ha-Noded* (Halchmi, 1995, pp. 97-126, 134-139). The first artistic-dramatic-plot movie of Palestine came out in 1932 (*Va-Yehi Bimei*, "And it came to pass in the days of"). It was a silent movie, a short comedy that took place in Palestine and focused on the individuals described in the movie, with their problems and weaknesses. The success of this movie encouraged the making of *'Oded Ha-Noded ('Oded the Wonderer)*, the first artistic-dramatic, full-length, plot-based movie in Palestine. This small budget 1932 silent movie (movies with sound had been introduced in 1927) was based on Zvi Liberman's (Livnei) short story (see Liberman, 1932). It is an adventure story that draws on Daniel Defoe's *Robinson Crusoe* and carries the message that Jews in Palestine are bringing with them skills and cultures and thus will contribute to the progress that will help make peace with the Arabs.

190 producers made 407 full-length plot movies in Israel in the years 1932 through 1994 (see Shniz er pp. 15-29), not including short films, documentary movies (except few), foreign productions in Israel, and made-for-television movies. Some brief and general observations about Israeli cinema will be offered here, and then some landmarks in the history of Israeli cinema will be briefly presented.

Only 16 movies, all small budgets, were produced in 1932 through 1960. These movies supported Zionist ideology, the Jewish settlement in the land of Israel and the in-gathering of the exiles, as well as the creation of the State of Israel in 1948. In the first decade of the State of Israel, government agencies intervened in the field of Israeli cinema by applying censorship and controlling financial support. Thus it was difficult not to adhere to Zionist concepts.

Most of the above-mentioned 16 movies concentrated on compelling social issues in Israel. For a long time they voiced Zionist messages, glorified Israeli fighters and the returning of Jews to their homeland. The serious messages were presented often in high, sometimes distanced and artificial style. Within time, the movies adopted spoken Hebrew, and Hebrew colloquialism suited the portrayed characters.

The Bible, which encouraged producers of many movies outside Israel, inspired very few movies in Israel (Gross, pp. 247-250). Perhaps the preexisting Biblical movies with their elaborate budgets and world-renowned actors were an intimidating factor.

Similarly, the assertion of Jewish tradition in Israeli movies is relatively marginal. This may be the result of the fact that Zionism collided with Jewish traditions. Israelis are not connected with their distanced historical past; secular and religious Jews do not live in peace with each other in Israel.

Israeli cinema in general did not give weighty expression to the Holocaust and to the Jewish experience in the 1940s. From 1946 through 1953, there were some movies about the Holocaust and its survivors. The emphasis was on the Zionist present with its "new" heroic Jew, resulting in a lack of attachment to the "old" Diaspora Jew who went "as sheep to the massacre." The relatively few movies about the Holocaust, which were made in Israel at later stages often depicted troubled Holocaust survivors, affected by their pasts.

Comedies seem to be a very successful Israeli-film genre. They sometimes attract spectators regardless of their artistic quality. Many of these comedies are based on the Ashkenazi (for example, *Luppo*. 900,000 Israelis saw Shenei Kuni Lemel, "Two Kuni Lemel"!), or on the Sephardi origin (for example, *Kasablan and Salmoniko. 1,200,000 Israelis saw Salah Shabbati!)* and presented humor, customs, manners of speech, ways of life, characters and wisdom that attracted many spectators. Menahem Golan, later an internationally acclaimed producer, was particularly successful in Israel in melodramas based on Jewish-community origin *(Eldorado, Fortuna, Kasablan and others)*. But not all comedies were based on Jewish-community origin. For example, over 1,300,000 Israelis saw the youth comedy *Eskimo Limon* ("Lemon Eskimo Bar").

War can be an attractive theme for film. Hollywood was interested in Biblical wars (*The Ten Commandments, David and Bath-Sheba*) and historical movies (*Shlomit, Ben-Hur).* Israeli movies were also made about the pre-State Israeli wars, such as *Havura she-Kazot* ("Such a Company," 1962) and *Hu Halakh ba-Sadot* ("He Walked in the Fields," 1967) and about the underground Israeli movements, such as *Za'am ve-Tehilla* ("Fury and Glory," 1984) and *Hannah Senesh* (1987). One of the television movies about the Israeli pre-State underground movements is "Winter Games."

Movies were made about all of the Israeli wars: The War of Independence (1948), The Sinai War (1956), The Six Days War (1967), The Yom Kippur War (1973) and The Lebanon War (1982). One finds various expressions of these wars in the literary works and movies discussed in this book.

In addition to Israeli-war movies, Israeli movies were made about various military operations between the wars, such as *Ha-Sayyarim* ("The Patrol Soldiers") and *Ha-Milhama she-A'harei ha-Milhama* ("The War after the War").

30 war and military movies were made in Israel in the first 30 years of Israeli independence. Some of these plot-based movies are considered artistic achievements, such as *Kol Mamzer Melekh* ("Every Bastard is a King"), *Maz or* ("Siege") and *Mivz 'a Yonatan* ("Jonathan's Operation").

The war situation in many movies was predominantly about the Israeli man. The mainline Israeli movies were about introverted macho men who avoided tears, belittled the pain of the individual when compared with the nation's needs, and prevented the melodramatic. Melodramatic movies were made by some producers but usually did not achieve wide recognition as quality movies. Contrary to the active man who often takes charge of his life, the Israeli woman appeared in many movies as the widow of the hero soldier, carrying his memory, or dependent upon men and manipulated by them.

While military service has a weighty place in Israeli cinema, and is often connected to serious social messages, it also provides one of the frameworks for comic movies. There are also Israeli movies that criticize the Israeli Defense Force, such as *Massa' Alunkoot* ("Stretcher Military Drive").

70 of the plot movies made in Israel in the 1980s are about the Israeli wars and the Israeli army. These movies deal with the social and psychological impacts of war on individual soldiers and do not focus on the heroic-Zionist model. Other movies are love stories between Arabs and Jews. After the rise of the Likkud party (1977), the Lebanon War

(1982) and the Intifada (1987), Israeli films attempted to present complicated facets of the Israeli-Arab conflict on both sides.

Burshtein's book (1990) provides an opportunity to see, in close-up, the faces of various characters in Hebrew and Israeli films in the years 1911 through 1990. The faces represent the local culture. The close-up, affected by the acting, photography, editing and sound, is considered in the book as the most human and intimate expression in film.

Nitzan S. Ben-Shaul (1998) studied the subject of war and the Israeli-Palestinian conflict and the Jewish inter-ethnic conflict as it is expressed in Israeli cinema. He divides the history of Israeli cinema, since 1948, into periods according to the expression of siege in Israeli cinema. Many Israelis believed that the whole world was against them, and the notion of siege is a prominent factor in Israeli films. Economic and political changes resulted in a cinematic shift away from this belief.

The genre of children's movies was minor in Israel.

LANDMARKS OF ISRAELI CINEMA SINCE 1948

The years **1948 through 1953** were years of meager and technically poor productivity (for detailed historical accounting see Gross, p. 182-383). Filmmakers struggled to establish the movie industry in Israel and made efforts toward achieving recognition of the importance of Israeli cinema. Some full-length Israeli-plot movies were made in these years, among them the 1950 movie *Hafuga* ("Cease-Fire"), which is the first plot movie made in the State of Israel. It is a sentimental movie about a romantic triangle, a mix of love story, documentary and Zionist ideology. Six of the first ten movies produced in Israel portrayed the Israeli warrior of the 1948 War of Independence, who was ready to sacrifice his life for his country. Other movies about this war are *Himmo, King of Jerusalem* (made in 1987), which takes place at the end of that war and *Hill 24 Does Not Respond* (made in 1958).

Hollywood producers were also intrigued by this war, making *A Sword in the Desert*, 1949; *Exodus*, 1960; *Judith*, 1966; and *Cast a Giant Shadow*, 1956.

From **1953 through 1958** the status of Israeli cinema improved, the government and the Israeli Workers Union adopted the use of documentary movies; and a new law regulated various issues relating to short movies and documentaries. The movie-industry employees became unionized. During this time, some plot movies were made, and two contests for the best Israeli short movie took place, one in 1953 and the other in 1955.

The first Israeli-plot movie that received recognition and distribution out of Israel was *Giv'a 24 Enah 'Ona* (*Hill 24 Does Not Respond*). It was made in 1958 and was composed of four short dramatic stories about volunteers, warriors and a young Israeli woman who died on the hill. The movie focused on a national subject — the War of Independence. The budget for the movie was high, and the producer was English.

The years **1959 through 1962** were productive years for Israeli film, including the Israeli-plot movie; some of Israel's most famous movies were made at that time, due to the growing Israeli economy and a new attractive tax-return policy for Israeli movies. The Hebrew-speaking audience grew. A modern movie studio was established (*Geva*). *Exodus* was filmed in Israel in 1960-1961. *I Like Mike*, a simplistic comedy drew a relatively substantial number of viewers. In 1963, a Biblical movie of the story of Joseph and his brothers was produced (*Ba'al ha-Halomot*, "The Dreamer"). The Israeli movies at that time also explored various themes: the Holocaust (*Ha-Marten*, "The Basement"), the Bible (*Ba'al ha-Halomot*, "The Dreamer"), adventures (*Holot Lohatim*, "Scorching Sands") and war (*Sinaya*)—giving an expression to the 1956 Sinai War (*Sinaya*, 1962).

The number of plot movies produced in Israel increased gradually in each one of the years **1963 through 1970**. In 1963, three young producers began film careers: Menahem Golan (*Eldorado*), Efrayim Kishon (*Salah Shabbati*) and Uri Zohar (*Hor ba-Levana*, "A hole in the Moon"). All the three left their imprints on Israeli cinema. The 1960s are characterized by an involvement of experienced theater individuals in Israeli films. They knew Israeli audiences and produced movies that suited them.

For a long time, beginning with the movie *Salah Shabbati* (1964) and throughout and after the seventies, Israeli cinema highlighted the Sephardi-Ashkenazi encounter. 1,200,000 people saw *Salah Shabbati*, which is, relative to the Israeli population, one of the world's largest audiences (*Eskimo Limon* and *Kasablan* are the only other Israeli movies seen by more than one million people). In these movies, a rich and insensitive Ashkenazi was confronted with the socially inferior, shrewd Sephardi, while the spoken Hebrew — especially as spoken by the

Sephardi caricature — provided numerous occasions for humor. This generated a genre of movies that are often referred to as the ""Burekas" movies, after the name of a popular Sephardi pastry. In these movies the Askenazim (Jews from Central or Eastern Europe, Jews who are not Sephardi) dominated the Sephardi (Jews of Spanish stock, including Jews from the Middle East). The Ashkenazi was depicted in these movies as economically comfortable but unhappy, and often enjoying high social status and success — even when he was unqualified for success — because he was well connected to officials in various government agencies. The Sephardi had the street smarts and wisdom that made him enjoy life in spite of his poverty. When the confrontation between the Ashkenazi and Sephardi characters escalated, the conflicts were often defused by a nostalgic, ceremonial, traditional event in the Jewish life cycle (such as circumcision, Bar Miz va a celebration of a Jewish boy of thirteen assuming the religious obligations, or a wedding).

In parodying movies such as these, there are many entertaining situations and amusing characters. Sometimes the situations and the characters are vulgar and presented as illustrative of Israelis in general — for example, their impoliteness projected in the way the character eats or treats a woman.

Israeli legislation, and later television-orientation policy, encouraged the "Burekas" movies. The 1954 Israeli Statute for the Encouragement of Israeli Movies automatically subsidized any movie produced in Israel with government funds, matching the revenues received in movie theaters from ticket sales for the film. Producers were aware of both the popularity of the "Burekas" movies and of the coveted subsidy.

In 1968, about fifteen years behind western European countries, Israel broadcast television began. Israeli television, to a high degree, disregarded the expression of Sephardi culture but nurtured the expression of European culture. The 1954 law and television's orientation — both the result of policy — encouraged the continuous production and prosperity of the ""Burekas" movies. Television did not cause a decrease in these movies' ticket sales.

These movies (see Shohat) often treated the Sephardi-Israeli Jew in a stereotypical, belittling way. Often these films used funny pronunciation, poor verbal abilities, ragged clothing, disgusting drinking habits and playing backgammon in a comic, exaggerated, mocking way to portray the Sephardi Jew. Time and again in these movies the Sephardi Jew was portrayed as limited and devoid of any intellectual ability. Nevertheless, due to his powerful sexuality, he could charm women.

In the late 1960s, some movie producers attempted to place the world of the individual instead of nationalistic themes in the center of their movies. This attempt was the result of various Israeli internal and external factors, such as the national Israeli elation that resulted from the victory in the 1967 Six Days War, the French "New Wave" movies, the "flower generation," and the protest of the Vietnam War. One of the movies discussed in this book, *Three Days and a Child* (1967), can demonstrate the shift from the social-national theme to that of the individual.

The Israeli victory in the June 1967 Six Days War, with the Wailing Wall and other territories recaptured by the Israelis, nurtured a nationalistic pride and again inspired the making of movies about the Israeli-born warrior who sacrificed himself for his country. In addition to foreign movies, several Israeli-plot movies were made about the Six Days War, including *Kol Mamzer Melekh* ("Every Bastard is a King"), *Loa ba-Yom ve-Lo ba-Layla* ("Not during the Day and not at Night"). This also was the time that the famous 1948 novel of Moshe Shamir, *He Walked in the Fields* — a novel expressing the boundless commitment of the young Israeli born to the Jewish people and their land — was made into a film. In his book about the Israeli cinema of modernity, Schweitzer (1997) focuses on the period beginning in the Six Days War to the 1973 Yom Kippur War and suggests that it blazed a trail for the Israeli cinema that came later.

In the **1970s,** some producers continued to be drawn from national toward individualistic themes.

It took a long time before the traditions, costumes and absorption problems of Sephardi Jews were represented in a respectful way in Israeli cinema. The change was the result of various factors, among them: the demonstrations of the "Black Panthers" against discrimination of Middle Eastern Jews; the protest of Israeli singers of Middle Eastern origin, whose themes and melodies were influenced by the music of their homelands; the singers' protest against their exclusion from Israeli media; the outcry of Israeli intellectuals, who used literary (Hakak, 1981), sociological, historical and other disciplines to point out the discrimination against Sephardi Jews and the distortion of their image.

In **1977,** the Likkud party defeated the Labor party for the first time in Israel. The new spirit, recognizing the need for corrective measures toward Sephardi Jews in Israeli, did not support the "Burekas" movies anymore. The 1954 Statute for the Encouragement of Israeli Movies was modified, and the fund subsidizing the "Burekas" movies was reduced to the degree that these films became no longer profitable. The Jews from the Middle East became participants in the government, which lessened frustration. The need for "Burekas" movies as an outlet for deprived people lessened and the monetary incentive to produce them ceased to exist. The impact of the political scene on movie production was evident. In 1980, The Public Fund for Encouragement of Quality Movies was founded, and its name describes the change it brought about — encouragement of movies on the basis of their artistic qualities and not due to some automatic and quantitative criteria.

My Michael (1975), discussed in this book, is an example of those 1970s movies in which there was some protest of the strain inflicted on the individual by his milieu. Some movies portrayed the life of homosexuals in a society that appreciates combat skills and nurtures heroic myths.

The image of the Israeli-born romantic fighter, portrayed time and again as young, strong, popular, optimist and well-liked by young women, was reexamined in Israeli movies as he was in the 1970s. He was questioned, mocked and exposed in his weakness (*Mez ez im,* "peeping;" *Le'an Ne'elam Daniel Wax,* "whereto did Daniel Wax disappear"?). Only the nostalgia remained (*Eskimo Limon,* "Lemon Eskimo Bar").

The Antebe Operation (1976), in which Israeli soldiers rescued, — in a stunningly heroic military action — the passengers of an airplane hijacked by a Palestinian organization, generated an Israeli movie (and two American movies).

The 1973 Yom Kippur War traumatized the Israelis in spite of their victory, and did not stimulate movie making. Some movies made in the 1970s shattered the myth of the macho Israeli-born hero who is ready, willing and able to serve nationalistic needs without hesitation. The setting of the movies *Shellshock* (1988), *On The Fringe* (1987) and *Don't Give a Damn* (also 1987) is in the wake of the 1973 Yom Kippur War. Israeli movies in **the 1980s** illustrated the price of Israeli wars by showing the painful and baffled condition of an invalid Israeli soldier. Many of them no longer presented an Israeli soldier who had confidence in his objectives and assignments and was willing to sacrifice his life for his people and country. National consensus increasingly became a problematic concept. Some movies clearly expressed objection to a non-inquisitive acceptance of the old concepts of war, sacrifice, collective demands and expectations.

In June 1982, Israel invaded Lebanon, and this invasion triggered some Israeli movies. Zionist ideas were challenged and the national consensus of war's necessity was questioned in some movies that presented tired and skeptical solders. *Burning Memory* (1988) is set after the Lebanon War. After the 1982 Israeli invasion of Lebanon, some Israeli movies commiserated with the Palestinians. Movies of the 1980s, such as *Hamsin* ("Heat-Wave"), pointed out the Palestinians' point of view and their suffering. Their condition reflected some of the moralistic blemishes of Israeli existence and the need for a peaceful resolution to the conflict. The image of the Arab became more human, and the treatment of his character became more empathetic.

The May 1977 political change (the first-time loss for the Labor party) was strongly felt in the 1980s. Various Israeli movies focused on Israel's social and political issues. The Arab became the subject of several movies (to name a few: *Hamsin,* "hamsin," "heat wave;" *Gesher Z ar Me'od,* "A Very Narrow Bridge;" *Hiyyukh ha-Gedi,* "The Smile of the Lamb;" *Me-Ahorei ha-Soragim,* "Beyond the Grids") while the Israeli soldier was depicted as broken, beaten physically and psychologically, estranged and subdued. (To name a few films: *Lo Sam Zayin,* "I Don't Give a Damn;" *Ot Kayin,* "The Sign of Cain;" *Bez illo shel Helem Kerav,* "In the Shadow of a Battle Shock.")

Himmo, King of Jerusalem was made at this stage (1987), uncovering the tragedy, the pain and wounds of the fatally wounded Israeli soldier in the 1948 War of Independence. The myth of the Israeli-born soldier who sacrifices his life for Israel without any question was presented by its price. The center of the movie is not the hope, vitality and heroic victory of the Israeli War of Independence, but despair, withering and death. Other Israeli movies in the 1980s related to other Israeli wars and their impact on soldiers, such as *Helem Kerav* ("Battle Shock") and *Resisim* ("Splinters"). The focal point of *The Lover* (1986) is not the Israeli hero who does not question the war and is willing to sacrifice his life for his country. War veterans (such as Adam), orthodox Jews and military defectors do not participate in war.

At the end of 1987, when the Intifada (the name of the Palestinian revolt) broke the Palestinian stopped being a popular subject for Israeli movies. Instead of nurturing the Israeli-Arab dialogue, the Israeli-Arab conflict was prominent in movies such as *Sadot Yerukkim* ("Green Fields," 1989). The background of *The Deserter's Wife* (1992) is the Intifada.

In the 1990s, visual effects became more important than before. The night and night people and burdensome urban life are the subject of some of the movies (*Sippurei Tel-Aviv,* "Tel-Aviv Stories;" *Ha-Hayyim 'al-pi Agfa,* "The Life According to Agfa;" *Hesed Mufla,* "A Splendid Act of Grace").

During the Intifada insurrection, the peace process intensified. There was a significant immigration of Jews from Russia to Israel. In 1992, the Labor party won in the Israeli elections and came back to political power. In 1996, Yitzhak Rabin, the pro-peace Prime Minister of Israel was assassinated, and there was a political overturn again. The political pendulum continued to swing and, in the 1999 elections, the Labor party came into power again. According to Ben-Shaul (pp. 128-129), recent films about war reject the belief that the world had negative intentions toward Israel.

Various authors studied Israeli cinema. For English readers, some books written in English may be of special interest. Arzooni (1983) wrote about *The Israeli Film: Social and Cultural Influences: 1912-1973.* The book presents the people of Israel and the contributions of Jewish heritage to Israeli film; film and stage in the years 1905-1973, the years the Israeli film went public; and an analysis of six Israeli films.

Ella Shohat wrote *Israeli Cinema: East West and the Politics of Representation* (see bibliography). Her book presents the beginning of Israeli cinema in the Jewish population in the Land of Israel, the post-1948 heroic-nationalistic genre, "Burekas" and the Sephardi representation, personal cinema and the politics of allegory and the return of the repressed Palestinian. Of special interest is Shohat's analysis of the Burekas films, which she argues,

> ...had an impact on the general image of Sephardim far beyond the cinematic framework.... The dominant ideology that marked these films even penetrated prejudices embodied in the films..." she argues (Ibid. p. 136).

In 1996, Amy Kronish published his book, *World Cinema: Israel* (1996). Kronish describes the Zionist period of Israeli cinema, the heroic period during the early years of the state, the beginning of an indigenous film expression, the post-Six Day War period with its return to heroism, the "Burekas" movies as an expression of ethnic portrayals and escapism. Other chapters probe into artistic movies made by young filmmakers in Israel, old myths that face new realities, the challenges and traumas of war and the expressions of tensions and ties between Jews and Arabs. Women in Israeli film, the search for ethnic roots and the individual in society as depicted in the new wave films are the subjects of other chapters.

The above books, along with their analytical, informative and evaluative aspects, provide specific information that the reader may find of distinct interest. For example, Appendix III in Arzooni's book (p. 376-377) presents the "best Israeli films in the opinion of persons connected with the film industry." Kronish's book includes "useful addresses" (pp. 250-251) in the world of Israeli cinema. It has a listing of Israeli feature films and provides credit information; it includes documentaries, shorts and television productions, which have been discussed in the book. The three books have an extensive bibliography.

As of now, six Israeli movies were nominated for Academy Awards in the category of "Best Foreign-Language Film" (*Operation Thunderbolt, Salah Shabbati, I Love You Rosa, The House on Shlush Street, The Policeman, Beyond the Walls*). The Israeli producer Moshe Mizrahi was internationally recognized when he received the Academy Award in 1977 for his movie *Madame Rosa* (*La vie devant soi*, France) as the "Best Foreign-Language Film."

In 1972, Israeli actor Hayim Topol was nominated for an Academy Award for his role as Tevia, the milkman in *Fiddler on the Roof*.

In September 1999, *Yediot Aharonot*, the most popular Israeli newspaper published, a special issue titled, "The Dreamers," about Israeli cinema. Central producers, actors, directors and screenwriters, some of which we will come to know through the movies presented in this book, discussed the past, present and future of Israeli cinema. The wide range of issues gives some current insight into the world of Israeli cinema. "Is the [Israeli] cinema the medium of the next decade and what should be done so that it happens?" was a central question (see Amir). The answer was positive on the condition that Israeli cinema would underscore themes related to the big drama of Israeli identity and existence (Amos Gittai), and because television had already consumed its topics But, what is needed is money (Moshe Ibgi). Israeli cinema is now in line with French and Italian cinema, and it will be the medium of the next decade through television (Asi Dayan). Israeli cinema will die unless there are drastic changes in government attitude (Menahem Golan). It will be possible to make Israeli cinema only when many Israeli movies are produced every year and Israelis begin to see Israeli movies on a regular basis (Mikhal Bat-Adam). The future of Israeli cinema will be great because new Israeli filmmakers have far better intellectual and professional foundations than previous generations (Rafi Buk'ai, a director and screenwriter). Israel has the talent and the technological knowledge and, with government support, Israeli cinema will become a central medium in Israeli culture (Uri Barabash). The crisis in Israeli cinema will pass because of Israeli talent (Gila Almagor, an actress). Israel will have to produce movies that will be a synthesis of quality, relevance and communication (Katriel Shehori, Director of the Cinema Foundation).

Now, in Israel, there are 10 institutes for cinema studies and 250 high school classes, specializing in film studies. These programs educate a total of 10,000 students. A journalist (see Hofshtein) reports that a student in Tel-Aviv University burned down his parents' house in order to achieve total authenticity in a scene of a house on fire in a movie that he directed.

"We, crazy people," is how Mark Rosenbaum defines filmmakers in Israel after he himself produced 20 movies. Hayyim Buzgalo described how, when he made his first movie in 1989 (*Fictitous Marriage*), there was a scene of a fisherman coming out of the Jaffa port with fishing nets loaded with fish that he could not afford to pay for. The crew bought only a few fish and put cardboard under them to create the illusion of abundance. The movie was an artistic success, yet Buzgalo had to deal with debts and liens for many years. The filmmakers describe their traumatic experiences — having to deal with bureaucracy, lack of endurance, distrusting audiences and tiny budgets (see Cohen). But an argument was strongly made (see Ingbar) that Israeli cinema can strongly succeed by emphasizing local color problems and Israeli identity, and by ceasing to adapt everything that comes from overseas.

The smallest budget for a movie in recent years was under $150,000, and the highest budget for an Israeli movie was $2 million.

BIBLIOGRAPHY

Almagor, Gila. *Under the Domim Tree*. Traslated by Hillel Schenker. Simon & Schuster, School and Library Binding, 1995.

_____. *The Summer of Aviya.* Translated by Hillel Halkin. London, Collins, 1991.

Bar-Kadma, 'Immanu'el. "Sifrut mi-Ba'ad la-'Adasha." *Moznaim*, Vol. 70 No. 2, Nov. 1995, pp. 8-9.

Beja, Morris. *Film and Literature.* New York, Longman, 1976.

Ben-Amoz , Dan. *Lo Sam Zayin.* Bitan, Tel-Aviv, 1973.

Ben-Ezer, Ehud. *Ha-Mahzeva.* Am Oved, Tel-Aviv, 1965.

Ben-Ner, Yitzhak. "A Dime Novel," in *Rustic Sunset and Other Stories.* Lynne Rienner Publishers, 1998, pp. 91-123.

_____. "Winter Games," in *Rustic Sunset and Other Stories.* Lynne Rienner Publishers, 1998, pp. 5-26.

_____. "Atalya." In *Aharei ha-Geshem.* Keter, Jerusalem, 1979, pp. 40.

Ben-Shaul, S., Nitzan. *Mythical Expressions of Siege in Israeli Films.* Studies in Art and Religious Interpretation, Volume 17. The Edwin Mellen Press, 1998.

Benaya-Seri, Dan. "Elef ha-Nashim shel Siman Tov." In *Zipporei Zel.* Keter, Jerusalem, 1987, pp. 9-78.

Bluestone, George. *Novels into Films.* Baltimore, The Johns Hopkins Press, 1957.

Burshtein, Yigal. *Panim Kisdei Kerav: Ha-Hisitoria ha-Kolno'it shel ha-Panim ha-Yisraeliyyim.* Hakkibutz Hameuchad, 1990.

Chatman, Seymour. "What Novels Can Do That Films Can't (and Vice Versa)." In *Critical Inquiry*, Autumn 1980, Volume 7, Number 1, pp. 121-140.

Esner, A.G.S. *Filmed Books and Plays, 1928-1986.* Gower Publishing Co, England, 1987.

Gertz, Nurith. *Sippur me-ha-Seratim: Sipporet Yisraelit ve-'Ibbudah le-Kolnoa'.* Ha-Oniversita ha-Petuha, 1993.

Giddings, Robert, Selby, Keith and Wensley, Chris. *Screening the Novel: The Theory and Practice of Literary Dramatization.* Macmillan, 1990.

Grossman, David. *Hiyyukh ha-Gedi.* Sifrei Siman Kri'a, Hakkibutz Hemeuchad, Tel-Aviv, 1983.

Hofstein, Avner. "Lo Raziti li-Gmor kemo Misken." *Yediot Aharonot, 7 Yamim*, Dec. 24, 1999, pp. 40-43.

Kaniuk, Yoram. *Rockinghorse.* Translated by Richard Flantz. Harper & Row, 1977.

_____. *Himmo, King of Jerusalem.* Translated by Yosef Schacter. Anthenum, New York, 1969.

_____."Ha-'Etym." In *Layla 'al ha-Hof 'im Transistor.* Hakkibuts Hameuchad, Tel-Aviv, 1979, pp. 134-162. Reprinted in *Arba'a Sippurim ve-Shir.* Hakkibutz Hameuchad, 1985, Tel-Aviv, pp. 65-88.

Kenan, Amos. *The Road to Ein Harod.* Translated by M. Hutzpit. Al Asqi Books, London, 1986.

Kenaz, Yehoshua. *After the Holidays*, Translated by Dalia Bilu. Harcourt Brace, 1987.

Liberman (Livnei), Zvi. *'Oded ha-Noded.* Kuppat Sefer, Tel-Aviv, 1932.

Linur, Irit. *Shirat ha-Sirenot.* Zemora-Bitan, Tel-Aviv, 1991.

Lupack, Barbara Tepa, Ed. *Vision/Re-Vision: Adapting Contemporary American Fiction by Women to Film.* Bowling Green Satte University Popular Press, 1996.

McFarlane, Brian. *Novel To Film: An Introduction to the Theory of Adaptation.* Clarendon Press, Oxford, 1996.

Matalon, Ronit. *Sippur she-Mathil be-Leveya shel Nahash.* Dvir, Tel-Aviv, 1989.

Mayne, Judith. *Private Novels, Public Films.* The University of Georgia Press, Athens & London, 1988.

Miller, Gabriel. *Screening The Novel: Rediscovered American Fiction in Film.* Frederick Ungar Publishing Co., New York, 1980.

Oz, Amos. *My Michael.* Bantam Books, 1972.

_____. *Black Box.* Vintage International, 1989.

Richardson, Robert. *Literature and Film.* Indiana University Press, Bloomongton, London, 1969, Chapter 6, pp. 79-90.

Ron-Peder-Amit, Galila. *Nadia: Sippurah shel Talmida 'Araviyya.* Tel-Aviv, Milo, 1985.

Ropars-Vuilleumier, Marie-Claire. *De la litte'rature au cine'ma.* Paris, Armand Colin, 1970.

Ruppert, Peter, edited. *Ideas of Order in Literature & Film.* University Presses of Florida, Tallahassee, 1980.

Shabtai, Yaakov. *Zikhron Devarim.* Hakkibutz Hameuchad, Sifrei Siman Kri'a, Tel-Aviv, 1975.

_____. *Namer Habarburot.* Hakkibutz Hameuchad, Sifrei Siman Kri'a, Tel-Aviv, 1985.

Shamir, Moshe. *Hu Halakh ba-Sadot.* Merhavya, Sifriyyat Po'alim, Tel-Aviv, 1948.

Sinyard, Neil. *Filming Literature: The Art of Screen Adaptation.* Croom Helm, London & Sidney, 1986.

Zalka, Dan. *Kefafot.* Am Oved, Tel-Aviv, 1982.

Yehoshua, A.B. *Three Days and a Child.* Peter. Owen, London, 1970.

_____. *The Lover.* Translated by Phillip Simson. Doubleday & Co., inc. Garden City, N.Y., 1978.

_____. *Mr. Mani.* Translated by Hillel Halkin. Harcourt Brace & Company, 1993.

Yizhar, S. "The Story of Hirbet Hiz'ah." Tr. By Harold Levy (a condensed version, an excerpt). In Sonntag, J., ed. Caravan: a Jewish Quarterly Omnibus. New York, Y. Yoseloff, ap62, pp. 328-334.

Chapter 3

ADAPTATION OF PROSE FICTION INTO FILMS
The Case of Modern Hebrew Literature

Some Israeli movies are adaptations of works of Modern Hebrew literature. Many authors hope that their literary works will be made into films. Through the medium of film, the author's message may reach many more people and new readers may read the literary work itself after seeing the movie.

There are many reasons for the adaptation of prose fiction into film. The particular prose fiction may have captured the imagination of a filmmaker. He may identify with its ideas and want to present them to a wide audience or feel a need to deliberate them. A novel may be adapted to the screen because it brings cultural respectability to the screen. It may inspire the creation of a new original work and influence it, or inspire the need to faithfully present it in another medium. The success of a novel may also catalyze its adaptation into a film because it increases the number of expected viewers.

In Israel, which is a small country with a small audience, the potential monetary benefits of an author whose literary work becomes a movie are insignificant because the payment he may get is meager. Thus it appears that Israeli authors' aspirations for movie adaptations of their literary works are not the result of financial considerations but of artistic ones. When 'Irit Linur protested the movie made on the basis of her novel *The Song of the Sirens* (for the literary works see the Bibliography; also Bar-Kadma, 1995, p. 8), and when A.B. Yehoshua expressed reservations about the movie based on his story, *Three Days and a Child* (Yehoshua, 1970. N.B. whenever a literary work is available in translation the year relates to the English translation) their reactions were based on artistic judgment. This judgment may change within time as it happened in the case of A.B. Yehoshua: *Three Days and a Child* was considered, time and again, as one of the best achievements of Israeli cinema, and A.B. Yehoshua himself grew to like the movie.

Kronish in his important book discusses (1996, pp. 158-159) literary adaptations which feature portrayals of Israeli women and briefly discusses Ben-Ner's *'Atalia*, Kaniuk's *Himmo King of Jerusalem*, Yehoshuas *The Lover* and Oz's *My Michael*. He concludes that "in these literary adaptations women are all victims of their surroundings; they suffer as a result of the men in their lives and find unique means to overcome the anguish of their realities" (p. 159). This is a highly debatable view.

Hebrew prose fiction's tradition of adaptation to the screen began in Palestine with *'Oded ha-Noded ('Oded the Wonderer)*, the first artistic dramatic, full-length movie in Palestine. The small budget, silent movie from 1932 was based on Z vi Liberman's (Livnei) short story (see Liberman, 1932). It is an adventure story that draws on Daniel Defoe's *Robinson Crusoe* and carries the message that the Jews in Palestine bring skills and a culture that contributes to the progress that will help make peace with the Arabs.

Among the Israeli literary works that were adapted into films is *He Walked in the Fields*, the 1948 novel of Moshe Shamir, which was made into a film in 1967. Mikhal Bat-Adam made into films *The Lover* of A.B. Yehoshua, Dan Benaya-Seri's *The Thousand Women of Naftali Siman Tov* and *Spots Leopard*, Yaakov Shabtai's play (1985). Yaakov Shabtai's play, *Protocol*, was also made into a film, as were A.B.Yehoshua 's *Three Days and a Child* and *The Lover* Dan Wolman made two movies on the basis of two literary works — Amos Oz's My *Michael* and Dan Zalka's *Gloves*. Oz's *Black Box* was also made into a film. Gila Almagor, an important Israeli actress, wrote two stories about Holocaust survivors — *Under the Domim Tree* and *The Summer* of *Aviyha*. Almagor also produced and acted in both films. Ram Levy made four television movies based on three literary works: "Dime Novel," a short story by Yitzhak Ben-Ner (Ben-Ner, 1998), S. Yizhar's *Hirbet Hiz'ah*, the play, *Keter David*, by Yaakov Shabtai and A.B. Yehoshuas novel, *Mr. Mani* (translated into English), which is considered Israeli television's most ambitious dramatic project (see Hofshtein). Ben-Ner's "Winter Games" and "'Atalia" are two other short stories by Ben-Ner that were made into films. Four movies were made on the basis of Yoram Kaniuk's literary works: *Rockinghorse, Ha-'Eetim* ("The Vultures"), *Himmo, King of Jerusalem* and *Grossman* (German television). Many works of Efrayim Kishon, the world-renowned humorist-author, were made into films. Amos Kenan's *Ha-Derekh le-'En Harod* was translated (1986) and adapted for the screen. The same is true of *Aharei ha-Haggim* ("After the Holidays") by Yehoshua Kenaz (1987).

The works discussed in this book are Israeli prose fiction that were made into films and also translated into English. These requirements limit the number of potential literary works that come under this scope.

Morris Beja (1976, p. 81) presents some of the frequent questions raised when prose fiction is adapted into film:

> How should a film-maker go about the process of adapting a work of written literature? Are there guiding principles that we can discover or devise? What relationship should a film have to the original source? Should it be faithful? Can it be? To what? Which should be uppermost in a film-maker's mind: the integrity of the original work, or the integrity of the film to be based on that work? Is there a necessary conflict? What types of changes are permissible? Desirable? Inevitable? Are some types of work more adaptable then others?

Before we look for definitive answers to the above questions, Giddings, Selby and Wensley (1990, pp. 23-24) remind us of some of the other specific problems in the adaptation of prose fiction into film:

> The question of objective and subjective viewpoints; the presence or absence of a narrator; time — past, present and future; verbal and visual descriptions; and liberty and visual imagery. In addition, sociological issues such as the methods of production, distribution, and consumption of the novel and the film are relevant, as well as consideration of the effects of film and television adaptation upon the understanding and appreciation of the original novel; does the adaptation add to

> the body of interpretation, criticism and analysis of the text,
> or does it in some way damage or replace the experience of
> reading?

In the frame of this discussion, I will briefly touch upon some of these problems. Literature and film are adjoining neighbors in many respects, they both are story-telling arts, they employ similar devices of narrative and they are the dominant artistic expression in the creation of aesthetic responses. They influence each other. Beja (1976) argues that written stories and filmed stories are two forms of the single art of narrative literature, which is any work that recounts a sequence of events, a story.

Literary adaptations have been studied for a long time by analyzing specific literary works made into films and by studying theoretical aspects related to film adaptations of literary works. Enser in his *Filmed Books and Plays, 1928-1986* lists nearly all of the books and plays from which American or British films have been made. He includes books and plays made for television viewing only, as opposed to those made for the cinema (Enser, 1987). Enser lists more than 4,500 such films!

According to Beja (1976, p. 78), 20- to 30-percent of American films were derived from novels, many of the highest-grossing films are literary adaptations and three-quarters of all of the Academy Awards for best picture were given to literary adaptations.

There is also a process of "novelization," transforming exhibited films into novels. Richardson (1969) is one of many who have discussed the impact of film upon modern literature.

It is agreed that a film adaptation of a novel renews the interest in the novel and increases its sale. In general, it is agreed that the majority of viewers of an adapted film did not read the literary work. This opinion does not apply perhaps to Israeli reality, where the number of readers of literary works is relatively high, and where many of the viewers of Israeli screen adaptations see the movies, not with the expectation that it can compete with the world's best cinema, but because it represents local culture.

There are no "worldwide" accepted principles that one has to apply when one examines a prose narrative adapted for the screen. There are no definitive answers to the questions that are raised about the adaptations. Presenting a detailed view of the wide range of theoretical and critical works and the growing diversity of critical approaches to film and literature is beyond the scope of this book. These approaches include

feminist criticism, myth criticism, semiotics, structuralism, poststructur-
alist criticism and formalistic criticism to mention a few. Film study has
developed a meticulous theoretical framework and analysis of film as a
signifying system. One may find fascinating specialized studies in the
field of literature and film, some of which will be briefly mentioned.
Lupack (1996) edited essays about adapting contemporary American
fiction by women, looking into the extent to which filmmakers adopt,
retain, or erase the feminist content of the fiction upon which their films
are based.

Few issues related to fiction made into films will be briefly touched
upon here. Ropars (1970) published a significant study prior to contemporary film studies. Ropars highlighted the fact that films and novels share
many common denominators as narrative forms, and suggested that
evaluating cinematic adaptations is necessary in order to study how the
encounter between cinematic adaptation and its literary source creates a
commentary on the narrative process. Miller (1980) examined eight
neglected American novels and the films made from them. The primary
concern of Mayne (1998) is how examining the films' relationship to the
Western middle-class novel can illuminate the social function of
cinematic narrative. Ruppert (1980) focused on the relationship between
literature and film as narrative, recognizing the richly eclectic and cross-
disciplinary nature of literary and film studies. The first part of *Novel To
Film* of Brian McFarlane (1996, pp. 1-30) presents an articulate background, issues and new agenda in the field. Nurith Gertz (1993) published
a study of Israeli fiction in film.

Bluestone (1957) thought that when a filmmaker undertakes the
adaptation of a novel, the modifications are inevitable. The filmmaker
views the novel as raw material and does not convert it but adapts a
paraphrase of it. "Changes are inevitable the moment one abandons the
linguistic for the visual medium," argues Bluestone (Ibid. p.5). The
language of a novel is organic to it, it is inseparable from its themes, but
the filmmaker disregards this fact and looks to characters and incidents,
detaching them from language. According to Bluestone:

> We often find that the film adapter has not even read the
> book, that he has depended instead on a paraphrase by his
> secretary or his screen-writer... In the fullest sense of the
> word, the filmist becomes not a translator of an established
> author, but a new author in his own rights (Ibid. p. 62).

When novel and film intersect, they are almost indistinguishable but, when they diverge, they lose resemblance to one other. At the farthest point from one another, "what is peculiarly filmic and what is peculiarly novelistic cannot be converted without destroying an integral part of each," argues Bluestone (Ibid. p. 63). He concludes:

> An art whose limits depend on a moving image, mass audi-
> ence, and industrial production is bound to differ from an art
> whose limits depend on language, audience and individual
> creation. In short, the filmed novel, in spite of certain resem-
> blances, will inevitably become a different artistic entity from
> the novel on which it is based.

There were modern writers who were fascinated by the medium of film and probably felt that film could free them from some responsibilities of the novelist, such as entertainment and precise observation of everyday trivialities. While for other authors, cinema was the enemy that under-mined the book and literacy subjected art to popular culture, to industry and to the denominator of mass taste (Sinyard, 1986).

In their laudable overview of the literature/screen debate, Giddings, Selby and Wensley (1990) present their opinions as well as a wide range of various opinions about a number of issues related to screen adaptations from literary texts. The diversity of opinions about these issues is thought evoking and proves again that we should not expect "universally uniform" principles that one has to apply when one examines a prose narrative adapted for the screen. The authors remind the reader that novels are written by individual writers and are read by a relatively small, literate audience, while films are the product of groups and are viewed by a mass, diverse audience. The production of a film is highly expensive and the expected audience must be large. The commercial considerations explain some of the differences in the requirements of a novelist and from those of a filmmaker. The film image is iconic, specific, precise, while the words in a novel are symbolic: "not 'room', but a specific room" (Ibid, p. 6).

Various attempts were made to classify types of adaptations of literary works. Critics found adaptations that are faithful to the original works and preserve their integrity; other adaptations retain the core of the original work but significantly re-interpret it, while another kind of adaptation is by itself an original work and the source text is treated as raw material (ibid. pp. 10-12). The study of Giddings, Selby and Wensley analyzes problems of transfer from literary texts to screen adaptations, including points of view, time, imagery, psychological realism and selective perception (Ibid, pp. 13-28) and presents these problems through the works of various theoreticians. However, in the frame of this chapter, the issues will be simplified and presented in brief.

As to point of view, the perspective from which a story is told, some of the modes of points of view, which are available for an author of a novel, are not available for film. The first-person point of view in a novel does not have an equivalent mode in a film.

Another problem of moving from literary text to screen adaptation is the screen's limited ability to convey time. Literature has three tenses while the screen displays the present, a happening act and not its account.

Also, transferring symbols and metaphors from a literary text to the screen may be difficult. Language can be used in order to compare one thing to another, but it is impossible to transfer the precision of verbal image to a picture. Even when the viewer understands that a certain picture in a film implies a metaphor, the implications are not made in the picture itself. Similarly, symbols are a distinctive quality of the imagination.

As to perception, cinema presents a visual image while narrative literature presents a mental image. Visualizing something we read about is different from seeing it in a picture.

In fiction, a writer can address invisible psychological states of his characters, such as thoughts, memories, dreams and imagination, which may be difficult to do in a screen adaptation. For example, the film cannot show us thoughts and, if a thought is transferred to a picture, it is no longer a thought. The camera can show us appearances, but cannot show abstract concepts; it can show us a happy man but not "happiness." In narrative literature, explanation is linked to description, while in a film the explanation is often missing and is replaced by viewer inference.

Seymore Chatman asks "What Novels Can Do That Films Can't (and Vice Versa)." Chatman explains how the peculiarities of the novel and of film explain the striking differences between them in form-content and impact and compares the features of description and point of view of these two media. In a novel, when we read a description, the narrator asserts the details, the timeline of the story is interrupted and frozen, and events are stopped though our reading is continued. Film does not describe but rather depicts and renders in pictorial form; film presents a vast number of details, but the frames go by quickly and do not allow us to dwell on many of them. As to point of view in its perceptual sense, authors have greater range and flexibility than filmmakers because most novels and short stories are told through the voice of a narrator. The narrator does not have to account for his physical position — he may comment on the front, sides and back of a character, enter its body and describe it, all in the same glance. The filmmaker, by nature of his equipment, encounters restrictions with the visual point of view being fixed precisely because the camera is placed somewhere. Such limitations encourage artistic solutions.

The time needed for reading most novels is usually longer than the time needed for viewing most films. The individual reader of a novel can decide to take a break from reading, to skip ahead, or to repeat his reading and check back. While in films, there are no breaks and no opportunities to review what happened at earlier stages of the movie; the viewer is part of a group.

While the majority of issues in the literature/screen debate relate to "visualization" and apply to film and television, there are still some differences between the two visual media. The videocassette recording gives the viewer some of the flexibility that the reader enjoys: the viewer can pause at will and go forward and backward through the film.

The reader of a novel controls his linear progression in the book. In film, the words also follow each other, but the other elements come at the viewer simultaneously.

The films made from the literary works studied here were responsible for increasing the popularity or publicity of these literary works. This can be specifically illustrated by S. Yizhar's *Hirbet Hiz'ah*, which was part of the mandatory high school curricula in Israel and did not provoke public anger but, once it was screened, it generated a national debate.

When we view the films made from novels, which are presented in this study, it is important to remember that we bring to our viewing our preconceptions based on the novel, while a viewer who is not acquainted with the novel approaches it without its comparative value as an adaptation.

There are some common practices of the art of adaptation in the movies discussed in this study. As a general rule, the filmmakers have facilitated the scope of the literary works they adapted. Subplots and secondary characters were removed or reduced in order to present a simple, smooth plot, intensifying central characters in the fast pace of the film narrative. Through the linear succession of images, film depicts its themes and characters directly and quickly. For example, Haddasah, the protagonist's friend and a peripheral character in *My Michael*, was eliminated from the movie.

The sophisticated, rich metaphors and symbols of some stories are not presented well sometimes in movies. For example, much of the symbolic quality of the literary works is eliminated, such as the symbolism of the red cross in *Himmo King of Jerusalem*, of the thorn-cactus and the animals in *Three Days and a Child* and of the car in *The Lover*.

Sometimes the thematic aims of the films are different from their fictional literary counterparts. In *The Lover*, Yehoshua made a hard statement about the disintegrating Israeli society, the film lost the social-political depth and became a family melodrama. The Israeli-Palestinian problem was also lost. This movie can also illustrate a change in a character. In the movie, *The Lover*, Asya is depicted as a sensual woman, contrary to the novel. This was meant to be a device for attracting viewers.

BIBLIOGRAPHY

Almagor, Gila. *Under the Domim Tree* Traslated by Hillel Schenker. Simon & Schuster, School and Library Binding, 1995.

_____. *The Summer of Aviya*. Translated by Hillel Halkin. London, Collins, 1991.

Ben-Amoz , Dan. *Lo Sam Zayin*. Bitan, Tel-Aviv, 1973.

Ben-Shaul, S., Nitzan. *Mythical Expressions of Siege in Israeli Films*. Studies in Art and Religious Interpretation, Volume 17. The Edwin Melon Press, 1998.

Burshtein, Yigal. *Panim Kisdei Kerav: ha-Hisitoria ha-Kolno'it shel ha-Panim ha-Yisraeliyyim*. Hakkibutz Hameuchad, 1990.

Cohen, Bo'az. "Anashim Meshuga'im Anahnu." *Yediot Aharonot*, Sep. 10, 1999.

Gross, Natan and Ya'cov. *Ha-Seret ha-'Ivri: Perakim be-Toldot ha-Re'inoa' ve-ha-Kolnoa' be-Yisrael*. Published by the authors, Jerusalem, 1991.

Grossman, David. *Hiyyukh ha-Gedi*. Sifrei Siman Keri'ah, Hakkibutz Hemeuchad, 1983.

Halachmi, Yosef. *Vihi Ma: Perakim be-Divre Yemei ha-Seret ha-Arziyisraeli*. Steven Spielberg Jewish Film Archive, 1995. English excerpt: pp. III-VII.

Har'el, Yehuda. *Ha-Kolnoa' me-Reshito 'ad ha-Yom*. Yavne, 1956.

Hofshtein, Avner. "Dor Shalem Osei Kolnoa'." *Yediot Aharonot*, Sep. 10, 1999.

Ingbar, Nahman. "Tash'iru et *Tarantino* be-*Amereica*." *Yediot Aharonot*, Sep. 10, 1999.

Jacob-Arzooni, Ora Gloria, O.G.J. *The Israeli Film: Social and Cultural Influences, 1912-1973.* Garland, New York & London, 1983.

Kaniuk, Yoram. *Himmo, King of Jerusalem.* Translated by Yosef Schacter. Anthenum, New York, 1969.

Klausner, Margot. *Ta'siyyat ha-Halomot: 25 Shana le-Ulpane Hasrata be-Yisrael, Herz eliya (1949-1974)."*

Kronish, Amy. *World Cinema: Israel.* Fairleigh University Press, 1996.

Liberman (Livnei), Zvi. *'Oded ha-Noded.* Kuppat Sefer, 1932, Tel-Aviv.

Schnitzer, Meir. *Ha-Kolnoa' ha-Yisraeli: Kol ha-'Uvdot, Kol ha-'Alilot, Kol ha-Bamma'im ve-Gam Bikkoret.* Kinneret, 1994.

Schweitzer, Ariel. *Le Cine 'ma Israe 'lien de la Modernite'.* L'Harmattan, 1997.

Shamir, Moshe. *Hu Halakh ba-Sadot. Merhavia Sifriyyat Po'alim,* 1948.

Shir-Ran, Shaul, and Zimerman, Moshe. "Bereshit Haya ha-Re'inoa': Perek Rishon bi-Skira Mekuzeret 'al Toledot ha-Kolnoa' veha-Re'inoa be-Erez Yisrael." *Cinematheque,* No. 40, May/June, 1988, pp. 10-13.

Shohat, Ella. *Israeli Cinema: East/West and the Politics of Representation.* University of Texas Press, 1989.

Yehoshua, A.B. *Three Days and a Child.* Peter Owen, London, 1970.

The Lover. Translated by Phillip Simson. Doubleday & Co., Inc. Garden City, N.Y., 1978.

Yizhar, S. —. "The Story of *Hirbet Hiz'ah*." Tr. By Harold levy (a condensed version). In Sonntag, J., ed. *Caravan: a Jewish Quarterly Omnibus.* New York, Y. Yoseloff, ap62, pp. 328-334.

Zimerman, Moshe. "Aggadot ha-A'him Aggadati." *Cinematheque,* No. 42, Sep.-Oct, 1988, pp. 21-25.

_____. "Ha-Kolnoa' ha-'Ivri Lomed le-Dabber." *Cinematheque,* No. 41, July-August, 1988, pp. 14-18

_____. Ha-Kolnoa' ha-'Ivri: Shnot Periha." *Cinematheque,* No. 43, Nov.-Dec., 1988, pp. 28-31.

_____. "Kolnoa' 'Ivri la-Kis ve-Laregesh." *Cinematheque,* No. 48, July-Aug., 1989, pp. 25-27.

_____. "Kolnoa' Neged ha-Zerem." *Cinematheque,* No. 49, Sep.-Oct., 1989, 00. 28-30.

_____. "Lamma Axelrod? Perek Hamishi: 1936-1945." *Cinematheque,* No. 44, Jan.-Feb., 1989, pp. 20-24.

_____. "Tekufat ha-Mashber: 1936-1944." *Cinematheque,* No. 45, March-April, 1989, pp. 32-34.

_____. "Zipor ha-Hol." *Cinematheque,* No. 46, May-June, 1989, pp. 30-31.

Chapter 4

"WINTER GAMES"
BY YITZHAK BEN-NER

LIFE OF THE AUTHOR AND HIS
WORK IN ENGLISH

Yitzhak Ben-Ner was born in 1937 in a village called Kefar-Yehoshua in Israel, to a family of farmers After his military service, he studied literature and drama at Tel-Aviv University. He is an author of short stories and novels, a radio broadcaster, film critic, journalist and storyteller. Some of his works were adapted for film, television movies and stage. In 1981, he received the Agnon Prize.

Ben-Ner's literary work is realistic. It allots a special attention to realistic details of various settings. Some of his characters and settings are tragicomic and bizarre. The main characters are often isolated and solitary; they confront a historical situation with pain, love, honesty and bravery.

Ben-Ner's first book was published in 1967 when the works of authors such as A.B.Yehoshua, Yoram Kaniuk and Amos Oz were known, including their non-realistic expressions. Ben-Ner's first book was the novella *Ha-Ish mi-Sham* (translated as *The Man from There)*, a story about a young Israeli who returned wounded from Egypt when the War of Independence began. He was stuck in an Arab border town and was taken in by an enlightened Arab physician. After this novella, Ben-Ner published two volumes of short stories: *Sheki'a Kafrit* in 1976 (translated as *Rustic Sunset and Other Stories)* and *Aharei ha-Geshem* ("After the Rain") in 1979. In *Aharei ha-Geshem* ("After the Rain"),

Ben-Ner included three stories; the three main characters of these stories have a feeling of the coming end, but they do not submit to it. Ben-Ner's *Erez Rehoka* ("A Distant Land") was published in 1983; it includes six stories about Israelis that together make a novel set mainly in 1977-1979. In the 1986 *Protocol*, the Zionist establishment confronts Anti-Zionists Communists. In 1987, Ben-Ner published *Mal'akhim Ba'im* ("The Angels are Coming") about Israeli reality, with its violence, suspicions and estrangement and its Orthodox Jews and their power. It is a sophisticated, sad and funny parody that has both realistic and fantastic elements. Ben-Ner's 1990 *Ta'atu'on* ("A Little Delusion") is a novel composed of four different monologues of four Israeli men that were thrown into complicated events in Israel (The *Intifida,* the name of the Palestinian revolt which broke at the end of 1987). Sometimes they contradict each other, and sometimes they supplement each other.

Ben-Ner's realistic stories are strongly attached to Israel. Often the places are geographically ascertainable and the times and the events are known from the history and the daily life of Israel, which yields authenticity to the literary works. Through various literary devices, Ben-Ner prevents his stories from becoming non-fiction and mere reportage. The individual characters are independent thinkers, and their feelings and philosophy about the national and private arena are individualistic.

Rustic Sunset includes eight stories that Ben-Ner wrote after the Six Days War in 1967 until 1976. Not only "Winter Games," but also the other stories in *Rustic Sunset* are strongly connected to their time and place. "Nicol" and "Eighteen Months" relate to the Yom Kippur War of 1973. In "Winter Games," the place is a village near Haifa and Haifa itself. The time is that of the British Mandate with the Jewish underground. The story mentions specific, well-known locations: the radar in the Stella Maris army camp (p.11) and the Jeleme Checkpoint (p. 12), the oil refineries of Haifa (p. 11) and the petroleum camp (p. 12).

Ben-Ner stated that what motivated him to write "was in the first place the core of the plot" (Oren). Ben-Ner emphasized his desire to present a compelling plot. If morals and ideas would also be an inseparable, non-prominent part of the plot, it was acceptable to him. He was not interested in literary theories. After one year of literary academic studies, he left the university because he felt that interesting literary works became boring when analyzed in the lectures halls (Gutkind, 1977).

Like many other literary works of Ben-Ner, the dominating sentiment in "Winter Games" is sadness. Like many of these works it is

written as a monologue in which the narrator is a witness and a participant. His style discloses his character as much as his acts do and, like
other characters in these works, the narrator is a unique person with
unique views when confronting tragedies and death (Shaked, 1998) that
he cannot prevent.

Through the eyes of the perceptive boy, the Yemenite is central to
the story, while Yemenite Jews are not central in the Zionist history. The
author brings the unrecognized Yemenite to the center of the story from
the margin of history, contrary to the attitude toward him by the villagers
and by the Zionist history. The official Zionist story is questioned without
an explicit protest, for its lack of credit to Sephardi Jews who were central
to some of the needs and actions of Zionism but who were pushed to the
margin of the Zionist tale. The big hero in "Winter Games" is not
Starkman but the Yemenite.

Robert Weitehill thinks that in Ben-Ner's stories, the situations and
characters are "often bizarre, always real, with sensuous portrayals of
sexuality and honest presentations of love, of dying, of day-to-day living"
(Ben-Ner, *Rustic*, p. 1).

Ben-Ner's books in English translation are: *A Man From There*
(Sabra Books, 1969), *Rustic Sunset and Other Stories* (Lynne Reiner
Publishers, 1998). *A Man From There* was also translated into French and
Japanese.

THE PLOT

"Winter Games" is one of several of Ben-Ner's stories that are
linked to the Israeli wars. It relates to one of the underground movements
at the time of the Mandatory regime in Palestine. It takes place mainly in
a village that is apparently close to Haifa, the city in which part of the
story takes place. The loud boom from the direction of Haifa sounded in
the village, and the villagers could clearly see the "large mushroom of
smoke and dust" (p. 10). The location is well known and non-fictitious:
Haifa, the well known of Haifa (p. 11) and the petroleum camp (p. 12).
The hatred of the members of the underground, as well as the explosion,
correlates with facts.

"Winter Games" is a story of a human crisis and what it generates.
Death is a central experience in the literary works of Ben-Ner and, in
"Winter Games," witnessing the death of the Yemenite was a major life
experience for the narrator.

A young Yemenite man was a member of the LEHI (Lohmei Herut Yisrael, Fighters for the Freedom of Israel), one of the underground movements at the end of the Mandatory regime in Palestine. He came to the village where the narrator lived as an 11-year-old boy. The Yemenite was found with the 15-year-old daughter of one of the village inhabitants while she was in her underwear. She was battered and bruised, and the Yemenite was smuggled out of the village. At a later point, the narrator found the Yemenite again in the village. One day there was a big explosion in Haifa and, afterwards, the narrator found the Yemenite wounded at the back of his barn, in the strewn and rotting straw. The narrator tried to help the Yemenite young man by offering him food, visiting him, not telling anyone about him (so that the Yemenite will not end up at the mercy of the British soldiers) and bandaging him. When all this did not help, he solicited the help of the girl with whom the Yemenite was found. She came and stripped the Yemenite, tore her own dress, and cleaned his panting, sang him a song, embraced him, clung to him tightly, moved up over him and on him to bring warmth to his torn body. Nevertheless, he died. The narrator and the girl lifted him into a wagon and laid his body in a ditch.

THE NARRATOR AND HIS
POINT OF VIEW

The events took place when the narrator was 11. At the time he tells the story, he is an adult. The reader encounters the question from what point of view is the story told — the narrator as a boy or as a grown-up man? What style is employed in the story — that of a boy or a grown-up man?

The ability of the first-person adult, experienced, perspective narrator to emotionally identify with his feelings and views as a child prevents treating any of the events in a belittling manner.

"That winter, in January, my brother had a bitter quarrel with Father, but I can't remember what it was about" (p. 5) - the opening sentence makes it clear that the event happened in the past, possibly a very long time ago. It is "that winter," which took place in the past, and the narrator forgot the subject matter of the bitter quarrel in his family. "I was eleven then," (p. 8) he mentions to us when he describes his angry, impulsive acts against Starkman (p. 8). "My father was a good man. Tall. I remember him well now — tanned and thin" (p. 22). The style is of memoirs, relating to self-history, not to the present. "In the flickering yellow light, the wounded man opened his eyes and groaned in a voice that I still hear to this day" (p. 24) — the long time that passed since it happened is evidence of the deep imprint the groaning made on him.

The narrator is aware of the implications of his age and remembers how, as a child, he was sometimes sensitive to it. This happened, for example, when he asked Adina about her relationships with the Yemeni and with the Yemeni's friend, and Adina responded: "What do you care, little boy?" and later: "How old are you, anyway?" Attracted by her, he lied to her: "Thirteen, pretty soon" (p. 24). "I was a child to them, and they didn't answer" (p. 19), perhaps his self-perception was different from the way he was perceived by his neighbors who did not answer his question. When he tried to persuade his older brother to rest for one day after the explosion, he described himself as "being as mature as I could be" (p.15).

Referring to the narrator's age points out the gap in years between the time of the telling about the events and the time they happened. While in some parts of the story the point of view is that of the child, in other parts the point of view is from the perspective of the adult narrator. "One man's success is always another man's failure" (p. 9), he tells the reader in summation, using epigrammatic language. And than he proceeds to tell us how his brother's success at work, by his doing the work of two Arabs, was the failure of two Arabs who were dismissed from their work and the beat up his brother. In another instance, the narrator presents the direct speech between his father and Menashe (p. 15). The father said: "Leave him alone today... it's better for him to rest" (Ibid.). Then the narrator adds in a perspective, explanatory way: "My father had the habit of talking with the Sephardim in their own way and with the others in their own way." This sentence, which clearly takes us from the time of the direct speech to the time of telling about it and adding a comment is indicative of perspective point of view and was omitted from the translation.

If the narrator thought at a certain point that the 29-year-old, single Starkman "was in heat and had gone out to the whores in Haifa" (p. 7), later he learned that Starkman indeed went to Haifa for his underground activity.

In most parts of the story, the style is not of an 11-year-old child, but when a direct speech is presented, the style, the rhythm, intonation and the content are representative of the boy's age. To a large extent, this is preserved in the translation. "You're one lousy prick!" — he said to Starkman after Starkman shot the mule. "I wish *you* were sunk up to your ass in mud and they were shooting you! I wish!" (p. 8). At home, still outraged at Starkman, the narrator said to his father: "You will break his head, Papa. Right? You'll break that lousy murderer Starkman's head. Right, Papa? Right?" (p. 8). The emotional style, with its repetitions and questions, joins the childish wishes.

The narrator's father is aware of style nuances, and the narrative was aware of this. "My father was accustomed to speak with the Sephardim their ways and with the other their way" he tells us after his father asked Menashe to let his son rest that day. The style of the monologues and of the dialogues strives to be representative of the characters.

The direct speech revitalizes the past by presenting it in a present tense; it dramatizes the conflicts and other emotionally intense moments, and explicates the boy's world. The dialogue is mimetic in its level of style; the spoken Hebrew expresses the character and is part of the characteristics of the realism in the work of Ben-Ner.

THE VILLAGE

The story takes place mainly in an Israeli village before 1948. The story is clearly set before 1948 in Israel, and it does not support the romantic view of united Jews who are guarantors (responsible) for one another, not even the myth of fighter's comradeship.

Whitehill writes the following about the setting of Ben-Ner stories (Ibid.):

> Setting is the core strength of Ben-Ner's stories. His charac-
> ters are convincing, tragicomic figures. His plots, ostensibly
> a series of independent incidents, are unified and strong, yet
> artistically subtle. The movement is fast; the dialogue,
> controversial and reflective of various social and ethnic
> groups. Still, setting is the supreme factor...

The title of the book in which the story is included is "Rustic Sunset" (the Hebrew title is *Sheki'a Kafrit*). The sun setting may lead the reader to expect a description of beauty of nature, but the Hebrew word "sheki'a" is not only sunset, it also means sinking, decline, decadence, degeneration and all these terms may correctly apply to the described village. The rural decadence refers to the villager's apathy, men and women, young and old alike. Their lives are dominated by the absence of a chance for loving relationships and the absence of self-dignity and hope.

The village ambiance is of decay, evil, old age, suffocation and death. It is a village of "lost souls" (p. 13). The realistic descriptions of the village reflect Ben-Ner's style — it is not a style, which strives for beauty and attention for itself independently, but it is a carefully selected style that serves to advance the story. The story is realistic, yet the village is not identified by specific external details that correspond with any specific village in Israel. Throughout the course of the plot we find, however, clear realistic objects illustrating the life at that time in Israel. For example, the narrator's father loaded his milk pails onto his little cart, hitched his donkey to the cart and went to sell milk (p. 10, 15). This is how milk was sold in Israel in the fifties, too (sometimes with tricycles instead of a cart). In the morning, the father prepared "chicory coffee on the burner" (p. 10, the Hebrew word is "petiliyya" in the original story, a "kerosene cooking stove"). The Yemeni had a crumpled pack of cheap Maspero cigarettes in their soft box in his pocket (p. 24).

The reader becomes acquainted with the condition of the village already in the second paragraph of the story: A barn with cracked tin walls, moldy and rotten fodder and heat of aging (p. 5).

We learn something about the medical, educational and transportation services in the village. The doctor comes only on Thursdays and one of the villagers serves as a nurse (p. 18). The two schoolteachers did not come to teach, because the village payment for the teachers did not arrive and also because someone wrote on the board "Mania the Maniac" about the teacher Mania. The male teacher did not return because he was beaten up, and those who beat him were not punished. What caused them to stop teaching may suffice to explain the educational qualities. In the destroyed classroom there are now bird droppings. The children cannot be acquainted with the world anymore, "the world map was torn to shreds," now they can only "learn" from the village life, and strong rain cut the village off from the rest of the world (p. 16).

It is an "accursed village" (p. 6, 16), a village with few cows and thus, according to the narrator's father, its "last breath was gone from its lungs, doomed to chock to death" (p. 10). "There were always lots of sick people" (p. 11) in the village, "whose twenty years of life had been twenty years of old age" (p. 6). Many of the young men and of the farmers left the aging village (p. 7, 16), and many of those who stayed left their agricultural work for day work in Haifa (p. 6). Unlike them, Niasi came from the city to the village to make a living from sickness and death. He bought sick fowl at a low price so that he could slaughter it and sell it (p.16).

Physical abuse seems to be part of the lifestyle. When Adina was found with the Yemeni and his roommate in her underwear, half of the boys of the village "demanded their blood" (p. 6); they were beaten up and bruised. One of the teachers was beaten up (p. 15). Women threatened Starkman, and his mother burst into their circle and struck them (p. 11). The narrator and Starkman exchange blows with each other (p. 8), Mrs. Dvash hit her filthy rioters' children (p. 13) — to mention some examples. Ben-Melilla is a "giver" — he gave the narrator sweet toast that tasted terrible and laughed when the galled boy threw the bread at his window (p. 13).

In a village such as this, love brings pain and, only when one completely disregards the societal attitude and its possible outcome, may love provide some relative relief. This is demonstrated in Adina's loving acts at the end of the story. The girl's emotional and social maturity, her courage, love and compassion disregard the people around her: "I don't care what everyone says" (p. 23), she tells the narrator, "the village ought to be burned, or all the people here ought to drown in a flood — all of them." The drowning/clean-up wish was somehow granted at the end of the story with the heavy rain. She risked her life and exposed her reputation to further damage when she did not give into the villagers' attitude, but she followed her heart.

The Yemenite is a tragic character; he sacrificed his life for those from whom he had to hide, whom he did not trust that they would try to keep him alive. Many did not appreciate his unconditional and unqualified dedication to his people, but this did not discourage him because of his strong values and beliefs, which were not contingent upon any expectation of a reward or recognition. The Yemenite's name is unknown. He is the anonymous soldier.

The first part of story describes the return of the Yemenite to the village, while the narrator remembers the details of the killing of the mule by Starkman and what happened afterwards. This structure may allude to the Yemenite's destiny. Starkman is heavily involved in the killing of the mule and in the death of the Yemenite. He killed the mule and refused to give any help to the Yemenite even though he was the last hope for saving the Yemenite's life. The ironic name of the mule — Chaya — (Hebrew: life, spirit of life, alive) only makes death more perceptible. The sequence of the story encourages connecting the death of the mule with the Yemeni. The narrator describes the vultures pecking holes in the mule's carcass, and his naturalistic description focuses on its swollen belly and the "creaky breath issue from the oozing, swollen body" (p. 16). He now discovers the Yemeni "gasping to breath" (Ibid.), "his head half-buried in the ground" (p. 17). From now on additional animals will be connected with the Yemeni's death: a headless body of a chicken after her head was cut off, sick cows, torn apart chickens (Ibid.), wounded cows (p. 18) and a wounded mongoose (pp. 17, 19).

Like the mule in the story that was shot when it was helpless and stopped being of a benefit, the Yemenite, too, is buried in an unknown place once his service to his people ended.

Fear dominates many characters in the story. The villagers are insecure and do not trust the people around them. The Yemeni is afraid to have the boy seeking medical help for him. Starkman tells the boy, who came to ask him to help the Yemenite, his fellow in the Lehi: "Everybody's out there to ambush me" (p. 22), because "they are all traitors and quislings here" (p. 21). The boy concludes: "All you freedom fighters are more afraid of each other than you are of the British" (Ibid.). Risking life for the same worthwhile cause does not guarantee comradeship. Similar fear and suspicious attitudes characterize other people in the village, "our accursed village" (p. 16).

Similar to the Yemeni, Starkman risked his life for the Jewish people but, when he comes back from Haifa injured and shaking, he is called "Polack pig" (p. 12) and surrounded by hate.

The people of the village are busy with gossip, slandering and disparaging each other, being angry at each other. "In our village everyone quarreled with everyone about everything" (p. 5), we are told in the second sentence of the story. "The last elections had been without result, due to the quarrels between the Sephardim and the non-Sephardim and everyone else" (p. 14) — the narrator tells us ("and everyone else" is the translation of the Hebrew "and between the Sephardim and themselves and the non-Sephardim and themselves").

"Stories were told about everyone in the village" (p. 6). People were victims of rumors and in the absence of social compassion and responsibility they were degraded. "All the people of the village were always angry when they spoke about their friends" — we are told in a sentence that was omitted from the translation (p. 7). "The village boys had called him 'Yemeni' derisively" (p. 5) — perhaps because of his origins. The village guys spoke about the Yemeni and his roommate "with scorn, and rumors circulated" (p. 6). The villagers called Adina's mother "an Arab," "due to the rumor she used to lock herself in the house" (p. 23) and the boys called Adina "Arab whore" (Ibid.). About Starkman, "the village boys said in ridicule that he was in heat and had gone out to the whores in Haifa" (p. 7) even though the rumor did not make any sense (see p. 9, he went for a whole month). The villagers called the Sephardi boys of the Dvash ("Dvash" in Hebrew means honey) family "Dvashits" (p. 13, "Drashits" is a printing error) when they saw the boys going on Saturday morning with their father to the synagogue "with their weekday clothes still wet from the wash" (Ibid.). This is not a praiseworthy attitude toward poor children, making efforts to appear in the synagogue neatly, out of respect for the synagogue and Saturday.

The village and its people represent the reality that will lead to a troubled Jewish national existence in Israel, devoid of any positive promise for the future of Zionism.

LITERARY DEVICES

Ben-Ner strives to tell a story that is, in the first place, enthralling and its ideas and in which morals are of secondary importance. In one of his interviews he said:

> I want very much to be a storyteller more than an author. I want to tell an interesting story, to be a 'story teller', like a Medieval Troubadour who can gather around him the local people and to mesmerize them with bygone plots and deeds, and if while doing that philosophical and moralistic ideas are formed and are interwoven — this is fine, on the condition that they become an essential, inseparable, non-conspicuous part of the story itself (Gutkind, 1977).

In "Winter Games," we may find many virtuous ideas, but the story is not structured to give them a dominating place. It is a story of courage, love, crisis, conflicts, compassion, fear and death. The British-Jewish conflict, the deterioration of Jewish brotherhood, the deterioration of the fulfillment of Zionist-pioneering agricultural ideas are all in the story, but not central to it. The narrator's attraction to Lehi, which was considered a more extreme underground organization than some other ones, is not well-founded ideologically, but merely a childish attraction to the heroic-romantic. He even misspells the name of the organization and writes it on the walls as "Fighters freedom of Israel" (Hebrew: "lohamim herut yisrael," the English translation on p. 13, "LEHI-ISRAEL FREEDOM FIGHTERS" does not reflect the child's delightful and smile evoking misspelling).

This is a story told in first person from the boy-narrator's subjective point of view. The boy is a reliable narrator. He tells his story with a restrained tone, sometimes passionate; he is one of the characters in the story, a witness and a participant.

The narrator tells the reader of his experience, impressions, feelings and thoughts. He does not look down on his reader and does not use a high style that distinguishes him from the reader. He does not admonish him, and does not make ethical demands of him (Barzel, 1979, pp. 11-17).

The language is unequivocal and unambiguous. The reader is engaged with the indifference, love, sacrifice and death story. One situation causes the other, and the various situations portray the human souls going through emotional experiences. Even when there is some scolding (the narrator scolds for example Starkman, "you're a fucking coward!... You're a disgrace to this lousy village," p. 22), the scolding is not central to the story and does not come from a moralistic authority that is higher than the reader. This is accomplished by the age of the narrator and by his cussing style. In this way the narrator continues to engage the reader in the plot without separating and distinguishing himself from the reader.

Sometimes, without any transition, the narrator's style shifts to a high-poetic style, with Biblical allusions, and the point of view becomes authoritative and experienced. One can read these paragraphs as narrated by the implied author only, or by both the boy and the implied narrator.

For example, the last paragraph of the story is told in a high, dramatic, poetic style, dominated by Biblical allusions. It describes the morning after burying the Yemeni:

> The next morning the heavens poured down heavy rain the likes of which had not been seen since the birth of this accursed village. The entire valley becomes a lake. The water rose and increased upon the land and our village was closed and shut in; no one went out, and no one came in, forty days and forty nights. And then came spring (p. 26).

One may read this paragraph as the voice of the implied narrator, or as his voice, combined together with the voice of the boy. Either way, the point of view, the authority of the speaking voice, is higher than that of the 11-year-old boy and enriches it. As in many other emotional-dramatic situations, in this situation, too, Ben-Ner employs Biblical allusions. The words "the likes of which had not been" (the word "seen" is not in the original Hebrew text of Ben-Ner's story), describing the heavy rain in the village, reminds us of the hail, which was one of the plagues on Egypt, hail "of which had not been" in Egypt (*Exodus* 9, 18, and 24). The rain in the "accursed village" was a plague, not a blessing; it may allude to the sins of its people. The water rose, and the village was closed "forty days and forty nights." The punishments (plague of hail, flood) of the sinners in both Biblical cases are diverted to the punishment of the village people. The 40 days and 40 nights of heavy rain on the village are not a reminder of those 40 days in which the Lord gave Moses the two tables of the covenant (*Deuteronomy* 9,9) for his chosen people, but 40 days and 40 nights of the flood destruction. During the flood (*Genesis* 6), "the water rose and increased upon the land…forty days and forty nights" — the allusion to the flood story with its sin and destructive punishment is clear (*Genesis* 7, 4; and 7, 18). The words in Ben-Ner's story describing the village in Hebrew are the precise words describing Jericho: "Now Jericho was straightly shut up" (*Joshua* 6, 1), translated in our story as "closed and shut in." The Biblical story again tells the story of the fall of Jericho, which was given by the Lord to the Hebrews, now, ironically, the Jewish village, is under the same siege.

The story has very little dialogue, and demonstrates critical points and feelings.

Adina plays the role of a woman and a mother with the Yemeni. "She sang him a song with words I could not make out; maybe her mother had taught it to her on some rainy night two centuries ago" (p. 25). The womanhood, femininity, motherhood, go from one generation to another; they are never old and the world needs them at its hardest moments. The words are not important. "mmmlll…" whispered the Yemeni (p. 25) and the girl interpreted it as "now," with her womanly instincts she knows he is calling for her, and the time is running out. Like prophets in the Bible, she is willing to give him everything she has — only this way her expression of love is complete. The entranced boy, witnessing the "desolate mirage" (p. 25) of the bodily contact of the girl and the hero also noticed how death, love and smile can be united when he notices the smile appearing on the sealed lips of the Yemeni.

One may read the end of the story as expressing reconciliation and resolution after the loss (Shaked, p. 428). The last sentence of the story is: "And then came Spring" (p. 26). Life went on; the village was resurrected. It seems to me however that the message is that the spring came and the Yemenite was forgotten. The spring is only a dramatic reminder of the unappreciated and forgotten life sacrificed by those who were marginal to the Zionist establishment. In other literary works, Ben-Ner also disapproved of injustice in Israeli society.

The hero that sacrificed his life did not even receive a dignified, traditional Jewish burial. He was not brought to a Jewish graveyard, and his place of burial is unknown; he is forgotten from national memory. He was buried somewhere in a ditch, out of a Jewish cemetery. Only the heavy rain was a cry and mourning for him, the rain being a punishment of a society that does not even dignify some of its heroes who give their life for it.

While Eros and death are the climax of the story at its end, the girl makes sure to instill the power of love and life in the narrator-boy: "She touched me, and I was startled. She was quiet in the darkness, and her hand passed through my hair" (p. 25). Both of them are united with the secret of the Yemenite's terrorism, injury and death. Both of them provided him with care and trustworthiness.

THE MOVIE

Director: Ram Levy. Producer: Barukh Abuluf. Script: Dita Gerry, Meir Doron, Gil'ad 'Evron, Ram Levy (literary adaptation. Based on Yitzhak Ben-Ner's story). Photography: Yehiel Cohen. Editing: 'Era Lappid. Cast: Gal Yohas, Moshe 'Ibgi, Konstantin Anatol, Dov Navon, Rae Roz, Mani Savir, Ruth Geller, Tuvia Gelber, Arie Elias, Yig'al Na'or, Yasha Einshtein, Varda Ben-Hur, Yaniv Bishari, Tom Carmi, Edi Mukhtar, Mike Altman, Yehuda Cohen, Nahum Shallit, Ania Buguslava, Zipi Sobol, Rahel Amran, Shula Ben-Moshe, Josh Ivin, Amiram Bukshpan. 1988, The Israeli TV. Color. 90 minutes.

Eli (Gal Yohas) as the narrator-child, and the Yemenite (Moshe Ibgi) are the two characters who play the major and most touching roles in the movie. Moshe Ibgi starred other Israeli movies: *Cup Final, Bread, Night Movie, Big Shots, Shuru, Max and Morris, the revenge of Itsik*

Finkelstein, Dreams of Innocence and *Lovesick on Nana' Street* Additional characters in the movie are Eli's father the wise Mr. Weiss (Konstantin Anatol); Eli's older brother Yig'al (Dov Navon, acting also as Asa in *Himmo, King of Jerusalem*); the romantic, seductive and mischievous Adina Hadari (Rae Roz); and her devoted father Mr. Hadari (Mani Savir); the bitter, loving, frustrated and strong Mrs. Starkman (Ruth Geller); and her son (Tuvia Gelber); Niasi (Arie Elias), who made his living by buying and selling sick fowl and whose role is expanded in comparison with the story; Menashe Menashe (Yig'al N'aor) as the Sephardi employer of Yig'al; Mrs. Dvash (Varda Ben-Hur-Elbaz), whose role is also expanded in comparison with the story and two of her children, Tshayik Dvash (Yaniv Bishari) and Beni Dvash (Tom Carmi); and some other villagers, such as Mr. Babayof (Edi Mukhtar); Mr. Cohen (Yehuda Cohen); the village policeman (Nahum Shallit); Mr. Pen, the village storekeeper who was responsible for the affairs of the town (Yasha Einshtein); and British Officers (Mike Altman, Josh Ivin, Amiram Bukshpan); as well as other characters. Ram Levy, the director, was also the director of *Hirbet Hiz'ah*.

In "Winter Games" themes such as trust, love, kindness, altruism and heroism are contrasted in the movie with themes such as betrayal, hostility, heartlessness, egoism and cowardice.

We are exposed to the neglected, rundown village, which the movie specified to be near Haifa in 1946. Brown areas of dry shrubs appear time and again. The village represents the despair of the villagers and their bad relationships with each other, their lack of energy and their indifference to their place of residence.

The houses inside and outside are also neglected, rundown, without any attention to aesthetics, and with an emphasis put on survival.

The verbal communication is informative, non-emotional, often lacking warmth and softness. Poverty can be blamed, but the movie takes even this excuse away. An Arab father passes through the village with his little boy on his humble carriage. They too appear to be poor, but there is love, harmony, pride, tenderness and trust between the two. The Arab child can experience the essence of childhood in spite of his poverty, while the Jewish village children seem to be deprived of childhood. Starkman's mother is domineering and castrating and, only when Starkman comes back from Haifa, can she show him in one sentence her care and love.

Only a few times, for a short while, happy sights accompany happy moments in the village. Such moments are Eli's first moments of milk-selling and Adina's memory of the Yemenite when Eli teased her about it. The music is jolly, and the fields are full of freshness and colors. Another happy moment is when Yig'al returns to work at the side of his father. In these moments the photography captures the beauty of a colorful blossoming nature, and they only make the strongly dominant atmosphere more painful.

The photography grasps details of nature that shape our mood: first rain drops fall on a dry stone; cows are deep in mud; endless fields of poppies; birds flying from a coming storm; lush green fields and mountains surround a grave; a wounded, old mule is taking its last steps on this earth, while the last showers of life spewing from her breath; winter flies soaring and circling the mule's dead body; birds circle above it.

In the movie we hear various languages used by the villagers — among them are Hebrew, Yiddish, English; these languages are not instrumental in improving the communication among the villagers but are evidence and illustrations of the separation and estrangement among them. The same is true about silence in the movie; it is not the expression of mutual human understanding that does not require words, but rather the expression of loneliness.

Young and old in the village are busy with quarrels. The characters lead lonely lives; only rarely do we see some unity, but even this unity represents hostility and lack of brotherhood. For example, men are united in a violent whipping of the Yemenite, and men and women are about to attack Starkman when he comes back from Haifa after the explosion.

The movie modifies Ben-Ner's story. The modifications are not substantial, and they do not change the messages, ideas, relationships and the main stream of the plot. Some of the modifications are humorous; others tighten the plot and strive to sharply exhibit the characters, their situations and relationships. Some of these modifications of the original story will be briefly presented, and I will refer to some more in the presentation of the movie plot. The changes of Ben-Ner's story can be described objectively, while the effects on the viewer are subjective.

Mr. Dvash in the movie disappeared, and Mrs. Dvash seeks intimacy with the narrator's father. While in Ben-Ner's story, her husband is around (p. 13); he takes his children to the Sephardi synagogue on Saturday and goes to Haifa to look for his son. The modification of this situation makes possible some amusing and possibly somehow erotic scenes related to Mrs. Dvash.

In Ben-Ner's story, the narrator does not know the spelling of the Lehi underground organization; the movie takes the error further: The narrator spelled the underground name as "Lekhi — fighters freedom of Israel." "Lekhi" means "go away" (second person feminine singular imperative), as if the narrator demands that the underground organization he admires go away — all because of the lack of education in the village...

In Ben-Ner's story, a British officer appeared and stopped in the front of the grocery store, went to see the storekeeper Pen, left him quickly and returned to his Land Rover and moved along the mud patch (p. 14). This becomes a long scene in the movie — the officer dances, breaks and smashes groceries with his shoes. He begins with a cheerful dancing to the sound of music; the spectators of the dance enjoy the dance, but soon, when the destructive dancing steps begin, it becomes clear that encouraging the audience was a misleading device that meant only to shock and sadden it afterwards. Children are exposed to horror and helplessness — the child attempting to follow the dance of the officer is a touching reflection of the poverty, hunger for joy and contrast between the destructive, cruel, shiny officer to the poor helpless childhood stuck in mud.

Niasi's role is expanded in the movie in comparison with the story. The veteran actor Arie Elias as Niasi is involved in some scenes and dialogues that were not in the story. His work, his views of the village, his clothes and his odor deject.

Another change of Ben-Ner's story is the narrator's bringing the gun of the Yemenite to Starkman when he asks him to help the wounded Yemenite. Starkman does not know where to hide the gun and refuses to help. He is exposed with his cowardice, lack of comradeship, bravery, maturity and resourcefulness. This change only increases our sympathy for the Yemenite. In Ben-Ner's story, the narrator's father made the rounds among the village houses to sell milk after his older son, Yig'al, went to work in Haifa. In the movie, Eli did that once, giving us an opportunity to see Eli's friends and to witness little Eli being deceived by a villager, Mr. Cohen, who paid only half-price for the milk he bought.

In the story, it was Weiss who grabbed Starkman "by the collar, as if threatening to wrench the truth out of him" (p. 11) after the explosion. In the movie, the father remains a moderate man.

The movie, unlike Ben-Ner's story, presents the events in an easy-to-follow, chronological order. For example, only after about 50 minutes into the movie are we at the point of the beginning of the written story: we see the Yemenite on his way to the village after he was battered and chased out of it, and he meets the narrator near the corpse of the mule.

The movie begins with the tense, dramatic, introductory scene. There was arson in the village, which could spread out and burn down the villagers' property. It was an act of the Jewish underground. This fire is not in Ben-Ner's story, and it takes a little less than 10 minutes in the movie. This scene sets an emotional situation in motion that displays the relationship of the Jews with the British and the relationships among the Jews themselves.

Soon the British soldiers arrive; they treat the villagers brutally, and men and woman, young and old receive the same rough treatment. The absence of harmony between the villagers is exposed already in this scene when Starkman asked the Jewish guard appointed by the British to sit in the village police office who called the British, and he received from the Jewish guard, Ezra Pardo, an evasive answer.

The fire is still on, while the sex element is introduced to the movie and added to Ben-Ner's story: a British soldier entered the hiding place of the Yemenite where Adina and Eli were, too. The soldier urinates and seems to be concentrating on his pleasure while looking at Adina, who responds to him with a flirting smile. The flirt charms the soldier; he forgets his search, leaves satisfied, and this is how he forgot to look for the Yemenite.

We soon are introduced to Mrs. Dvash. The day is nice, the birds sing, the radio broadcasts happy English songs. Mrs. Dvash is cleaning the floor with a rag and, of course, missing the pole that holds it, which forces her to bend down while sweeping the floor. She cutely dances her substantial rear end to the fast jolly rhythm of the song. Now we hear from her more about the villagers when she talks to Eli, and she shatters the myth of the Israeli hero when she says that the men in the village are not men at all, but the man who set the fire is a man.

Another scene hits us: Starkman asks his mother to give him the hammer so that he will do a man's job, but his mother refuses to do so because she doubts his skills. (It is ironic that his name is "Starkman," which means "strong man.") A physical struggle ensues between the two — another addition to Ben-Ner's story — and the son prevails. The struggle is long and disrespectful of the mother as a woman, a mother and an old person. He soon injures his finger in the presence of his loving, bitter, frustrated and offensive widow mother. The second generation was not made for farming.

Starkman's lack of interest in farm life and the existing generation gap will be expanded in other scenes. Yig'al, Eli's brother, wants to find work outside the village like other young villagers did, because he has nothing to do in the village. His negative views of the village will be expanded in other scenes.

The scene of killing the mule is faithful to the original. Starkman does not have the maturity to understand the trauma of the little boy, Eli, at the sight of the killing, and he reacts to him without any sympathy.

The movie sharpens the comparison between the Yemenite and Starkman. Contrary to the Zionist myth, it is the Yemenite who is courageous, charismatic, innovative and wise, while Starkman is problematic. In a meeting between the two, the Yemenite tells Starkman that his activity is problematic — "it is not good Starkman, before it was the fire and now it is your mother" — referring to Starkman's knowledge of the Yemenite. Starkman's gun is old, and he needs another one, "everything is hard with you Starkman," the Yemenite tells him. When Eli is found in the room — Starkman panicked, but the Yemenite is charismatic and calm. The movie accents the predominance of the Yemenite over Starkman, the Sephardi over the Ashkenazi, contrary to the way the Zionist story is told. The implied author protests the marginal role given to the Sephardi Jews in the struggle for the State of Israel; the marginal Yemenite becomes central and the traditionally central Starkman is questioned as to both abilities and comradeship.

Except Adina and the Yemenite's loving acts, the movie, like the story, does not present much tenderness and love between the genders. One meeting between Adina and the Yemenite ended with the clubbing of the Yemenite and expelling him from the village and another one ended with his death. Eros does not have proper ground to prosper when there are wars, hatred and fear. In the movie, Mrs. Dvash's attempts to seduce Mr. Weiss and to pursue him are also futile.

Mrs. Dvash has an expanded role in the movie; she is wise, strong, direct, courageous and yet motherly. Mr. Weiss is decent, ethical, clever, responsible and correct, but only rarely does he demonstrate compassion.

Seeing his bitten and bruised brother enraged Eli. When Eli went to ask for revenge through the Yemenite, the Yemenite tells him to never seek his help and to conduct himself by the rule that they do not know each other. Eli sees, in the meantime, Adina partially naked and hears her cry. He is humiliated twice. This situation or Adina's father's intent to call the British and tell them about the disappearance of his daughter, or both of these, explain why Eli was the informant, who divulged where the Yemenite was. Ben-Ner's story does not tell us that the narrator disclosed where Adina was; in the movie he is the tattletale and the above humiliations are the cause.

The scene of hitting the Yemenite is relatively long. It is a protest of how sometimes the old settlers treated their most dedicated heroes but, due to their idealistic views, these heroes did not change their devotion. The words "kill him," the spitting, the Hebrew and Yiddish negative exclamations, Starkman's silence at the sight of his brutalized friend, all these only reinforce the implied statement about hatred in the village.

Adina is mostly courageous, loving and ethical when, amidst all the hostility and battering, she screams that the Yemenite is not guilty. This is an addition to the movie and makes her character standing even taller among the people of her village.

In another scene, a Yiddish-speaking villager complains to Weiss that they will cry for a hundred years because the terrorists will cause the British to leave Palestine and they — meaning the Ashkenazim — will end up being with the "wild animals," which was a common way of describing the Sephardi Jews. This of course only makes the sacrifice of the Yemeni purer.

The boy takes clever initiative and goes to Adina. "Did he ask for me?" she asked. "He asked for Adina. Of course" — the boy creates a white lie, another modification of Ben-Ner's story. She decides to help.

In the background, when Adina is united lovingly with the Yemenite, we hear doves cooing. It is not the time for crows.

The only people who pay the Yemenite last respects are the boy and the girl. Fear did not corrupt their pure souls.

The fields are wide. The mountains around them are eternal. Wind whistles. There is a sight of one lonely tree. There are no spoken words. The landscape is dim. Everything is dream-like. The sound of digging a grave is clear. In a moment, Adina will not be able to hold the dead Yemenite's hand anymore.

"And the Lord said unto him [unto Moses]: 'This is the land [of Israel]...I have caused thee to see it with thine eyes, but thou shalt not go over thither'" (*Deuteronomy* 34, 4). The Yemenite, like the rest of those who sacrificed their lives for Israel, will not see the day in which Israel was founded. "...And he was buried in the valley...and no man knoweth of his sepulchre unto this day" (Ibid. 6). New generations had their redeemers, too, and no man knows of their sepulchre.

BIBLIOGRAPHY

Barzel, Hillel, edited and wrote introductions. *Megamot be-Sipporet ha-Hovei: Ha-Sippur he-Havuy.* Yahdav, Tel-Aviv,1979.Ben-Ner, Yitzhak.

Ben-Ner, Yitzhak. *Rustic Sunset.* Translated with introduction by Robert Whitehill, Lynne Reinner Publishers, 1997.

_____. *Sheki'a Kafrit* Am Oved, Tel-Aviv, 1976.

Gutkind, N'aomi. "Siha 'im ha-Mesapper Yitzhak Ben-Ner." *Hazofe*, 22 Kislev, 1977.

Hakak, Lev. *Yerudim ve-Na'alim: Demutam shel Yehudei ha-Mizrah ba-Sippur ha-'Ivri ha-Kazar* Kiryat Sefer, Jerusalem, 1981, pp. 82-85.

Oren, Yosef. "Interview With Yitzhak Ben-Ner." *Kol Yisrael*, Aug. 25, 1967, also quoted in Shaked (below), p. 421.

Shaked, Gershon. *Ha-Sipporet ha-'Ivrit 1880-1980*, Vol. 5, pp. 410-445. Hakkibutz Hameuchad and Keter, 1998.

Chapter 5

HIRBET HIZ'AH
BY S. YIZHAR

LIFE OF THE AUTHOR AND HIS BOOKS
IN ENGLISH TRANSLATION

S. Yizhar was born in Rehovot, Israel, in 1916, to a family of immigrant-writer-farmer-political activists. He graduated from a teachers' seminary, taught in various schools and studied at the Hebrew University of Jerusalem. Yizhar was an educator, who taught both literature and education, and he also fought in the 1948 War of Independence. This war deeply affected his views and his literary works. From 1948-1967, Yizhar was a member of the Israeli Keneset ("parliament"), first with Mapai. Then, when David Ben-Gurion left the Labor party to establish and lead a new party ("Rafi"), Yizhar joined him.

Yizhar's first story, "Efrayim Goes Back to the Lucerne Grass," published in 1938, made Yizhar the first of the first Israeli born authors' generation to receive literary recognition. Receiving critical acclaim, this story gained Yizhar the reputation as the first of the first Israeli-born authors to achieve literary recognition. He wrote prose for children and adults, garnering the highest Israeli literary awards: the Brenner Prize, the Bialik Prize and the Israel Prize. Yizhar was a pioneer in successfully using both spoken and literary Hebrew. He was an original author when he expressed the experiences of the generation that fought in the 1948 Israeli War of Independence, and he enhanced the aesthetic achievements of the literature of his generation (see Miron, S. Yizhar, pp. 257-258).

Yizhar wrote about the Jewish settlement before Israel was established in 1948, about farmers and pioneers, about the 1948 War of Independence and about the soldiers. His stories focus on the inner life of his characters, and his style is lyrical. Detailed descriptions of Israeli nature appear often in Yizhar's work with love and awe, giving emphasis to sensory effects. After thirty years of a literary silence that began in 1963, Yizhar published two novels, *Mikdamot* (1992) and *Z alhavim* (1993). In *Mikdamot* (*Foretelling*), he wrote about the early time of pioneers in Israel. Yizhar's 1999 *Gilluy Eliyyahu* also focused on Israelis and war.

Yizhar's literary works assert powerful, ethical considerations and question the pioneering heritage and the practices of wars. Repetitive themes in Yizhar's work are the issues faced by Israelis in their land; the landscape of Israel; the Israeli-Arab war and the moralistic issues that it generates; the conflict between the united group of soldiers and the sensitive, inquisitive, individual soldier. Yizhar focuses on the human soul, the inner struggle, but not the outer elements of the war.

His work, *Midnight Convey and Other Stories*, (see Yizhar) appeared in English translation. The English translation of *Hirbet Hiz'a*h is a condensed version of the Hebrew tale. "Hirbet" in Arabic means "the ruins of." "Hiz'ah" is a name given in the story to a fictional Arab village. Published in 1949, it is a short tale in prose, which was written at the end of the 1948 War of Independence, and it deals with moral and humanistic issues.

Yizhar's accounting of the War of Independence elicited a vehement public debate. The story focuses on the lyric description of the human soul and of the landscape more than it does on the events. It presents the tension between the group and the individual, the war and its impact on the narrator, the values of the soldiers and their acts, the fancy pompous military terminology and devices and the surrendering Arabs.

The narrator does not accept that the nation, which itself was exiled, is now exiling others. Hebrew literature has many stories about exiles of Jews. History changed and, for the first time in thousands of years, the Jews became the conquerors who expelled other people. The war conditions produced actions that were cruel and brutal. The narrator in the story protests, exposes and denounces these acts. He is a reliable narrator. The Jewish people bitterly related to their exile and the narrator wonders rhetorically: "What really had we done here today?" (p. 330). In other words: "Two thousand years of Galut [exile]. What did not happen? Jews were killed. Europe. Now we are the masters" (p.332).

THE PLOT

A group of Israeli soldiers was ordered to conquer the Arab village Hirbet Hiz'ah, destroy its houses and evacuate its inhabitants. The soldiers carried out the order. Their conduct was unfeeling and cruel. The Arabs of the village were not equipped to fight back and defend themselves and indeed they did not fight back. Those who could flee from the village did so at the sound of the first bullet. Among those who stayed in the village were many old people, women and little children. They were obedient, yet the soldiers treated them badly. The narrator, a sensitive individual, was a participant and a witness to the conquering of the village. He reports to us well-organized, illustrative details that he remembers from the military mission and presents the strong moral doubts he has about the mission. He presents poetic, equivocal, emotional descriptions of the Arab villagers whom he considers both his fellow human beings and his enemies. He does not take any bold act to stop the expulsion of the Arabs. The questions he asks relate to the human and moral meaning and implications of the War of Independence.

Triggered by external events, the narrator's internal journey is composed of detailed responses to the external plot (stream of consciousness). The internal struggle of the narrator delays the progress of the plot and is the core of the story.

THE TIME, THE PLACE, THE NARRATOR

The time and place of the story as well as the characteristics of the story's narrator are similar to other stories by Yizhar (Miron, *Arab'a* pp. 175-192). Yizhar developed artistic intensity and depth, mastering limited scopes of time, place and characters. The thematic scope of his work can identify him as an Israeli local author. Since the publication of his first story in 1938, and until 1950, Yizhar employed the same style — he persisted in depicting the protagonist's repetitive main characteristics. In these stories we find a similar treatment of the Israeli landscape and a presentation of a documentary-like plot as if it were non-fictitious.

The time of the events *in Hirbet Hiz'ah*, like in many other Yizhar's stories, is the War of Independence. The events are explicated without an inclination toward a wide historical perspective. Some historical perspective is found in references to Jewish exile and to the expulsion experience. The story focuses on the specific experience but refers to Jewish history in order to illuminate the narrator's feelings (*Gallut* and *gola* — exile and Diaspora*)*. The story of the expulsion begins in the morning and ends in the evening. Many other stories take place from sunrise to sunset.

The place where the events happen is Israel, particularly centered around the southern landscape (the detailed descriptions of the landscape were eliminated from the translation). The landscape frequently is open fields, uncultivated nature, sand, desert, mountains and hills. With his poetic expression, Yizhar describes the heat and cold, darkness and sunrise, insects and wild plants, wind and stars, sky and earth.

The characters are the combatants of Israel. The soldiers bring technology — such as vehicles and weapons — into the pure, open fields. Their aim is to conquer and destroy nature. In this environment, the vulnerable soldiers struggle for survival, they are estranged from the nature that encircles them and, lacking shelter, they feel loneliness, horror and physical pain. In addition to the soldiers' conflict with the enemy, their conflict lies with nature.

Yizhar's characters are young, the majority being in their twenties, and many of them come from the kibbutz or agricultural settlements. The narrator in the story has common characteristics with other characters in Yizhar's stories. Yizhar's hero is both part of a group yet strives at the same time to distinguish himself from it. He is an observer of the events and a participant in them. As an observer, he looks at the people, landscape, situations and events in a lyrical way. He deeply feels in a unique way — with dissent or consent — the experiences in which he participates, and he debates internally and sometimes verbally their moralistic nature as if he were an outsider. He is conscious of his uniqueness and relates to it with both pride and self-mockery. He strives for action that is dictated by his convictions, but he toes the line of his friends and goes with the flow of the majority.

The narrator in *Hirbet Hiz'ah* is typical of some of Yizhar's main characters. He is sensitive and perceptive, a romantic humanitarian. He has an inquisitive mind but cannot find the answers. He knows what the orders are and what the ideology is, but he still questions the justification of the events in which he participates. The narrator is ethical and rejects the arguments, conduct and morals of the group.

The protagonist-narrator is an individual who does not identify with the acts and claims of the group. However, his protests are emotional, and they take place internally, while in his actions, he obeys orders and follows the group.

The narrator's protestations shed some limited light on his character in general. Irony and self-irony are employed to address the fact that the narrator disagrees with his group, but he is helpless amidst the over-whelming majority. He does not take any action to disrupt the group's activity. Therefore, the ideological clash between the narrator and the group does not become more dramatic. Only a soldier called Shlomo agrees with the narrator, the rest of the soldiers disagree.

THE CRITICS AND THE MESSAGE OF THE STORY

The story leads the reader to certain moralistic conclusions. A victory in the battlefield may constitute a moral defeat. The story questions the necessity, justification and manner of the expulsion of the Arabs from their village. The Jews were expelled themselves; they suffered for thousands of years and condemned human oppression and cruelty, and now the Jewish soldiers in the story act mercilessly. The message of the story was particularly hard coming from an author who was committed to the pioneers' Zionist ideology. The story represents human deterioration in war conditions.

The soldiers are identified by their common, Biblical names, to remind us of the Jewish moral code and to create a conflict between Jewish values and the soldiers' conduct. The Arabs are not identified by names in the story but by their deformity or helplessness: wailing women; old men; a weeping, pleading woman; a sobbing woman carrying a thin baby girl; a strong-headed woman holding a little child by the hand and who will later become a poisonous serpent; a wailing woman in blue garments and white veils; blind folk. Yehuda's explanation that "they are like wild animals" only reflects on him and on his attitude toward these poor village inhabitants. The claim of "a few against many" which is typical of Israeli descriptions of the War of Independence is inapplicable here.

The military action does not involve a serious danger or risk. There is no battle over the village. The Arabs respond with tears, astonishment and surrender to the sudden conquest and destruction. The narrator's conscience is awakened by his encounter with the sudden disruption of the transported Arabs' peaceful life. The narrator's sensitivity and shock are highlighted by the insensitivity and brutality of the other soldiers who invade the landscape and shatter the Arab villagers' pastoral life. The narrator's feelings are central to the story.

The narrator in *Hirbet Hiz'ah* does not feel inferior for having different feelings from the rest of the soldiers. He is proud of his ethical uniqueness even when he asks: "Why, in the devil's name, was I the only one here to get excited? What sort of useless staff was I made of?" (p.333). His internal monologue represents his hardship in accepting the acts of the group due to his sensitivity and moral superiority. In the monologue, a "stream of consciousness" is used to record the unbroken flow of thoughts and awareness in the waking mind, the flow of the character's sense perceptions, thoughts, memories, associations and feelings.

The ideological point of view of the narrator in the story triggered the responses of the critics, who addressed not only the aesthetic literary aspects of the story but also its political and moral message. While many critics praised the literary accomplishments of Yizhar, some disagreed about its message (see details in Nagid, pp. 16-20). The political, moral problem remained unsolved.

When the story was published, some of the critics pointed out the author's commendable moralistic outcry, his humanitarian care, his condemnation of human indifference and insensitivity, his dedication to a positive military and national image and his artistic freedom. It was argued that Yizhar protested against inhumane, indifferent conduct, but did not argue that the War of Independence was unnecessary. The critics praised Yizhar's recognition that war is a most dreadful situation. "The voice of conscience spoke loud" in this story. "Yizhar succeeded to warn against the dullness and wickedness, ruthlessness and sadism, which were covered with patriotic talks" ('Aukhmani, pp. 364-365). It was argued that Yizhar was not showing wicked Jews and righteous Arabs but that he only pointed out what was closest to his heart — the fault of his own people, and his recognition of the fault of his people might contribute to peace between Arabs and Jews. Other critics emphasized that we must differentiate between Yizhar the personal author and the narrator of the story.

Other critics argued that the narrator of the story takes a strange position regarding the Jews' struggle for survival. It was argued that Yizhar's humanistic approach did not have deep foundations, and he lacked the courage needed in order to face the necessary war. Yizhar looked at reality from a childish point of view, and "it is impossible to encompass scope and depth through children's eyes and by identifying with childish views" (Luz, p. 67, see also pp. 53-67). Yizhar's characters "refuse to depart from their egocentricity of childhood" (ibid. 55) in their point of view. In *Hirbet Hiz'ah,* the narrator is not insisting upon his opinion because he is too weak to make a moral decision; he is affected by ever-changing sensitivity and not by well- structured values (see ibid. p. 57). There is no room for such an outcry considering the fact that what was at stake was the fate of the Jewish people and their homeland. Yizhar's humanitarian outcry was premature — it came to the world while the Jews were suffering bloodshed themselves, and Yizhar's outcry may be abused for political gain, while it is the duty of an author to serve the public needs. Already in 1950 there were critics who doubted the humanitarianism in Yizhar's story for what they considered as a lack of moralistic courage to accept the inevitable consequences of war (se Shalev).

Critics pointed out the skeptical position of Yizhar's characters toward the group they are part of, and wondered about the underlying moral, social and Zionistic concepts of the author (See Kariv, Kena'ani, Aukhmani, Kurzweil, Schweid). According to some of these critics, the reader remains often confused as to the position taken about the problem raised by the story's narrator because of the complexity of the issues and of the merits of conflicting arguments. It was argued that Yizhar's stories and their main characters lack a clear value system. The narrator in *Hirbet Hiz'ah* did not dare take any action because he is indecisive, and most of the time he argues and struggles within himself and not with the other soldiers. The narrator's human sensitivity is not supported by courage and moral confidence. Schweid (p. 196) thinks that the reason why the narrator does not act is not his being one person out of an entire group, but the absence of his certainty that he has the absolute truth, truth being more important than anything else. Therefore the narrator in *Hirbet Hiz'ah* escapes from action — he leaves the work of expelling for his friends and leaves the judging of the soldiers to God. Furthermore, the story tells us that the narrator "did not know how to say something sensible and practical" (p. 331). The position of the alien narrator is solid, yet one can trace some ambivalence in it.

Due to their historical role, the soldiers as a group ignored their personal perspective and accepted their acts. The narrator could not do that.

It is noteworthy that, in recent times, Yizhar again debated the issue of the justification and meaning of war. In his 1999 published book (see Yizhar, *Gilluy Eliyyahu*) about the Yom Kippur War of October 1973, Yizhar deliberates this issue with friends and soldiers and within himself in a bitter protest of the loss of life. War is an incongruous situation in which people kill each other instead of negotiating and settling their disputes.

STYLE

Some critics addressed the "difficult," vague style of Yizhar, but other critics considered it original and organic to the story (see Shaked, *Ha-Sipporet*, pp. 195-198). Some critics had reservations about the quality and authenticity of the style (see Zemah and Kurzweil), but it is well accepted that Yizhar's native Hebrew proved to be rich and powerful in depicting the human soul and describing the landscapes. Yizhar tells his story with a rich Hebrew vocabulary, which draws only a little on early Jewish sources for allusions, while he coins new phrases and gives a uniquely sonorous expression to the landscape. For the first time, the Hebrew language provided detailed, rich descriptions of the landscape of Israel. I will not present the stylistic achievements of Yizhar through our substantially condensed version of the translated text (the Hebrew story is several pages longer) of one of his stories, especially when the landscape descriptions in which one finds Yizhar's most remarkable stylistic gifts are omitted in this version. The selected passages in the translation can, however, present the core of the dilemma of the story.

Yizhar's style is poetic and exalted. His syntax is sophisticated. The addressee of his stories, the implied anticipated reader, is a well-educated Israeli (see ibid. pp. 195-201). Yizhar's high, poetic style, with which he wrote about common characters and events, was a device for casting glory and heroism on the characters. The high style includes neologisms, archaisms — including Biblical — synonyms, long sentences with sophisticated syntactical structure and poetic metaphorical language. It casts beauty on the landscape and stature on the documentary, on the reportage and on the chronicle. The fact that some of Yizhar's literary work is based on specific events and sites (see Ma'apil) does not detract from Yizhar's glorification.

The dialogues are written in a spoken Hebrew and are distinguished from the high style of the narrator's thoughts.

Biblical verses are used in a serious way only, as demonstrated by the following examples. One of the village inhabitants "took off his shoes the better to pass through" (p. 329) the pool of water. Yizhar's use of the Biblical words ("nashal na'alav meraglav"), while Yizhar had Modern Hebrew words available, alludes to God calling Moses out of the midst of the bush that was burned with fire but was not consumed. God instructed Moses to take off his shoes because Moses was standing on holy grounds (*Exodus* 2, 5). In addition, God tells Moses that he has seen the affliction of His people in Egypt, has heard their cry and knows their pain, and he is coming to rescue them (ibid. ibid. 7-8). Now, the miracle is gone; the afflicted people are afflicting others in the Promised Land. An angry echo of footsteps of exiled Jews came to the narrator, it was as angry as Jeremiah, the prophet who was born in Anathoth and his prophecies expressed his anger against those who exiled the Jews.

Hirbet Hiz'ah is described as a place "which we removed and to which we then moved," free translation of the original Hebrew text "we expelled and also inherited," which alludes to "has thou killed and also inherited" (*First Kings*, 21, 19). Ahab, king of Israel, wanted to purchase the vineyard of Naboth or to exchange it, and when Naboth refused the King's offer, the king's wife Jezebel plotted the death of Naboth and then told the king to take possession of the vineyard. The Lord came to Elijah and instructed him to ask the king: "has thou killed and also inherited?" The context is a conviction of the soldiers who expelled the inhabitants of the village, which will become a Jewish settlement.

In another allusion, the soldiers are the wicked who will be punished. The narrator thinks about the future when Jewish settlers "would strike root here like a tree by a flowing brook. On the other hand the wicked ones..." (p. 332). It is the righteous man who "shall be like a tree planted by a flowing brook" (Psalms 1, 3), "...not so the wicked; but they are like the chaff which the wind driveth away" (ibid. ibid. 4). Moyshe's idyllic description in the story of the Jewish future settlement in Hirbet Hiz'ah is the source of the anger and sarcasm of the narrator, who anticipates God's punishment. Moyshe is not an inspiring leader, but rather a shallow soldier, who is certain of the war's cause and of the values it represents, but who is incapable of questioning the ethical propriety of his acts.

The narrator wants to address his feelings to his friends but wonders, "To whom could I speak and be listened to?" This evokes the language of Moses to Israel: "so I spoke to you, and ye listened not" (*Deuteronomy* 1, 43).

"When they reached their enforced destination it would already be night. Their clothes will be their only covering to lie down in. All right. What can be done?" (p. 330). The humanitarian Biblical law instructs that, if one takes a garment from a poor man as a pledge, he must return it when the sun goes down, "for that is his only covering, it is his garment for his skin; when shall he sleep? And it shall come to pass, when he crieth unto Me, that I will hear; for I am gracious" (*Exodus* 22, 25-26). The use of the Biblical verse implies, in this context, a warning that God the gracious will punish those who expelled the village inhabitants. The sentences: "All right. What can be done?" are spoken Hebrew, drawing the narrator away from the abstract law to a current situation, from a futuristic God-judgment and to the present options to help, if any.

The closing paragraph of the story is particularly dramatic. Yizhar's sublime style, the silence disrupted by the cries, and the Biblical allusions are three of the dramatic devices. *Hirbet Hiz'ah* ends with the idea that "...when silence would blanket everything...God would come down to the valley to see if the deeds that were done matched the cries" (p. 334). Like all the other silences in the story, this silence, too, is an outcry. In the Biblical situation, God decided to look into the grievous sins of Sodom and Gomorrah himself: "I will go down now, and see whether they have done altogether according to the cry of it" (*Genesis* 18, 21). As a result, he "caused to rain upon Sodom and upon Gomorrah brimstone and fire" (Ibid. 19, 24). The allusion refers therefore to the gravity of the sin in Yizhar's story. The sound of the cry joins the sounds we have already heard in the story: the sound of wailing, a whimpering child, villagers who were weeping loudly, a silent village, walls which will cry, the sobbing of a child, long wailing, the whine of the wagon ("lorry"), a cow lowing. Sounds and silence express the pain.

The word "wagons" (Hebrew: "keronot" was translated as "lorries") may evoke hard associations in Jewish history, especially when the narrator remembers: "Jews were killed. Europe. Now we are the masters" (p. 332).

I will attempt to point out some characteristics of Yizhar's style in his descriptions of the landscape (which are eliminated almost totally from our translation). In one paragraph, we read, "The pool of water had already become still and the wavelets that passed across its surface quivered back over the reflection of the sky" (p. 331). Nature is connected to people. The soldiers invaded the calm nature (pool). One of its elements is the pool of water through which the Arabs walked in order to get to the lorries. As a result, the still pool of water, through which the Arabs passed became unsettled. The Arabs walked through it "splashing their bare feet in the water...as if there was nothing special about passing through a pool" (p. 329). They are an organic part of nature. The narrator thinks that they are "like cattle" (ibid. ibid.), but we may see their innocence and purity. When the pool stopped being invaded, nature returned to its original state, the pool became still. In the still pool the sky is reflected again. The sky, heaven (in Hebrew it is an identical word — "shamayim") is watching all the time, only sometimes it is not reflected on earth. When nature is not invaded, it can go back to its loving and harmonious condition — the wavelets "quivered back over the reflection of the sky." A more correct translation might be: "The pool of water had already become clear and the little wrinkles that passed across its face doted upon the reflection of the sky." The pool of water is personified — it has a face and wrinkles and it is doting upon the reflection of the sky. The use of personification in landscape description — particularly personification that reminds us of a woman — is prominent in Yizhar's work, often reflecting the spirit of the soldiers who long for women.

The sun silhouetted in the treetops "sharp silent shapes that were deep in mediation, and knew much more than we did, and gazed on the silence of the village" (p. 332). The personification of these shapes appears immediately after explicating the narrator's deep guilt feelings. Man may ignore the implications of his act, but nature preserves them. The shapes know that the silence of the village hides the forthcoming wailing storm. Nature relates to man's feelings, and the beholder views it subjectively in accordance with his feelings.

The metaphoric language is not merely decorative but it also supports the message. The silence of the village is "as of a dead's man body" (p. 332). The village stops being simply inanimate, and the act of expelling becomes an act of inflicting death. The expelled Arabs are "startled flock of sheep" (p. 333) — the image reminds us that the expelled people are part of nature.

The narrated monologue or represented speech, where a speech of a character is presented through the narrator's discourse, is used as an ironic statement for the intelligent reader who is associated with the narrator and is not taken by the ostensible meaning. For example, Moyshe said to the narrator who protested the "filthy war" (p. 331): "To Hirbet, what's-its-name, immigrants will be coming. Are you listening? And they'll take this land and they'll till it and everything here will be fine" (ibid.). Now the narrator thinks:

> Of course, what then? Why not? Why did I not think of that at first? Our Hirbet Hiz'ah. There will be problems and housing and absorption. Hurrah, we shall build houses and absorb immigrants, and then we shall build a grocer's shop, we shall put up a school, perhaps also a synagogue... Who will dream that once there was a place called Hirbet Hiz'ah, which we removed and to which we then moved in? We came, we shelled, we burnt, we blew up, we pushed and we shoved and we sent to exile (pp. 331-332).

The narrator in this paragraph first speaks for himself, then he speaks ironically in the name of the group and then again for himself. At the beginning of the paragraph, we hear the voice of the narrator alone. Then the narrator represent the speech of the other soldiers — with its intonation content and syntax — and his voice and their voice become one. But the reader knows of the narrator's disagreement with the others and this apparent unity is only an ironic device and even a parody (Gertz, 1993, pp. 132-137). The narrator's implicit meaning intended is, however, different from what he ostensibly asserts. The explicit attitude implies a different attitude. The narrator treats with anger and mockery the shallow attitude of his friend concerning what is done in Hirbet Hiz'ah. At the paragraph's end, the voice of the narrator separates from his friends' voice; the style is emotional, mocking, dramatic and self-accusative. It is charged with many verbs that expose the fault of the soldiers; the rhythm is fast. The use of "we" in the last sentence only highlights the narrator's loneliness.

While the narrator does not identify with the other soldiers' discourse, he identifies with the conjectured speech of the Arabs. The Arab boy was "tight-lipped, as if to say, 'what have you done to us?'" (p. 330).

One of the literary devices Yizhar used to distinguish between the narrator and his friends is differing dialogue and monologue styles. The colloquial Hebrew of the soldiers, their short utterances, with the simplistic content only accentuates the high, poetic, sometimes archaic, sophisticated style of the narrator and the complexity of his world. "Well...what do you want" (p. 331) Moyshe asked the narrator. "You, you are starting again," (p. 333) he said to him later. Yehuda said to the Arab woman who wept and pleaded: "Yallah, yallah, you also" (p. 329). Such language and shallowness of expression are compared with the depth and richness of the narrator's language and spiritual struggle.

THE MOVIE

Director: Ram Levy. Producer: Yosi Meshulam. Script: Daniella Carmi (Literary adaptation. Based on S. Yizhar's novel). Photography: Meir Diskin, Arik Rubinstein. Editing: Tova Asher, Rachel Yagil. Cast: Dalik Volinets, Shraga Harpaz, Gidi Gov, Amira Polan, Avraham Sidi, Amos Tal-Shir, Yitshak Aloni, Avi Luzia, Z vi Borodo, Rolf Brin, Bushara Kraman, Abu Se'ud, Madleline Bazly, Bishara Hamashta. Also Villagers from the villages Midia, Na'alen, Hirbeta Bet Or, Zafa. 1978. Color. 60 minutes.

Ram Levy, the film director of *Hirbet Hiz'ah*, is interested in issues such as discrimination, social inequalities, unemployment and hatred between people, war ethics and poverty in Israel. Levy also directed and co-wrote *Winter Games*. Levy studied filmmaking in London and joined Israeli television at its inception in 1968. In 1993 he was awarded the very prestigious Israel Award.

Hirbet Hiz'ah is among Levy's award-winning, well-known television films. Levy believes that films are efficacious in raising social awareness, spreading social and political insights, presenting hard issues and defeating fallacies (see Kronish, pp. 175-177).

In 1966, Levy wrote a short script for the movie, *My Name is Ahmed* The Arab-Israeli Ahmed tries to work in Tel-Aviv and to rent an apartment. He feels hated but has hope. *Hirbet Hiz'ah* is a 1978 literary adaptation of Yizhar's story. It took until 1986 before another literary adaptation was produced: the 1986 movie based on *The Smile of the Lamb* by David Grossman, a story about an old, semi-blind, semi-crazy, imaginative and wise Arab man and his political understanding. The old man's stories and wisdom captivate an Israeli soldier who tries to understand his own life. *Hirbet Hiz'ah* is a courageous movie, which was made when the discussion of some issues of the Israeli-Arab relations were hardly debatable. Shohat views this movie as "the first attempt at a relatively critical representation of the [Arab-Israeli] conflict" (Shohat, p. 238).

In 1972, Levy proposed to adapt Yizhar's story for television but Israel's authorities in charge of its sole state-operated television rejected the proposal. Israeli national television was not ready to present such a controversial topic in the history of Israel — the eviction of Arabs from their homes and villages. A few years later, Levy proposed the same idea again, and this time it was accepted. But even then it took a struggle to screen it (see below), and it took a workers-committee protest against Israeli television and an announcement that nothing would be transmitted in place of the movie to have the authorities agree to screen it. Ministers and members of the Israeli Keneset participated in the public debate.

The production of the one-hour film began in 1977, and was filmed over the course of several weeks in a village called Midia (near the site of ancient Modi'in). Arab villagers from four villages participated in the movie; Arabs also acted in roles such as the woman with a child (Bushara Kraman), an escaping Arab (Abu Se'ud) and the "mukhtar," who is the village headman (Bishara Hamashta).

At the time of production, the village Media did not have many technological features such as television antennae. When the crew and cast came to the village and told the villagers what they were doing and that the villagers would even "star" in the movie, the villagers gladly cooperated. The movie was scheduled for screening while peace negotiations were proceeding with Egypt. It is important to note that, at the time the movie was screened, there was only one television station in Israel, which was a state television station. Yitshak Shamir, later the Israeli prime minister, argued that as long as there was only one television station in Israel and it was state-operated, it was right to demand that it carry the nation's views as reflected by the Keneset majority.

The movie softens the story; the soldiers in the story are more brutal and more contemptuous. The movie includes dialogues that are not part of the story but mainly taken from another novel by Yizhar (*Yeme' Ziklag,* "The Days of Ziklag"). Dalia, the wireless operator, is a character taken from another Yizhar's work, "Midnight Convoy" (1949) to provide a romantic interest. Dally, the wireless operator in "Midnight Convoy," is an attractive and adored young woman. The reader does not learn much about her internal life (see Fuchs). When the public debate about screening *Hirbet Hiz'ah* began in Israel, it was mentioned that Yizhar was an intelligence officer with his brigade ("Giv'ati") and was instructed to conquer and evacuate several Arab villages. Yizhar's unit was in one of several units that were instructed to conquer a certain Arab village (near Yad-Mordekhai); he wrote his story in 1949, only two months after the event, and most of the details in it are authentic, with the exception of the name.

The movie begins with the whistling of a nostalgic, soft melody. In sudden contrast, the location changes to a military base, which is full of noise, youth, playfulness and enthusiasm. The soldiers load military equipment onto military trucks in preparation for their mission. Mikha, the story's protagonist, is carried on his friend's shoulders away from the crowd. In the background we hear the sound of a harmonica. Like the whistle, the harmonica is also a simple musical instrument, often connected over the years with camaraderie and singing around a bonfire. The movie begins and ends with a voiceover with excerpts from the story, the beginning of which focuses on the acts of the soldiers and the end on the expected punishment.

Dalia is young and smiling. She makes brief appearances; she has a sweet voice and sometimes her appearance is accompanied with a harmonica to express the romantic yearnings of the young soldiers. She appears more than ten times in the movie, as the subject of yearning and romance and dreams, without any in-depth characteristics, which is the case with many women in the thoughts of the soldiers in Yizhar's stories. On their way to carry out the orders the soldiers sing, but Mikha does not join in the singing, which begins portraying the differences between the united group of soldiers and the sensitive, inquisitive, individual soldier. This is a repetitive scene in Yizhar's stories. When the soldiers get off the truck, they begin to sing again. Suddenly they are silent and in ambush. Their plotting, military silence is the antithesis to the village pastoral silence. In the same way, their presence, military equipment and ammunition are antitheses to the villager's single donkey rider, who, in contrast, belongs to the place and its nature.

The dialogue about the arbitrarily and cruelly killed donkey strikingly contrasts the sight of the Arab riding a donkey and later to the sight of an old Arab using a donkey to carry his meager belongings. The technology belongs to the soldiers with their trucks and guns and the morals, simplicity and justice belong to the Arabs. Technology does not belong in that place; donkeys do. While two soldiers are immersed in a detailed description of donkey killing, we hear the innocent birds twitting in the village's groves.

The shooting at the village creates the expectation that the villagers will shoot back but surprisingly, their response is a silent one. When few Arabs are attempting to escape, the soldiers shoot at them, and they become immersed in their shooting abilities more than with the question of why they would want to kill. Mikha is silent and worried. Finally, he suggests that they leave the villages alone. The pastoral setting surrounding the soldiers strongly contrasts their cruel acts.

The soldiers bring guns, explosive materials and vehicles with them, which corrupt the pastoral landscape. Inside the village, there is a clear contrast between the village and the soldiers. Various scenes are filmed from the villagers' point of view. Other scenes are filmed through the Arab village's architecture — alleys, window frames, doorways and the village square. The simple stone houses with arches and alleys, which serve as the Arabs' homes, are peaceful and simple. Architecturally, they fit the nature around the village. These are homes with family trees and traditions; around them, we hear the barking of small dogs; we see and hear chickens, goats, donkeys and cows. Later, we encounter the gentle, sensitive, loving side of the soldiers when they see a pony.

The Arabic language is used from time to time by some of the characters; it contributes to the authenticity of the events. The Arabs appear in their traditional clothes, without any weapons of any kind.

The sounds of exploding houses are accompanied by the sound of the harmonica. The presence of the soft sound of the harmonica at the time of the explosion and at the times of romantic, tender yearning expresses the cruelty of the soldiers, who are destroying the existence of a peaceful Arab lifestyle that they themselves desire. Another sound that accompanies the explosions is an Arab woman's screaming, a desperate and lamentable outcry.

The camera focuses often on the villagers, their silence, their faces, their age. This is countered by the insensitivity of the soldiers.

When Mikha finally has an opportunity to have a very brief conversation with Dalia, she is driven away. He will last see her playing and being chased by the driver-officer in a grove, and his pain about the Arabs is aggravated by his personal disappointment. Mikha's attempts, time and again, to deliberate the soldiers' acts and to protest them meet with the slogans and shallowness of the soldiers who are sure of the propriety of the mission and their actions.

——————————

The reviews of *Hirbet Hiz'ah* heavily relate to the ideological issues of the story and less to the artistic achievements of the TV movie. The screening of the movie generated a public debate and was done in spite of the opposition of the Israeli Education and Culture Minister at that time, Zevulun Hamer. Yizhar, Levy and the screenwriter, Daniella Carmi, came under attack. Yizhar's story was part of the Israeli Ministry of Education's high school curriculum for many years, but it provoked public anger only when it was made into a film. The argument that the movie could be used for Arab propaganda was confirmed when Jordanian Television chose to broadcast it.

Some of the critics' opinions are thought evoking and demonstrative of the possibility that ideology may dominate artistic judgment. The public debate also represents a variety of political approaches in Israel and their possible impact on art (for detailed accounting of the political issues involved with the screening, see Alon). The differences between reading a book and watching a movie were also deliberated in the context of the public debate. It was argued that the story and any part of it can be read and re-read, while the movie flicks by in one session.

Minister Hamer postponed the TV screening of the film. This raised an a outcry among members of the Israeli Keneset, lawyers, authors and journalists who saw this act as conflicting with freedom of speech. In an interview (see Bashan), Hamer emphasized that he considered the screening of the movie a sensitive public issue. While Yizhar's story was only one of many points of view that an Israeli youth considered in high school studies about the War of Independence, the movie was an exclusive work shown in the context of the thirtieth anniversary of Israel's independence. In addition, it presented the majority of Israelis as people who committed unnecessary brutal acts against the Arabs and did not provide a correct view of Israelis. "The movie is done well from a professional point of view, but it is two-dimensional colors wise: Black and white, while the black is dominant, and in my opinion is far from reflecting the true facts of the War of Independence," Hamer argued.

One critic (See Glida'ai) found the movie boring and resented the shabby and sloppy appearance of the soldiers, including their commander. He claimed that the soldiers in the movie conducted themselves in a humane manner and, unlike the conquerors, did not apply violence toward the Arabs. Even when they shot at the escaping Arabs, they missed their targets because they did not intend to hit them. They did not interrupt the main character from offering water to the refugees, and one of them even offered food to an Arab. The main character did not have any answer as to what should otherwise be done. Also, they did not evacuate the Arabs to a difficult place. Yizhar, continues this critic, was the culture officer of the unit about which he wrote and, if he felt that other moral values should have been implanted in the soldiers but were not, it was his personal failure. To this critic, Yizhar rebelled against the possibility that the evacuation was not for the purpose of driving the enemy away but simply for capturing land for Jewish settlements.

Glida'ai presented the opinion that the screening of the movie may undermine the Jews' right for Israel. The story was part of the mandatory curricula for high school education in Israel, but reading a story individually did not resemble viewing it. Screening the movie in the course of negotiating peace with the President of Egypt Anwar Sadat (1978) implied that Israel did not belong to the Jews and the Israelis themselves admit it.

There were also some attempts to belittle the movie's artistic merits. Malkin (1978) objected to a movie being presented as a documentary while it was not one. Many claimed that the movie was an attempt to present inauthentic scenes as if they reconstructed history. The movie failed because the script did not reflect the personal story of the main character and did not make an emotional impact, while the film ignored the individual and presented a collective event, which its disconnection from historical context rendered meaningless. Yizhar's novella dwells on the narrator who participates in an unforgettable unjust act of evacuation, which affects him deeply, but the camera in the movie focuses on one character after another and one act of violence after another without reason and meaning. Yizhar's story focuses on the feelings of the character through which he witnesses the historical event. These feelings are ignored in the movie, and we see only the historical setting, without any context, including scenes that are ridiculously calm and show a fake indifference of the soldiers. Malkin further argues that the movie is an artistic failure because the context, atmosphere and feelings of the 1948 war were not reflected in it at all; the film has a setting for a story but not a story. It does not have any historical event in its context; it is an "as if" documentary, resembling a placard, which is removed from the truth, and it does not present the inner world and the personal reactions of a certain character to the historical events in which he participated. The film is a mere collection of pale photographs that pretend to reconstruct history. It is a movie, which was made without feelings of responsibility or closeness and sensitivity to the participants in the historical event.

Evidence was provided that the Hagana (means "defense," here a Jewish self-defense organization in Palestine during the British Mandate, established especially against Arab attacks) tried to convince the Arabs to stay in their homes whenever they were in Israel. The Religious Writers Association in Israel declared: "One does not give weapons to the enemy and present work which is imbalance from a national and public perspective." But the Hebrew Writers Association in Israel viewed the delay in the screening of the movie as limiting freedom of speech and twenty-five of them demanded that the Education and Culture Minister resign unless he rescinded his decision to postpone the movie's screening. Yizhar declared that the motive of attempting to prevent the screening was not military security but mere guilt and claimed that he was "offended as a human being by the violence he had witnessed" and "instead of covering what happened, we must atone for it." (See Giora and Siegel). It was felt that unless it was a "national emergency," the postponing of the screening was unjustified, and was "a blatant instance of attempted political censorship of the arts" (see "Who's afraid").

There were those who claimed that the Education and Culture Minister merely exercised a privilege granted him by the law when he ordered the postponement of the screening, and there is nothing undemocratic about it. There were those who contended that broadcasting the movie would mean handing out further anti-Israeli ammunition to the enemies. Other critics claimed that freedom of expression and democracy came first, and even the Bible did not conceal the fault of the Jewish people and their heroes. The objection to the movie is justified by the difference between the movie medium and the book. A reader can gradually absorb as he reads the various elements of a text, to modify them, put them in a context, examine them and criticize them. Making *Hirbet Hiz'ah* into a film requires that, by the nature of a film, by the way its message reaches the eye and the mind, it "becomes a political placard, a slogan, that the viewer either accepts or rejects in totality." *Hirbet*

Hiz'ah as a story perhaps was not a clich' in 1949, but at the time of the movie it was. Israeli television did not have the duty to transmit the message that the conduct described in both the novel and in the movie was typical of the soldiers. Democracy and freedom of expression do not mean "license to say anything anytime, anywhere," but "the best way to uphold democracy and freedom of expression is by exercising responsibility" (see Kohn).

Another critic who felt that the film was well produced (see Gillon) was attacked by his readers for overlooking the fact that the battle order included a specific reason for the attack: the Arab village was close to the border and was being used by terrorists. This critic points out the fact that the Israeli soldiers in the movie had repeating rifles and guns and a machine-gun, while the Arabs did not. This critic felt that it is a fictional movie with a message; it did not pretend to be a balanced documentary presenting all aspects of the conflict. It was unacceptable for this critic that human decency is automatically suspended when a nation goes to war.

BIBLIOGRAPHY

Alon, Gideon. "Ha-Kerav ha-Sheni 'al *Hirbet Hiz'ah*." *Ha'arez* , Feb. 10, 1978.

Bashan, Raphael. "Eneni Mukhan le-Hashlim 'im Yez irot she-Kol Kullan Akhila 'Az mit le-Te'avon." *Yediot Aharonot*, Oct. 2, 1978.

Fuchs, Esther. "The Enemy as Woman: Fictional Women in the Literature of the Palmach." *Israel Studies*, Vol. 4, No. 1, Spring 1999, pp. 212-232, in pp. 214-219.

Gertz, Nurit. *Hirbet Hiz'ah ve-ha-Boker she-le-Mohorat*. Hakkibuz Hameuchad, Tel-Aviv, 1983.

Glida'ai, Moshe. "Le-Ahar ha-Hakrana." *Zot ha-Arez* , March 3, 1978.

Gillon, Philip. *"Hirbet Hiz'ah* Revisited." *The Jerusalem Post*, Feb. 17, 1978.

Giora Zayid. "Hakranat *Hirbet Hiz'ah* Ka'et Yekhola rak le-Hazzik Lanu." *Haz ofei*, Feb. 2, 1978.

Grossman, David. *Hiyyukh ha-Gedi.* Siman Keri'a and Hakkibutz Hameuchad, Tel-Aviv, 1983.

Kariv, Avraham. *Iyyunim*. Devir, Tel-Aviv, 1950.

Kena'ni, David. *Benam le-Ven Zemannam*. Sifriyyat Po'alim, Tel-Aviv, 1955, pp. 94-135.

Kohn, Moshe. "The Placard Effect." *The Jerusalem Post*, Feb. 8, 1998.

Kremer, Shalom. *Hillufei Mishmarot be-Sifrutenu* Aguddat ha-Sofrim ha-'Ivrim le-Yad Dvir, 1959, 255-273.

Kronish, Amy. *World Cinema: Israel*. Fairleigh University Press, 1996.

Kurzweil, Barukh. *Ben Hazon le-Ven ha-Absurdi.* Shocken, Jerusalem and Tel-Aviv, 1966.

Luz, Zvi. *Me zi'ut ve-Adam ba-Sifrut ha-Erez Yisraelit* Dvir, Tel-Aviv, 1970.

Ma'apil, Avi. *I zuuv ha-Mez i'ut ba-Sipporet shel Yizhar.* Dissertation, Hebrew University of Jerusalem, 1988.

Miron, Dan. *Arba' Panim ba-Sifrut ha-'Ivrit bat Yamenu.* Shocken, Jerusalem and Tel-Aviv, 1962.

_____. "S. Yizhar: Some General Observations." In *Midnight Convoy and other Stories.* Israel Universities Press, Jerusalem, 1969, pp. 257-272.

Nagid, Hayyim, edited. *S. Yizhar: Mivhar ma-Amrei Bikkoret' al Yez irato.* Am Oved, Tel-Aviv, 1972.

Schweid, Eli. *Shalosh Ashmurot.* Am Oved, Tel-Aviv, 1967, pp. 185-201.

Shaked, Gershon. Ha-Sipporet ha-'Ivrit 1880-1980: be-Havlei ha-Zeman. Hakkibutz Hameuchad and Keter, Vol. 4, 1993, pp. 187-229.

Shalev, Mordekhai. "Sifrut ha-Milhama shel Medinat Yisrael." In *Sullam,* Vol.1, No.1 (1950), pp. 29-30. Reprinted as *"Mevukha ve-Sadism, Hirbet el Hiz'ah,"* in *S. Yizhar: Mivhar Ma'amre Bikkoret 'al Yezirato.* Am Oved, Tel-Aviv, 1972, pp. 47-51.

Shohat, Ella. *Israeli Cinema: East/West and the Politics of Representation.* University of Texas Press, Austin, 1989.

Siegel, Judy. "Public Outcry Over *Hirbet Hiza* Delay." *The Jerusalem Post,* Feb. 8, 1978.

Ukhmani, Azriel. *Le'ever ha-Adam.* Sifriyyat Po'alim, 1953.

"Who's Afraid of *Hirbet Hiza*?" *The Jerusalem Post,* Feb. 8, 1978.

Yizhar, S. *Sippur Hirbet Hiz'ah.* Sifriyyat Po'alim, Merhavya, 1949. Reprinted in *Arba'a Sippurim.* Hakkibutz Hameuchad, Tel-Aviv, 1959.

_____. "The Story of *Hirbet Hiz'ah.*" Tr. By Harold Levy (a condensed version). In Sonntag, J., ed. *Caravan: a Jewish Quarterly Omnibus.* New York, Y. Yoseloff, ap62, pp. 328-334.

_____. *Midnight Convoy and other Stories.* Israel Universities Press, Jerusalem, 1969.

_____. *Gilluy Eliahu,* Zemora Bitan, 1999.

Zemah, Shelomo. *Massa u-Vikkoret.* 1954. pp. 241-252.

Chapter 6

HIMMO KING OF JERUSALEM
BY YORAM KANIUK

LIFE OF THE AUTHOR AND HIS WORK
IN ENGLISH TRANSLATION

Yoram Kaniuk was born in 1930 into the cultural elite of Tel-Aviv, Israel Kaniuk served in the Palma'h (Pluggot Mahats, Striking Forces, the crack army unit of the war) a selected unit of the Haganah, a voluntary Jewish self-defense organization that was established in Palestine during the British Mandate. He fought in the War of Independence in 1948 and was wounded in the in a battle for Jerusalem. After his service, he worked on a ship bringing Holocaust survivors to Israel.

Kaniuk studied painting in Paris and then lived in New York (1951-1961) as a barman, tourists guide, journalist and artist. He began publishing short stories in 1949. Some of his works were made into films: *Rockinghorse, Himmo King of Jerusalem. Adam Resurrected* was made into a play. He first published short stories and was also a play critic. His literary work includes short stories, novellas, novels, journalistic articles, critiques and children's books (such as *The House where the Cockroaches Lived to Ripe Old Age*, 1976, *The Generous Thief*, 1980, *and Wasserman*, 1988).

Kaniuk's works are about the pioneering Israeli (*Aunt Shlomzion the Great*), emigration, the impact of the Israeli War of Independence and other Israeli wars, The Israeli-Arab conflict and the problematic Zionist justice (*The Acrophile, Aunt Shlomzion the Great, Himmo King of Jerusalem, His Daughter*). They also dealt with emigration from Israel to

America (*The Acrophile, Rockinghorse*); the Palestinian revolt (*His Daughter*); and the Holocaust, its victims and its survivors (*Adam Resurrected, Rockinghorse, Ha-Yehudi ha-Aharon* — "The Last Jew"). From 1961 through 1973, Kaniuk's stories (*Mot ha-'Ayir*, 1973, "The Death of the Young Ass") portrayed the loneliness of modern man in his city life at home, when he wanders from one place to another yearning for warmth, friendship and roots.

Kaniuk's attempt to react to Israeli reality is apparent throughout his literary works. *Ahavat David* ("David's Love," titled as "The Second Book of David") is a novel about the life and death of a national hero, and the 1997 *Nevelot (Ha-Sippur ha-Amitti)*, ("Bastards, the Real Story") is a black-comedy confession with intense activity that questions the destination of the Israeli myth, the meaning of friendship, and the meaning of killing all the time for just goals.

Kaniuk's attraction to the detective-story genre can be demonstrated by his thriller *Tigerhill* (1995) the plot of which includes a threatened woman, an explosion in a coffee shop in Tel-Aviv, a murder, a young criminal-cases reporter, a veteran police officer, a cynical and clever old friend, an aging writer (the author's self-parody), a ship called Tigerhill with clandestine Jewish immigrants that was stuck in 1939 on the shore of Tel-Aviv and more. In *'Od Sippur Ahava* 1996 ("Another Love Story"), Kaniuk created a sophisticated and complicated plot about a man in his "last third" of life in Tel-Aviv, whose son, daughter and friend participate in the story plot.

Kaniuk's newspaper stories and journalistic publications were compiled in books, too. A collection of them appeared in 1975 ('*Afar u-Teshukka*, "Dust and Desire"); a selection from his 1981 through 1983 journalistic publications appeared in 1983 (*Kemo Sippurim*, "Like Stories") and from his later journalistic publications in 1986 (*Sippurei Sofshavua'*, "Weekend Stories"). In many of these works there is an expression of Israeli reality. Kaniuk's work reflects his position that the Jews were victims and when they founded their state other people became victims. The Jews are culturally close to the western culture that almost annihilated them. Kaniuk's characters are irregular, yet they represent problems of their time and place. The protagonists in Kaniuk's novels represent the problems of their generation, emigrants, Holocaust survivors, fighters of the War of Independence, characters that desert the Zionist heritage, and the struggle between this heritage and others, such as the western European or the Sephardi cultures.

In Kaniuk's fiction, one can trace autobiographical elements, which are presented in a way that may give them broad implications and significance (see Shaked, pp. 190-191). For example, Kaniuk's parents and some of his relatives, memories of his childhood and the impact of the War of Independence appear in his fiction in one way or another. *Post Mortem* is a confessional story of autobiographical memories that focus on the relationships of the author with each one of his parents, who had a disastrous marriage. He also addresses his trauma from the War of Independence, his emigration to America and many other autobiographical memories that we also find in his other literary works such as *Rockinghorse.*

Kaniuk's style is dense and sometimes lyric-poetic. In some of his works he portrays the comedy within the tragic life of his characters. In Kaniuk's stories we find extreme human situations. Kaniuk's expressionism intensifies reality.

Kaniuk stated that he was influenced by South American literature and by Isaac Bashevis Singer (see Gingold), and that he loved the literary work of Yosef Hayyim Brener (see Bez al'ael). Indeed one may find the influence of some of the ethereal concepts in the literary work of the Hebrew author Yosef Hayyim Brener. Shaked (pp. 183-187) finds thematic or poetic closeness between the work of Kaniuk to other Israeli authors, Amos Oz, Yitzhak Oren, Hanokh Bartov, Pinhas Sade', Yehuda Amihai, Yaakov Shabtai and others.

In *Himmo King of Jerusalem*, the deformed moving character of Himmo demonstrates the consequences of the war. It seems that the high style even in dialogue, the dramatic plot, Himmo's condition and the message sometimes do not merely represent but also intensify the reality of war. The war and the warriors are not glorified and there are no winners in war. Where war claims its toll, Eros is unattainable.

Kaniuk's books were translated into fourteen languages, including English, French, Spanish, Swedish, German, Danish, Dutch, Slovak, Italian, Norwegian, Finnish and Portuguese. He received many literary awards. His books in English translation are: *Himmo King of Jerusalem* (Atheneum, Chatto & Windus), *Confession of a Good Arab* (Peter Halban, George Braziller and Paladin Grafton), *His Daughter* (Peter Halban, George Braziller), *The Acrophile* (Atheneum, Chatto & Windus), *Aunt Shlomzion the Great* (Harper & Row), *Rockinghorse* (Harper & Row), *Adam Resurrected* (Atheneum, Chatto & Windus, Harper & Row).

THE PLOT

The story takes place in the winter and in the spring of 1948, at the time of the War of Independence in Israel. Jerusalem was besieged, attacked, and its inhabitants were terrified. An old monastery in Jerusalem was converted temporarily into an emergency hospital for Israeli soldiers. The patients are wounded soldiers who fought for Israel and, as they lay injured, they constantly heard the shooting and the bursting shells all around. Fate brought them to one place, but they differed from each other in their background, education and character.

In one of the first paragraphs of the novel we see the rusty iron gate of the monastery; we hear the creaking groaning wicket. We smell the rancid smell of the courtyard and the fetid stench. We sense the air of deliberate neglect and squalor of the place (p. 5), and this serves as an overture to what we anticipate inside.

Hamotal, an 18-year-old woman whose boyfriend was killed in the war in the Galilee, volunteered to serve as a nurse in the old monastery. She was assigned to work in the "Bells Room," where inadequate food, water, medical care and medications made the work with the wounded soldiers difficult. Upon her arrival, Hamotal began developing relationships of sympathy and respect with the wounded soldiers, who are also attracted to her. But she dedicated herself more and more to Himmo, once a uniquely handsome and attractive man to suc a degree that he earned the nickname "King of Jerusalem" in romance, now legless, armless, blind and unable or unwilling to talk. Only his mouth remained beautiful. The pathetic hyperbolic description of the disfigured Himmo is macabre, horribly grotesque. (Kaniuk's inclination for the grotesque was possibly due to the influence of Yosef Hayyim Brener).

Hamotal's dedication to Himmo "the dummy," Himmo's repetitive request to shoot him ("reh bi, reh bi" — "shoo me, shoo me"), and his deadly wounds that were constant reminders of death spawned friction with the other wounded soldiers who were envious and needed Hamotal's care and attention, too. The envy of the soldiers resulted in their wish for Himmo's death.

Hamotal was attracted to Himmo and was full of compassion for him. She tried with all her might to protect and save him. But she came to the conclusion the best thing for him is to die, and she becomes his executor. Horror, fatal wounds and death become central to the life of the young soldiers at the peak of their blossoming.

THE CHARACTERS AND THEIR DILEMMAS

The characters are portrayed by general descriptions. We do not have an in-depth depiction of the characters' pasts and major parts of their basic constitution; their psychological world and background are unknown to us. Their inner world and history are brief and lack weighty perceptiveness. Due to the fact that often in this novel the reader is not provided with meaningful insights into the characters, some of the characters' feelings and actions may seem bizarre and even their dialogue at times sounds inorganic and unreal. Therefore, they do not fascinate the reader. Most of the characters are static, unlike dynamic characters that change throughout the course of a novel.

As a whole, the pride of the wounded soldiers in this anti-war novel was shattered. They were brave defenders but after they were wounded; they needed to be defended, but they felt helpless and useless. Their medical condition was insignificant when compared to Himmo's, the constant reminder of death and of the painful fact that death may be better than life in some cases. When we see the wounded soldiers silent in the darkening monastery at dusk, we are beautifully introduced to their inner life — the horror and fury.

Himmo, once the favorite man of young women, now begs to be shot because of his condition. He is only 19-years-old. (Himmo was born in 1929 and wounded in 1948, see p. 33). Except his two words requesting to be shot, Himmo does not say anything in the novel. We learn about his past only from Franji and Himmo's brother. He cannot fight for Israel anymore, and he is no longer handsome or heroic. He has no hope, and his loving brother Marco thinks that death will be better than life for him. Marco wants to help him to die. The more Himmo's past is glamorized, the more difficult his present and pain seem.

The medical condition of Himmo, who was a necessary sacrifice for the establishment of the State of Israel, is macabre:

> Right leg missing, left leg missing, one arm missing from the elbow, the other hand missing from the wrist; lacerated belly... crushed stumps of limbs... red, gasping wounds, and the stink of rotting flesh...The neck was twisted awry. Yes, his eyes were missing, too... (p. 34).

When compared with the glamour of his past by his old time friend Franji, this condition impacts us even more:

> Once he used to be King of Jerusalem. Himmo, King of Jerusalem, we called him... A real king he was. The girls used to faint all over him, heaps of 'em. That mouth of his, the Holy Mouth, they called it. He'd be walking up the street, just like that, with the lot of them chirping after him (p. 38).

Time and again we are reminded of Himmo's magnificent mouth that captivated Hamotal entirely (p. 62, see also p. 165) with its perfection:

> All else vanished, eclipsed by the fascination of that mouth...(to her last day, Hamotal would blush whenever she recalled how beautiful it was)... the mouth... turned into the acme of perfection.... Fate had here vouch-safed her its noblest gift, the rarest beauty, perfection on the brink of horror. *A mouth dripping kisses!* The king of mouths. A mouth made of flights of flashing angels. A thing of bright loveliness amid the ambient horror, like a solitary flower on a vast wall (pp. 35-36).

In the ambient of horror, Himmo's mouth reminds Hamotal of a flower. She also relates to herself sometimes as a flower. She saw herself "like one of those flowers...which bloom, proud and defiant, on the dung heap" (p. 23). During wartime, youth and beauty are disrupted, and they face the hardship of the flowers set in the composite of manure. While Hamotal sees the flower in Himmo, Franji sees the contact between Himmo and Hamotal as a contact between a stone and a flower as one may conclude from his ordering Asa to "draw two mouths kissing, one like a flower and the other like a stone" (p. 168) — the war turned Himmo's youthful, beautiful, "holy" mouth into a stone. Later Hamotal connects herself to her people's history and metaphorically to a flower, "she likened herself to an uprooted flower that has been restored by a fresh gentle breeze to its native meadow" (p. 149). One flower blossoms and another becomes a mere memory, but the tree continues its life, like a nation that loses individuals but continues to blossom.

Himmo is only one link of the 250-year history of his family in Israel (pp. 149, 161), in particular, and of the Jewish people in general. Himmo is called by the name of Himma, Himmo's great-great-grandfather's daughter who died in the 1837 earthquake of Safed (pp. 183-184). The price paid for Israel is heavy; nature and war get their victims.

In the name Himmo Farrah, Himmo is a shortened form of the Hebrew word "rahamim" which means mercy, while "farrah" comes from Arabic and means joy. This name may ironically remind us of our world in which killing someone may be the most merciful act we can do for him, and thus our hope that he lives a life of joy and that he brings joy is proved to be erroneous. (Some critics of the book missed the irony in Himmo's last name and interpreted the name as being "Perah" (flower) due to the non-vocalized Hebrew text and embarked with its interpretation and meaning as a flower.) Himmo's name reminds us that the anticipation of joy was premature and unrealistic in that merciless part of the world where death was Himmo's only merciful option.

Hamotal is a mature, responsible, thoughtful young woman with an irregular ability for perseverance. She is a pretty, efficient, diligent, serene, likable, polite, respected, amiable and her words "were reasoned and sound," "she was cold and controlled," admired "for her efficiency and straightforwardness" (pp. 18-20). Hamotal is a main character whose conduct generates the reactions of the other characters — Clara, the nurses, Himmo, Marco, the doctors and the wounded soldiers.

The reader can gather her appearance from strewn paragraphs in the novel. "She was young and attractive, with short black hair that accentuated her good looks" (p. 141). Hamotal yearned to tell Himmo "what she looked like, describe her graceful neck, her ebony-dark hair, her eyes which were sometimes hazel and sometimes green...She wanted to tell him about her firm, erect body, about her full, well-formed breasts that lay with her on her lonely pallet..." (p. 57). The people in the hospital were aware of Hamotal's "attractive appearance, her fine figure and her black hair which kept falling winsomely over her face" (p. 111). Asa in his anger and frustration described Hamotal as being "by no means ugly, but no raving beauty either, just average pretty" (p. 99).

Hamotal is of an Askenazi origin, different from Himmo's origin of the old Sephardi settlers in Jerusalem, "her father has been a pioneer who spoke Hebrew with a Slav accent and wore a Russian rubashka" (p. 181). Shaked (pp. 77, 192) claims that the novel presents the mental and social clash between Hamotal, who belongs to the beautiful Israel and to the beautiful Zionist norms on the one hand, and, on the other, to Himmo and Marco of the old Sephardi settlement, who sacrificed themselves for Zionism while Zionism did not recognize them. Hamotal prefers Marco and Himmo to her own social group. It is my opinion, however, that Himmo and Marco themselves "belong to the beautiful Israel and to the beautiful Zionist norms. "

Hamotal's childhood memories do not mount to a meaningful biography that would provide insight into her adult life. She "was born and grew up near the Tel-Aviv seashore" (p. 211) and later she differentiates between Jerusalem, the eternal city, and "Tel-Aviv, the ephemeral city of the moment" (p. 212).

Hamotal's womanhood and motherhood, the special treatment the doctors and patients accorded her, her attractive appearance, the clout of a boyfriend who was killed up in Galilee, her engaging modesty and her gentleness and her perseverance, evoked the nurses' jealousy. "Hamotal's capacity for caring so devotedly for the mangled human wreck that was Himmo must have aroused bitter envy of their femininely romantic young hearts" (p. 110). In short, "One simply can't help loving a person who never grumbles and who's never afraid" (p. 101).

Hamotal wants to understand the present and is curious about the past. Her life experience is limited, but her stamina is impressive. Marco tells her about his family, and Clara tells her about the monastery. Jews and Christians are attached to the land of Israel and to its history. Hamotal understood that Himmo's "roots were firm-set in the eternity of this city," Jerusalem; she saw the war in perspective and remembered:

> These wars and conquests had left behind many salient and martyrs... down to Himmo Farrah. Long and bitter and bloody had been this war for the heritage of Judah... Hamotal was gripped by a sudden fear, not for the blood that had been shed till now and the horrors and agony: she feared this might not be the final price.
> When Hamotal got up next morning, she unstitched the red cross from her coif (p. 160-161).

The War of Independence is a link in Jewish history; Himmo's blood is part of the price Jews paid and will pay for Jewish existence in Israel. The main characters and the setting of the novel are Israeli, and they are connected and viewed as part of Jewish history. This recognition evoked in Hamotal national feelings and identity; these feelings are demonstrated by her symbolic act of removing the red cross from her coif, the existence of which did not bother her until that moment.

Himmo's roots were firm-set in Jerusalem, and Hamotal is looking to lay down her own roots. It is possible that she develops an attachment to Jerusalem as an extension of her attachment to Himmo, who died for Jerusalem.

> Tel-Aviv, the modern city of her birth...now appeared to her a remote Levantine town...whereas the Eternal City...seemed to be drawing her down to plant her in its soil ...these very stones...were imparting to her, Hamotal, a sense of returning, of a lost daughter returning to her Hebrew birthright...(p. 150).

What draws Hamotal to the mutilated, "dummy," Himmo? Attraction? Pity? Or is it hatred and revulsion of others? Is it because her own "revulsion made way for a passionate craving" (p. 165)? Or perhaps it is an attempt to defy destiny and attain victory against all odds, which will be a proof of power? Is it guilt because she will live and Himmo will not? Pain because she could not save her boyfriend? The need to be needed? Is it obsessive attraction to death and helplessness? Maybe it was a strange physical attraction to his mouth? Did his previous status of king, the charismatic dream man of Jerusalem women intrigue her? Was it love, which is pure and "Platonic"? Was it an expression that the problems of the wounded Israelis have numbed her own problems and she decided to dedicate her life to them? Or perhaps coming from an Askenazi family she was attracted to the Sephardi Himmo — "there had been no Hamotal throughout Himmo's childhood. She was a Jewess from another world" (p. 181).

On the basis of his experience and on the basis of the text, the reader may explain the nature of the connection of Hamotal to Himmo in various ways, including the possibility that the psychological foundations for this attraction are feeble in the novel. Himmo cannot reciprocate Hamotal's love and devotion. Eros becomes grotesque during war.

Hamotal's dedication to Himmo brings about various feelings among the wounded soldiers, the jealous Asa wants to see her as "flesh and blood, a woman and no more...'she's just like you and me, no different'" (p 166) while Franji insists: "She's a woman who's... who's the Messiah... She's a queen, she is... A princess! That's what she is!" (Ibid.).

Hamotal's beloved had been killed in battle up in Galilee, an event that caused her to strive to feel a part of her surroundings (p. 16) and matured her (p. 18). The death of the boyfriend gave Hamotal clout (See for example pp. 58, 99, 111). The death as Asa described it was heroic: " He had been carrying a load of explosive and had set them off, turning himself into a living bomb, in order to save his comrades" (p. 21), but the narrator casts doubt about the accuracy of the heroic story. Hamotal and her betrothed were not about to get married and perhaps it was not he who detonated the explosive he was carrying (p. 25). Dr. Neuman heard a different story, and he asked Hamotal if it was true that her husband was killed up in Galilee (p. 29). Rumors have their way of adjusting the facts to suit a romantic tragedy and to dramatize and make myth out of certain situations.

The power of life is immense and, at the monastery within time, Hamotal's beloved became just a "blurred image...and vanished again into extinction" (p. 58); she has "forgotten all about him" (p. 60), even though "she had once — admittedly — loved" him (p. 119, see also p. 210). The death of her beloved impacted Hamotal, but life is far stronger than being just a memory.

The death of one adds flair to another. Facts get modified to fit human needs for understanding and for drama. As long as one lives — even if he is in Himmo's condition — he can impact others; once dead his power disappears. But people such as Hamotal are also honest and willing enough to expose the weakness of a beloved, dead friend. Her boyfriend "was really a fine boy, but he had one shortcoming I couldn't stand" (p. 206), she told Dr. Neuman. He was not in love with her but did not leave her so she would not get attached to someone else. Hamotal has experienced therefore the pain and sadness of a unilateral love.

Special friendship developed between Hamotal and Marco, Himmo's older brother. He had "infinite degree of patience" (p. 104), even in wartime "he was always immaculately dressed; ...he always turned out well-groomed...His courteous, flowery manner of speech, his polished, almost ceremonial manners smacked of a Levantine air... He must have been of Sephardic origin..." (p. 104-105), "there was a primitive nobility about him that rather surprised Hamotal when she found out he lacked any formal schooling" (p. 105). If we believe Asa, Marco commanded a military position in the Sheikh Jerrah sector (p. 104). He "loved his brother dearly" (Ibid.) and wanted to bring an end to his brother's torment.

By portraying Marco, Kaniuk attempted to portray not just an individual but also a "typical" young Sephardi from the old Jewish settlement in Jerusalem. In one incident Hamotal's thoughts related to Marco in quite a stereotypical way (Hakak, 1981) — being cautious with and suspecting of people, he was shrewd and sad; he was not culturally refined and had no formal education, but had "primitive refines" only; he was calm and overly polite:

> Marco doesn't trust people, she [Hamotal] mused, and he doesn't expect people to trust him, either. She had more than once pondered over his shrewd oriental characteristic in his make-up, this craftiness tinged with sadness. She had come to appreciate, even admire, his primitive refinement, his intro-verted calm, his exaggerated politeness — qualities that stemmed not only from his lack of formal education but primarily were rooted in the tradition of generations, a tradition that was lacking in her own past (pp. 217-218).

Asa and Franji are two other wounded soldiers treated in the monastery. Their wounds were not fatal and when "...confronted with Himmo all of them are well off compared to him" (p. 66). Like all the wounded soldiers they lived life without hope, "for hope was not allowed to intrude openly among the inmates of Emergency Hospital C" (p. 79). In the first chapter of the novel we find that fear dominates Jerusalem in general (pp. 4, 7), and later we find that the heroic soldiers too "lived in fear breathed fear, wet their trousers in fear, wept and moaned in fear" (p. 83).

In the battlefield Asa was heroic. He "pinned down on the roof of a mosque with a bullet in his leg, surrounded by a score of Arabs, continues shooting it out" (p. 83).

In Asa we have a thinker-soldier who feels and thinks intensely. Asa had the role of intermediary between the hospital staff and his wounded comrades (p. 3). He had a flair for painting, acting and pantomime (p. 75). But in the world of war and wounds with its grading, tacitly Asa was at the bottom of the social scale because he was comparatively lightly wounded and an "intellectual" (pp. 162-164), who talked eloquently about politics and social problems. Even his status as "king of the rumor-mongers" (p. 169) could not offset his "shortcoming" of being "intellec-tual." Both Dr. Abayoff (in p.93) and Clara (in p. 100) tell Asa that it was out of jealousy that he complained about Hamotal for her dedication exclusively to Himmo, and finally he was honest enough to admit it (p. 100).

Franji, a Sephardi, was at the top of the social scale in the hospital because he was one of the most seriously wounded and because he "alternated between brutality and tenderness according to his mood." (p. 162). Franji too was heroic in the battlefield, he "sprawled wounded on a cold Jerusalem mountainside" and saw "with his good eye how the vultures are swooping down on him while his other eye is spilling into his palm, and keeps shying stones at the birds to drive them off" (p. 83).

Himmo as a "king" "had always somehow made Franji aware of his own inferiority" (p. 163). He is aware of the complexity of the love-hate feelings he and Himmo had for each other, "just like brothers" (p. 178-179). This complex love-hate relationship may be the cause for Franji's brutal treatment of Himmo at times, it is a mix of jealousy, pity, pain, mockery, death, fear and frustration (see p. 186). He tried to bring Himmo to speak: "Hey, King... It's me, your bosom pal, Franji!" (p. 39) — he yelled and, when he did not receive any response, "he savagely jerked Himmo's pillow out from under his head" (Ibid.). Laughingly and ironically he continued talking to Himmo, calling him Abu Jilda, a notorious Palestine Arab bandit chief: "Hey, hero! King of the heroes! Abu Jilda!" (Ibid.). Pain is the strongest motive of Franji's brutal conduct: "He looked at his friend and pitied him" (p. 42).

Two doctors, Moshe Abayoff and Neuman (the latter to be discussed subsequently in this chapter), are portrayed in some detail. Dr. Abayoff was the head physician, "a shrewd little man, highly irascible and always tired" (p. 12), bitter, bristly and full of complaints against everyone. He was practical and strives to be fair, in a situation where "the fighting men needed their ration far more than the wounded who would not be able to fight any more" (Ibid.). His sarcasm and overtone are inappropriate and uncalled for, especially in a hospital where the young wounded soldiers need a fatherly touch.

When Hamotal complained against shifting Himmo to a pallet near the doorway, Dr. Abayoff attempted to ridicule her: "Should we perhaps let him have a drawing room with a balcony overlooking the sea?" (p. 51, see also p. 93) But he also tried to reason with her and, when Hamotal finally called him "a louse," he nodded his head and smiled: "yes, of course... that's what they all say" (p. 53). The response is that of a firm person sure of his sense of fairness.

Clara called Dr. Abayoff "degenerate," but Hamotal defended him: "Abayoff is a poor overworked man... If you'd only think of the crushing responsibility weighing him down day and night, you'd see the man's an angel" (p. 100), and on another occasion she thought: "It was a shame he was so bitter, for behind all his grievances and cynicism he was basically a principled man who followed the dictates of his conscience, and who therefore stood out as a landmark of decency in an ugly world..." (p. 133). While "Abayoff felt that he has been destined for greatness... "The nation was facing its greatest hour, and he had been condemned to miss it" (p. 132), because of his position (p. 132), "Hamotal sometimes mused that Dr. Abayoff didn't realize this was his hour of greatness. She saw him a mediocre little man, an insignificant third-rate doctor who had been elevated by the fortunes of war" (Ibid.). Had the novel provided the reader with significant insight into the doctor's character, the reader could formulate his own position about the doctor when facing the gap between the doctor's self-assessment and Hamotal's assessment of him.

We see Dr. Abayoff through his own eyes, the eyes of Hamotal, and those of the other characters. And we weigh the reliability of each character's view.

MERCY MURDER

The novel presents the questions if a life should be prolonged in all cases and if not who should decide what actions to take: The suffering person? The physicians? Those who love the sick person and witness his torment? Who is wise and fair — the person who will expedite his death or the person who will keep him alive regardless of his condition? Can life be so agonizing that death will be redemption?

Various characters in the novel debate the issue of euthanasia and raise major points about it. The general debate about mercy murder and its applicability to Himmo slows down the plot and builds up anticipations and suspense. Sometimes the novel style concerning the informal debates of this serious and painful issue is too high.

Based on Himmo's condition Franji thinks Himmo should be assisted in dying: "He wants to die, that's all. So why don't you let him, eh? Call yourself merciful? That's mercy, is it?" (p. 41). Marco thinks his beloved brother Himmo is "in a tight fix" (p. 54) and, under the circumstances, he is sorry "they won't allow it" (Ibid.) — the hospital authorities will not allow euthanasia in spite of Marco's "pleading glances at the doctors" (Ibid.). Instead Marco was closely watched so that he not end his brother's life. Hamotal's thoughts against such an act are well-founded:

> ...She remembered... that life was sacred and none had the
> right to take it. No matter how elevated the motives. There
> were no two ways about it...Regardless of what life was like,
> it must be preserved at all costs. What doctor was so infallible
> to pronounce all hope gone, to say that death was preferable
> to life? Who could be certain...that a person...really wanted
> to die? Perhaps he didn't really want to die... (p. 55-56).

Various doubts intervene in Hamotal's thoughts:

> If he really wants to die...who am I to stand in his way? But
> there again...why does his mangled body go on fighting with
> death? Why doesn't it simply surrender to the death? (p. 62).

Considering putting an end to Himmo's suffering, Hamotal wondered "whether what she really wanted was to break loose from him,
rather than help him break loose from his fate" (p. 192). When she felt
united with Himmo's heart she "feared that this feeling...was but the
shrieking of a murderer heart, decked out in false finery (p. 193).

The young Dr. Neuman exhibits human sensitivity and thoughtful-
ness in his dialogue with Hamotal about euthanasia. When Dr. Neuman
told Hamotal that there was some improvement in Himmo's condition, she
wondered: "What for?...What's the need, the urgency, this frantic
eagerness to prolong suffering?" (p. 197). Dr. Neuman responded that "a
man has the right to live because he wants to" (Ibid.) and he has other
reasons:

> If every doctor who saw his patient's end in sight hastened it
> on, where would that get us? ...We mustn't risk missing a
> single chance, and there is always a chance (pp. 197-198).

Dr. Neuman thinks that the doctors' work is gauged by their "ability
to prolong life, and not in finding some nobler content for life" (p. 198),
while Hamotal wondered "what about the suffering" (Ibid.). "In theory
there is hope for every man" (Ibid.), Dr. Neuman reminds Hamotal. He
thinks that a man who "is helped to stay alive a little longer may increase
the life span of others" (p. 199), the doctor does not know if Himmo's life
"for him is a blessing or a curse" (p. 200), but he thinks the prolonged
agony of Himmo may advance mankind toward the desire to have people
dying at an old age without suffering.

Concluding that there is no hope for Himmo, Hamotal became decisive: "Now it's clear there is no room for pity. Himmo's suffering must be ended" (p. 202). Dr. Neuman thinks that "it is precisely out of pity that we must not do this," but Hamotal thinks to the contrary that "out of pity we must not keep from doing it" (Ibid.). Hamotal claims that Himmo "wants to die...and you don't let him" (Ibid.), but Dr. Neuman claims, "only his mouth begs to die...but his spirit doesn't want to die" (p. 203). In this argument he is close to Clara who brings another idea to this dilemma of mercy murder. Clara states that Himmo was begging to be allowed to die, "when all he has to do is to stop...exerting the strongest will to live I have ever seen in my life" (p. 64), she doubts if "the heart knows what the lips mumble" (Ibid.). Even when one asks for death it is not always clear if he means it.

Hamotal, however, insists, "one can't lay down iron-clad rules in this matter.... I don't in the least doubt the existence of the powerful wish to live... Himmo doesn't want to live, and he is afraid, it's of what may be on the other side" (p. 206). Later Hamotal feels that she has been charged with the task of murdering Himmo (p. 223). But she needs the strength of rationalizing the task by a feeling of womanly humiliation after expecting Himmo to romantically do that which he can't do; she first slapped Himmo's face (pp. 236-237) and then inflicted death on him by giving him a lethal injection. This act frees her from Himmo and is the clue to her choosing life.

In the death scene three elements are most touching: Himmo's weeping and without uttering a sound begging to live, Hamotal's clinging to him with shut eyes and licking away the tears from his lifeless face, and Dr. Abayoff's taking Hamotal down from the bell-rope "with the most utmost gentleness...as though he was leading a bride to the strains of a wedding march" (p. 244). War turns Eros into death and potential weddings into mourning.

"You see, Miss Hamotal, death can bring peace to sufferings when there is no choice" (p. 186) — says Marco after telling Hamotal about Himma. Death as mercy, death as a redeemer — that is sometimes the only option at wartime. This is a most restrained and, at the time, a most powerful anti-war outcry. "Spring pervaded the blue sky" (p. 193) — and this only made Hamotal realize that out of pity she must put Himmo to death (p. 202). The siege and the war were coming to an end and the weather was improving. The world will continue, spring will come after spring, the living can't help but enjoying life, and those whose death is a better alternative for them than life should die. This, in the structural setting of the monastery, gives a gothic and macabre atmosphere to the novel.

SOME MESSAGES OF
THE NOVEL

Himmo was not "The King of the Jews," he was "The King of Jerusalem" only, but the king ended up dying a terrible death without significantly changing the ways of the world. He was sacrificed in the war for the establishment of the State of Israel.

Some of the messages of the novel are central to it. The anti-war message is strong, yet war awakens national awareness and belonging. Christians and Jews may have close friendships based on mutual respect and recognition of each other's virtues, but a religious missionary may create barriers and skepticism and emphasize differences. A pious person is not one who is unaware of the temptations of the world but one who is aware of them and struggles to resist them. Forgiveness provides repeated chances to correct human ways and achieve piety; forgetting is as important as remembering, because memories may be too heavy to bear and may disable us.

Humanity is involved with love, life, beauty, youth and care — but in wartime, such as the period in the novel, it wastes the young and beautiful. The story leads to an anti-war conclusion and to the understanding that there is no victory in war. At the same time, the story leads to the conclusion that mankind can find the most beautiful feelings of love and unconditional benevolence even within the worst of circumstances.

When one looks at the outcome of the Israeli War of Independence in national terms, the war was a great success because it made the founding of the State of Israel possible. The novel, however, does not focus on the national outcome, but on the consequences suffered by the individuals who paid the price of war. What was a victory from a national perspective, was a tragedy from an individual perspective. The establishment of the State of Israel was the answer to national dreams, at the price of creating problems or even causing death for some of the individuals who made the dreams come true.

The novel presents the tragedy of the wounded soldiers, who, at the end of their heroic acts, were wounded and felt "like scraps that have fallen from the table and are not worth picking up, a burden on the war machine... and each one sees himself a maimed, wretched hero" (p. 67).

Franji, describing how they were wounded and pulled out of the battlefield, bitterly wondered: "What for, I ask you? What did they have to pull us out for? So that we should be like dead for the rest of our lives? For that? We've got nothing that's worth anything any more, it's all gone with the ravens" (p. 179). When the soldiers can look on themselves in a tragicomic way, they speak of themselves as maimed future beggars, and as Asa put it, "for a moment we were heroes on the battlefield — redemption on a silver tray, rebirth of the nation, our reply to the ghettos of Europe, a two-thousand-year-old hope, and all that — and just look what's become of us!" (p. 115).

When weighed rationally, the attraction of Hamotal to Himmo is impossible; but when the human heart prevails, everything is possible — even Hamotal's complex feelings for the "dummy" with their infatuated distracted side. But even the most human and tender feelings are not likely to be fulfilled in a world of war. Hamotal "imagined Himmo — in her dream he had assumed Marco's form..." (p. 189) — in wartime, only if the impossible becomes possible; love has a chance.

War also may play a strong role in awakening and strengthening national awareness and bonds. The changing attitude of Hamotal toward the red cross on her coif (a lucid symbol of Christianity) in the novel is representative of her growing awareness of her Jewish identity. When Hamotal first observed the crucifixes set in the windows of the monastery, they "filled her with unease" (p. 8). Later, Hamotal wore the nurse uniform that was brought from a former British army headquarters. "The smart British nurse's uniform, with the red crosses stitched to the bodice of the apron and the coif, was most becoming to her" (p. 15-16). She did not attribute any meaning to wearing the cross. Hamotal insisted on wearing the coif even though she should not have and "the matter of the coif remained an imponderable mystery" (p. 16). When Clara noticed the coif on Hamotal's head, Clara's face grew serious and she fixed her wounded look "on the red cross that glowed bright against the whiteness of Hamotal's coif' (p. 27). Hamotal became self-conscious and straightened her coif; she felt Clara was mixing in her private affairs, it is doubtful that Hamotal thought about the red cross in religious terms, but for Clara it was not a private affair.

When Hamotal linked herself and the monastery to Jewish history, and remembered the blood that had been shed including Himmo's and the possible future sacrifices, she became attentive to the cross on the coif. "She unstitched the red cross from the coif" (p. 161).

The encounter between Judaism and Christianity is treated somehow further in the novel. Dr. Neuman tells Hamotal that Clara was sent to the monastery to look after the property, "but nobody seriously intends giving the property back" (p. 27). Clara indeed sees the monastery as abandoned property that belongs to her religious order, and the Jews took it only as a loan (p. 26). Dr. Neuman's view of the situation is different:

> Don't forget that all they want is to turn us into Christians, and that's what they're here for. We don't owe them a thing. They've always been and will always remain our enemies. Now it's war to the end — a two-thousand-year-old war that's now coming to a head...
>
> The religious order that sent her [Clara] over to us... has its head office in a building over there in the Old City, and on the roof of that building there are guns nests and emplacements that keep shelling us... (p. 28).

Dr. Neuman sees Christianity as constantly striving to turn Jews into Christians and therefore there is an ongoing war between the two religions. The Jews are facing therefore two wars: one, which threatens to extinguish them physically, and one, which strives to convert them spiritually. Once Hamotal hears the history of the monastery (Chapter 10) and thinks about the various nations and religions involved in conquering and losing it, she becomes very attached to it, and she thinks "what a terrible price they [the Jews] had paid in this house!" (p. 161) — the house signifies the entire country of Israel, and the price was paid by the Jews for claiming it from others who want it, too.

Clara, a nun and a "qualified nurse" (p. 26), "a permanent observer of life" (p. 128), has lived in the Holy Land for 35 years prior to meeting Hamotal. Jerusalem in her eyes is "a mad city... that consumes its inhabitants, spellbound by glory of its past, and as filthy as hell" (p. 25). Dr. Neuman admires Clara's energy and good spirit; he is also aware that she is strongly connected to Christianity: "all day long she is answering [error in the translation, should be "swearing"] and crossing herself" (p. 27).

Between Hamotal and Clara there developed a tender relationship and love (see for example pp. 44, 63, 119-110, 225-229), full of understanding and trust. This relationship grew to be relationship of respect:

"Hamotal was the only person who had ever got her to talk about herself... Clara found herself regarding Hamotal with unqualified respect" (p. 129). Religion does not seem to obstruct the two unique women from developing a close friendship.

While Hamotal wanted to understand many situations on the basis of personal relationships, Clara brought up the perspective of her faith to her perceptions. As to Himmo, Clara tells Hamotal: "If you believe in God... I would tell you that He had a hand in it..." (p. 63) and "it's God's own mystery why He keeps him alive" (p. 64).

Hamotal, as a secular Israeli, is pushed back to her roots not in spite but because of Clara's persistence in constantly bringing up religious issues in secular dialogues. Hamotal tried to associate herself with her own national history, "like a wayward son returning to the family hearth" (p. 149). She thought that Clara could never understand her, being that Clara is only "a missionary whose sole purpose in life was to save some shred of erring souls of Jews who had not yet seen the Light and the True Path" (p. 150). Clara's mission only brings Hamotal closer to Judaism and with the land of Israel, and she had "a sense of... a lost daughter returning to her Hebrew birthright, and that gradually she was becoming the real mistress of the house, regarding Clara merely as a housekeeper..." (Ibid.). Looking at history and remembering what Jews were willing to sacrifice for Israel make Hamotal feel that the "house" — the monastery as a symbolic tangible representation of the land that Jews fought for — belongs to her.

In the last dialogue between Hamotal and Clara in the novel, Hamotal illustrates the differences between their future activities, differences which are the result of their beliefs. Clara will go back to her missionary work to save erring souls; to handing out free meals and Bibles; to her monastery; to her matins, vespers and vows; to advance to the kingdom of heaven; and to confessing to sins she knows nothing of. Meanwhile, Hamotal will participate in building up Israel, the kingdom on earth, and she will "sin" (p. 228). Yet, love and friendship mark their feelings for each other (p. 228).

Hamotal may continue her charitable acts while she lives a secular and whole life, while Clara will continue her charitable acts in the frame of her religious order.

While there are human bonds of love, respect and friendship that, on an individual basis may be stronger than religion, a religious missionary may create barriers and skepticism and emphasize differences. It is in this light that one may understand Hamotal's anxieties expressed in dreams, "Jews are being burned alive in their synagogues. Clara appears from somewhere...laughing wildly..." (p. 190).

Clara told Hamotal about Hieronymus who translated the Bible into Latin and who, 1600 years ago, sat in the place where the monastery was. Clara described Hieronymus as a man who was God-fearing and who lived as a hermit, purifying himself. His lifestyle did not come easy for him, for "his heart longed for the rich, profane roman literature and civilization" (p. 47). Clara identifies with his awareness of temptations and his struggle against it: "Me too... I fight back the Devil... spit in his face... whereas you, you don't even acknowledge his existence" (Ibid.). In order to be a holy person one must encounter temptation feel its power and be able to resist it (see Bartana).

When, however, Clara told Hamotal that Hieronymus is the one who will shield her with his spirit, Clara became a stranger to her, "she felt a surge of hostility that snapped the newly formed bond of friendship" (p. 48) because of Clara's intrusions into Hamotal's faith.

In spite of the respect for those who sacrificed themselves for the founding and for the existence of Israel, life is compelling and the living go on. Twelve years after Hamotal put Himmo to sleep, Hamotal accidentally met Marco in Jerusalem without saying a word about the past. Marco's look said: "We mustn't, it is forbidden" (p. 245). "All was erased...He [Himmo] no longer exists" (Ibid.). But coffee shops, coffee and cakes, sugar, taxis, kiosks and ice cream do exist. "The burden was too heavy for any of them to bear: She knew that they, too, were being crushed under it" (Ibid.).

Sometimes we must remember in order to go on; sometimes we must forget.

HIMMO AND KANIUK'S
MEMORIES

20 years after the publication of Kaniuk's novel, when the movie based on the novel was in production, a unique public debate took place in Israel: Was Himmo a real person or only a fictitious character?

We keep in mind the liberty of the fiction writer, however, it is still worthwhile in this case to relate to that debate, especially because Yoram Kaniuk himself initiated it. As mentioned above, Kaniuk's literary works give clear expression to autobiographical events and characters. Kaniuk spoke about his injury in 1948 in the battle for the Old City of Jerusalem. He was hospitalized in the basement of the Italian Hospital in Jerusalem where he met another injured soldier:

> Near me lied down a young man called Amnon Vigolik, who murmured constantly that he wanted to die. I learned afterward that he was from Jerusalem and was considered the most handsome young man in the city. After he died there was a rumor in the hospital that the doctors put an end to his life. The days I was hospitalized next to him engraved his character in my memory, and I founded Himmo's character after him (see in *Kol ha-'Ir*).

This story was supported by Amira Bleiberg, the mother of the producer of the movie *Himmo, King of Jerusalem* She met Amnon Vigolik in 1946 in a youth movement and later, after he was wounded in the war, he was brought to the Italian hospital in Jerusalem where she was a nurse. About the issue of Himmo Farrah-Amnon-Vigolik she said:

> When I read Kaniuk's book, the first thing that I envisioned was Vigolik's character. The event itself is similar. Vigolic was severely wounded. His arms were amputated up to above his elbows. He lost his vision and his hearing in one of his ears. At the beginning he tried to be a hero, but when he started understanding his condition he became silent. The man who talked non-stop was retreated inside himself... Himmo can be Vigolik... Vigolik was a handsome man, very likable and with wonderful sense of humor. His fatal injury was the result of his heroic act. He was a commander of a military unit, which was attacked, and most of its soldiers were wounded. Vigolic volunteered during the fighting retreat to put mines in order to hold the Arabs up and one of the mines exploded in his face (See: Vered Lam).

After several months in the Jerusalem hospital, Vigolik was transferred to Tel-Aviv. He was sent to the United States for eye surgery but did not regain his eyesight. He demanded an additional eye surgery, which was dangerous, and he died during the surgery in Israel.

The social worker, who worked with Vogolik (Ora Kenat), and an artist, who was also hospitalized with Vigolik, remembered a nurse similar to Hamotal.

Amnon Vigolik's brother (Hayyim) objects to the connection between his dead brother and Himmo:

> Kaniuk describes as if they all waited all the time that Amnon will die... This is a lie. He also did not die there. He died in the surgery room. No one killed him. They did not kill wounded soldiers in the hospital at all... Kaniuk describes Amnon as a living corpse who did not talk and only murmured all the time: 'shoot me, shoot me'. In the memorial book published by the Ministry of Defense is written: 'With crushed limbs and helpless, without eyes vision and with his amputated arms bandaged, he was not discouraged and even joked with the nurses and those who cared for him and he encouraged the wounded soldiers who were groaning around him', and this is the truth. Amnon did not want to die, and did not ask anyone to shoot him... There was no nurse that fell in love with Amnon, and he did not receive any special treatment (see Ibid.).

One may conclude that Kaniuk employed a character that he met in the hospital when he was wounded, and used some of his strong characteristics and physical and mental conjunctures when he portrayed Himmo.

Needless to say that while the above information may satisfy the human curiosity of some readers, it clearly should not play any role in the evaluation of the novel and of its artistic achievements.

KANIUK ABOUT HIS NOVEL
AND OTHER ISSUES

In an interview (See Bez ala'el) with Kaniuk after the publication of *Himmo King of Jerusalem*, and in two journalistic essays, Yoram Kaniuk expressed some opinions that may be of interest to the reader. From these published pieces one may learn about Kaniuk's concept of a realistic novel, love, the attitude to Israel, his fascination with the history of Israel and with the Sephardim and the expression of his own personal War of Independence experience in the novel, *Himmo, King of Jerusalem*.

I will present some of his ideas:

> In *Himmo, King of Jerusalem* I intended to write a realistic novel. I did not strive for the reflections, but for the story, that lived inside me for many years. I wanted to describe love

under the less possible circumstances... I believe that love is always possible, that it is like a miracle of a meeting between two souls. The most beautiful miracle that can happen to a human being. Many told me that *Himmo* is an authentic book, that the types of people, the setting and the way of life in it are authentic, and at the same time I was surprised to hear that the situation in it is not realistic. People believed everything written in the novel, only not the love described in it, they did not believe this miracle that blossoms like a flower on a garbage pile, that gets ignited at the end of a deep wadi. This love of Hamotal to Himmo is like a step beyond the absurd... I consider it a failure that I did not convince the reader in this main point of *Himmo*.

And *Himmo* has a secondary theme: mercy murder. This is a hard problem that people faced time and again during the War of Independence, but was almost not described in Hebrew literature.

...About twenty years after this War, I tried in *Himmo* to write something else about that war. Not a story about the way of life. Therefore the plot was written intentionally in a very condensed way.

...In my attitude to Israel there is a contrast, in the autobiographical and the literary sense. On the one hand, I have strong yearning to Israel. The history of Israel is my hobby, not only the history of the Jews in it, but also the crusaders and the Turks, and to all the historical periods... I have yearning to roots deeper than Zionism; Zionism was insufficient for me in this regard. I always looked for the continuity of Israel, the tradition that passes from one generation to another. This is how I was attracted to Himmo's family in the book, a family that has lived in Israel for two hundred fifty years. On the other hand, it is strange that I from all people... lived for many years overseas.

...I do not have a defined attitude toward Sephardim except one thing: I find in them some nobility that other Jews do not have. They have a tradition of customs...that are richer than those of the Ashkenazim. This tradition is the one that is close to my heart...These Jews have deep roots in Israel, perhaps because they themselves came from the Middle East, and they did not experience the shock that the Jews from Europe experienced. The courtesy, their concepts of time...all this is well intertwined with the Eastern landscape and climate of Israel.

In a journalistic essay, Kaniuk (see: Kaniuk, *Ma'ariv*) wrote:

> ...One needs a long time in order to absorb these matters. You
> fight, your friends are killed...It took me fifteen years to write
> a book that its background is the War of Independence...
>
> A war is not necessarily an accelerator for a war litera-
> ture.
>
> War is, above all, a catastrophe. And we live in the
> shadow of catastrophe. When I wrote *Himmo king of Jerusa-
> lem* in which I intended to express my powerful experiences
> of the War I found out at the end that I left the War out of the
> story. Only its echoes came into the story...

In *Himmo King of Jerusalem*, Hamotal is interested in her roots and
in the history of Jerusalem. In one interview Kaniuk addressed some of
his feelings about Jewish history: "Everything I write about is affected by
this sense of historical weight" (see Furstenberg). Hamotal "was born and
grew up near the Tel-Aviv seashore" (p. 211) and later she differentiates
between Jerusalem, the eternal city, and "Tel-Aviv, the ephemeral city of
the moment" (p. 212).

> Tel-Aviv, the modern city of her birth...now appeared to her
> a remote Levantine town...whereas the Eternal City...seemed
> to be drawing her down to plant her in its soil ...these very
> stones...were imparting to her, Hamotal, a sense of returning,
> of a lost daughter returning to her Hebrew birthright...(p.
> 150).

> Like her Kaniuk has

> A sense of destiny, of blood ties, which is missing in the Tel-
> Aviv cityscape... Everything in Tel-Aviv is so temporary, so
> ephemeral. Nothing is sacred. Nothing has history...the
> younger generation doesn't seem to miss the historic sense...

THE MOVIE

*Director: 'Amos Gutman. Producers: Enrique Rotenberg and Ehud
Bleiberg. Script: Edna Maz'a (Literary adaptation. Based on Yoram
Kaniuk's novel). Photography: Horne Ureic and Amnon Salacity. Music:
Ian Wartburg. Editing: Siva Postal. Cast: Alona Kimahi, Dove Narvon,*

Amoral Gabriel, 'Amos Lave, 'Aliza Rosen, Yogi Garber, Offer Hibachi, Echo Vital, Adam Valleri Tal, Ya'acov Halperin, Avi Gil'or. 1987. Color. 84 minutes.

The impact of the Israeli-Arab wars, including their after-effects on the Israeli soldiers, is described in many movies. The physical and psychological needs of the wounded soldiers are well presented in the movie, *Himmo King of Jerusalem.*

Himmo King of Jerusalem is a 1988, 84-minute, color movie of war drama. A cable TV station acquired the rights to screen the movie in the USA and did screen it several times. It is a movie that puts emphasis on ambiance within a realistic setting. Yoram Kaniuk liked the movie and considered it a powerful film (see Lam), but some critics did not feel the same about it.

'Amos Gutman, the director of the movie who produced two movies prior to this one (*Drifting*, 1983 and *Bar 51*, 1986*),* is attracted to the world of the marginal, damned and outcast souls. The above two movies and *Amazing Grace* (1992), a movie about a young man dying of AIDS, explore problems of sexuality and homosexuality. He portrays people who are rejected by society and exist miserably, who lead hopeless lives, devoid of desirable choices and options.

Enrique Rotenberg produced three of Gutman's movies: *Bar 51, Himmo King of Jerusalem* and *Drifting*. Edna Mazi'a was 35-years-old when she wrote the script for the movie in 1986 and, in 1999 (see Cohen), she still remembered her trauma because of what she describes as the Israeli critics' hatred to the movie.

Alona Kimhi, a graduate of the school of fine arts Bet-Z vi, with little acting experience behind her, played the role of Hamotal, attempting to radiate innocence and compassion. Aliza Rozen was Clara, the big mother of all and Yosi Garber as Dr. Abayoff. Both of them were experienced actors. Clara's words are few in the movie, but she always hit the main issue in a truthful way. Yosi Garber as Dr. Abayoff performs as the curt, bitter, pessimistic, tactless and rude side of the doctor convincingly as well as the doctor's tenderness as it is expressed at the party later. Amiram Gavriel, as Franji and Dov Navon, as Asa, sometimes speak too long, yet their acting is poignant.

The film was made in the Monastery of the Holy Cross in the Valley of the Holy Cross in Jerusalem. The scriptwriter, the cameraman, the editor and the director are focusing their artistic energy inside the monastery where the outside world is reflected by memories, news, radio, visitations (such as Marco's), rumors and the sounds of shelling and shooting. There is no real plot to the movie. The tragedies of the wounded soldiers are emotionally effective. The script attempts to make an emotional impact through the soldiers' various changing dispositions. Death and the threat of death govern.

When Hamotal comes close to entering the monastery, the sight of the smoke from the shelling aggravates the sound of the shelling.

The threatening, terrifying sounds of war and the life inside the Greek Orthodox monastery where the movie was filmed provide the setting for the consequences of the war, on which the movie focuses.

The monastery becomes a place disconnected from the outside world for which the wounded soldiers fought and were injured. The life in it seems to be dream-like and fanciful. The exposition is intense and pathetic, and the restricted monastery atmosphere prevents possible vulgarization of the situation. The setting of the movie inside the monastery provides a restricted background for producing it. Perhaps this is why we listen to stagy speeches, dialogues and monologues from wounded soldiers instead of seeing the action itself. Telling rather than showing in the movie becomes burdensome, at times. The war is present with its sounds of shooting and shelling only, however the war's impacts on those who fought is central to the movie.

By various sounds and music, by a well-calculated play of light and darkness in the background, the monastery looks like a demonic, ghostly castle. Its walls are thick, and they shut inside the crying over the maimed soldiers, the fear of death and the grief over the dead close friends. The cinematographer, Gurevich, is known for his photography in movies such as *Himmo King of Jerusalem*, *Sara* and various short films. His photography reflects the tragic results of war; his camera lingers on shadows, ghostly scenes of nightmares, claustrophobia and light amidst darkness

The soldiers' moods change from one scene to another, the nightmarish monastery does not. It becomes a microcosm of a world impacted by a war and has in it pain, grief, fears, hopes, frustrations, bitterness and outcry of any place affected by war.

Flashback is not used in order to take us to emotional and tense events that took place outside the monastery. There are no battlefield scenes in spite of the dramatic scenes provided by the novel. For example, Asa's heroic fight, when he was "pinned down on the roof of a mosque with a bullet in his leg, surrounded by a score of Arabs, continues shooting it out" (p. 83) could provide a dramatic flashback but it is not part of the movie. Franji, too, was heroic on the battlefield, he "sprawled wounded on a cold Jerusalem mountainside" and saw "with his good eye how the vultures are swooping down on him while his other eye is spilling into his palm, and keeps shying stones at the birds to drive them off" (p. 83). But this dramatic, moving scene too was not made part of the movie through flashback. In another instance, Marco tells Hamotal the story of Himma's death, a story that includes earthquake, beauty, hopes, starvation and death. It was possible to begin the story of Himma's death by Marco's telling it to Hamotal near Himmo's bed, to continue it with Marco's voice over the main events of the story, and to show them happening. Then, we could have returned to the monastery and the Hamotal-Marco scene near Himmo's bed.

The movie emphasizes mood and atmosphere. Nuances of colors and light, sounds and silence are used to create atmosphere and various moods. Such use of nuances of light and darkness, sound and silence can be demonstrated by the first time it was Hamotal's turn to care for Himmo at night. The shout of Himmo is petrifying; it spreads throughout the monastery and becomes mysterious in the play of light and darkness at night, accompanied by intense music. In another instance later, light, focused on a window in the ballroom — with adoring wounded soldiers, the harmonica playing at the background, and a jealous nurse watching — surrounds Hamotal. Later in the movie, we see the same window bright again, but the sliders appear without Hamotal; they are watching her with anger and jealousy when she is with Marco and Himmo outside. The contrast between the two scenes at the window is expressive.

Understatements are preferred in the movie to overtone and therefore they become more effective. In one scene (which is not in the novel), we hear bells ring, representing an attempt to express something that the words cannot — death, pain, horror, protest and frustration — an attempt to speak to God when all the words exchanged on earth did not bring any solution. And we see a little girl (she is repeatedly attached to the gravedigger) wandering in the hospital with a one-limbed doll. War destroys childhood dreams, demolishes innocence, imposes itself on young and old and, while it cannot extinguish the yearning for continuous childhood, it makes only amputated childhood possible. The one-limbed doll is a metonymy to the soldiers and represents the world to which the little girl is exposed, while a doll with two arms would not represent it. As in the case of Hamotal, the little girl's psychic wounds are invisible.

The loud shuddering outcry of Himmo that echoes throughout the monastery is heard upon Hamotal's arrival. In the Bells Room, the room she was assigned to, we hear from the radio a soft, loving lullaby of a wishful mother, and we are compelled to compare the song with the condition of the wounded soldiers.

The repetitive appearances of the gravedigger and his daughter (in the movie only) add to the atmosphere of the monastery. The father drinks alcohol constantly, he does not talk; only sometimes his lips move. Like her father, the little girl does not talk. Words cannot express what they feel and see. At the party we see her tenderness and yearning for love and compassion when she dances with a chicken. She is neglected, lacking warmth and communication, and is exposed to an ugly world of death, melancholy and alcoholism. The absence of the little girl's mother is strongly felt.

Silence is used often as a statement and not just in the scenes with the gravedigger and his daughter. The soldiers' silence upon Hamotal's entering the Bells Room the day Himmo was transferred to that room can demonstrate one of the explosive silences.

Franji's memories of "king" Himmo are a device to intensify pain in light of the current Himmo, and the sobbing of the two expresses the unbearable pain. At night, when Himmo begs, "shoo me shoo me," the soldiers wake up and listen to him silently. In the erotic scene when Hamotal changes her clothes in the Bells Room in order to put on her pajamas, the silence is tense. The viewer sees Hamotal taking off some of her clothes, while the lonely wounded soldiers keep their eyes away from her. The silence significantly intensifies the erotic scene. Franji breaks the silence by two words: "Esther Williams," the name of the actress who is the object of his wet dreams. The scene was added in detail to bring an erotic dimension to the movie. Silence also heightens the night scene in which Hamotal responds to Himmo's hand and gets close to his body, while the wounded soldiers are watching secretly breathless.

Humor plays some part in the movie. Franji asks Asa during a sleepless night if Asa is asleep, and the "sleeping" Asa answers in the affirmative... Hearing Franji singing in his Sephardi pronunciation a famous lullaby in Yiddish and comparing his pronunciation with that of Asa who is singing with him may raise a smile, not only understanding of the yearning for home, safety, raisins and almonds ("rosinkei mit mandelin"). Marco's telling Hamotal that the woman on his pendant saved his life by stopping the bullet between her legs makes both of them smile.

The contrast between silence and noise draws attention many times in the movie. Upon Hamotal's entrance everything is silent, but all of a sudden the wounded soldiers burst with a frivolous noisy song attempting to overcome their fear of the shelling and their despair.

Some of the events of the novel, such as the party, take a larger part in the movie than in the novel. The script makes some changes in the novel text, for example, in the movie we see Asa making threats with a gun at the party, imposing Bach's mass instead of the romantic song asking for kisses ("Became mucho"). In another scene, Hamotal leaves the party and exchanges sensual kisses on the lips with Marco. In the background, the music may remind us of Klezemer playing Jewish wedding music, but the dialogue between the two is not of romance and commitment. The choice and the changes may be easily challenged. A few times in the movie the emotions escalate. Hamotal is forcefully grabbed by Asa or thrown to the floor by another soldier. It appears that these scenes are meant to depict dramatic situations. When the standupist failed and Asa took over the entertainment, Franji loudly says that Hamotal wants a cucumber. The vulgarization of the relationship between Franji and Hamotal is not in the novel. Dr. Neuman's opinion that the doctors' work is gauged by their "ability to prolong life, and not in finding some nobler content for life" (p. 198) is attributed in the movie to Dr. Abayoff in his dialogue with Hamotal who complained to him about placing Himmo near the door in the Bells Room. The idea seemed essential to the scriptwriter and presenting it there eliminated the need to introduce another character (Dr. Neuman).

It appears that the changes are meant to heighten the thespian, sensational, or amorous situation. Other changes were meant to present ideas and opinions concisely.

In the Bells Room we see the same two inner circles we found in the novel — one of Hamotal, Himmo and Marco on the one hand and, on the other, of the rest of the wounded soldiers, while Hamotal's care of Himmo increases. Hamotal stops being thought about by them as the loving caregiver figure, and she becomes the rejecting mother figure (see Loshitski). The obsessive Hamotal-Himmo relationship near death are also expressed by darkness and by the mysterious and dream-like structure of the monastery.

Like the novel, the movie script, too, strives to express pain and promote an anti-militaristic message. In order to deliver an all-anti-war message, the movie does not focus on reporting the specific historical events of the time of the plot. The War of Independence is only an incident, a specific local demonstrative human experience of war, destruction and sacrifice of young life throughout human history. All wars result in sacrificed young life even when they mean victory to the "winners." While death and physical mutilation are visible, injured souls such as Hamotal's are harder to see and comprehend. One may sustain deep emotional wounds from war while his body is completely intact.

National dreams demand sacrifices. The injured soldiers do not have any impact on the events anymore. Once maimed and rendered disabled to defend their country, they are doomed for a temporary life of fear and hopelessness in the monastery or to die.

The past, normal life, in which the sexy Hollywood actress Esther William was an object of desire, seems as distant from the wounded soldiers as happy Hollywood movies are distant from the monastery. Those who participated in making history are now immersed in their wounds, while historical perspective cannot provide comfort for their present suffering.

The movie shows the striving for the impossible: love without any chance, dreams that cannot be fulfilled, yearning that will not produce effective results, youth that evaporated in war wounds, bodily wholeness that became a memory. No love and care can restore Himmo's life and make living worthwhile for him.

The movie, like the novel, does not provide us with one clear motive for Hamotal's attraction to Himmo. The sexual tension between Hamotal and Marco, Hamotal and Himmo and Hamotal and the wounded soldiers is frequently present in the movie.

Hamotal is trying to do to Himmo that which was impossible for her to do for her boyfriend: to keep him alive. After the death of her boyfriend, she had pain and possibly irrational guilt feelings as the one who survived while a beloved person sacrificed his life for the nation. But she discovers that not everything depends on strong will, and neither dedication nor medical science can always guarantee results. Hamotal is a mystified character in the movie, as are the characters of Clara, the drunken moronic gravedigger and the little mute girl near him. Sometimes these characters may give a feeling of ghostly presence within a demonic castle.

That the national historical news may mean very little to a soldier who is going to live a life of a now-disabled person is eloquently shown in the movie. A soldier cahoots to get Franji's attention and tells him excitedly that David Ben-Gurion declared the establishment of the State of Israel. "For this you called me?" protests Franji.

Near Himmo's bed we see toward the end, the silent Marco and Hamotal. Marco tearing his shirt, it is a sign of morning in Jewish tradition. Possibly by the sound of tearing he tells Himmo that out of love he will see that Himmo's will to die is carried out. Due to the war, loving Himmo means killing him. Tenderly Marco kisses his brother on his beautiful mouth. Hamotal gives Himmo a lethal injection and takes Himmo's life. This is an exceptional solution for Israeli cinema that reflects Kaniuk's work. In the background is the same mass music of Bach. Hamotal pulls the bells' rope; we hear the ringing and the crying ravens adding blackness and death.

The Christian monastery will remain in the State of Israel, but Himmo will be gone. Unlike the "King of the Jews," the suffering Himmo, King of Jerusalem, will not be spoken of. Himmo is the sacrifice of the Jews for the recreation of the State of Israel.

The war ends. The soldiers go home. The music that accompanies this part is not of the movie; it is festive and joyful. A horn cries the same crying sounds that we heard at the time of the burial by the gravedigger. The scarred Hamotal watches them. In the monastery, the little girl wanders aimlessly and lonely, holding her doll upside-down by the doll's only leg. Even the gravedigger is not near her anymore. The Sephardi Himmo, who was not associated formally with the Zionist ideology, is the silver tray for the State of Israel, but will not be part of the official history of the State of Israel; he will be unspoken about and forgotten. The sad music that began the movie is repeated. The war is over; the lamentation of the killed young people is just beginning. Ravens cry.

BIBLIOGRAPHY

Alro'i, Yosef. "Ha-Tokhen — Ema; ha-Lashon — Ma'adanot." *Ha'arez*, Aug. 21, 1966.

Arad, Miriam. "Terrors of Death." *The Jerusalem Post*, August 5, 1968.

Avishay, Mordekhai. "Himmo Melekh Yerushalayim." *Al ha-Mishmar*, Oct. 7, 1966.

Bartana, Orzion. "Himmo Melekh Yerusalayim," in *Ha-Fantasia be-Sipporet Dor ha-Medina*. Papirus and Hakkibuts Hammeuchad, Tel-Aviv, 1989, pp. 62-76.

Bezal'el, Yitshak. "Re'ayon 'im Yoram Kaniuk: Ha-Sipurim, ha-Shorashim, ha-Goral." *La-Merhav*, Jan. 13, 1967.

_____. "Yoram Kaniuk." In *Ha-Kol Katuv be-Sefer.* Hakkibutz Hameuchad, 1969, pp. 108-115. Reprint of the above.

Carmi, David. "Shoshana be-Tokh Karhon." *Ba-Mahanei*, Sep. 14, 1966.

Cohen, Addir. "Himmo Melekh Yerushalayim." *Davar*, Sep. 11, 1966.

Cohen, Bo'az. "Anashim Meshuga'im Anahnu." *Yediot Aharonot*, Sep. 10, 1999.

Dotan, Rina. "Himmo Melekh Yerushalayim le-Yoram Kaniuk." *Devar ha-Po'elet*, Feb., 1967.

Furstenberg, Rochelle (interview). "Profile of a Tel-Aviv Writer." *Modern Hebrew Literature*, Spring 1959, No. 2.

Gal-Or, Ilana. "Gesisato shel Melekh Yerushalayim." *Yediot Aharonot*, 1966.

Gingold-Gilboa', Shulamit. "Yoram Kaniuk: Leta'el et ha-Mez i'aut le-Halom." *'Itton 77*, No. 55, September 1984.

Hakak, Lev. *Yerudim ve—Na'alim: Demutam shel Yehudei ha-Mizrah ba-Sippur ha-'Ivri ha-Kazar* Kiryat Sefer, Jerusalem, 1980.

_____. "The Image of Sephardim in Modern Hebrew Short Story." In: *The Sephardi and Oriental Jewish Heritage*, The Magnes Press, The Hebrew University of Jerusalem, Ed. By Isakhar Ben-Ami. pp. 297-310.

H.D. "Strange Relationship." *World Jewry* (London, England). July-August, 1969.

"Hamotal be-Erez ha-Maz leva." *Kol ha-Ir*, Sep. 19, 1986.

Kaniuk, Yoram. *Himmo King of Jerusalem* Translated by Yosef Schecter. Atheneum, New York 1969.

_____. "Dor le-Dor Moser— Herev u-Tehiyyot." *Ma'ariv,* April 25, 1969.

Lam, Vered, "Haya O Lo Haya." *Yediot Aharonot*, Oct. 2, 1987.

Loshiz ki, Josefa. "The Bride of the Dead: Phallocentrism and War in *Himmo, King of Jerusalem.*" *Film Literature Quarterly*, 21/3, 1993, p. 213.

Pryce-Jones, David. "The Quality of Mercy." *The Jewish Chronicle* (London, England), June 6, 1969. Republished in:

_____. *Jewish Affairs* (Johannesburg, South Africa), Sep., 1969.

_____. "Himmo, king of Jerusalem." *Hadassah Magazine*, April, 1969.

Raz, Avraham. *Kol Yisrael*, August 29, 1966.

Schnitz er, Meir. *Ha-Kolnoa' ha-Yisraeli.* Kinneret Publishing House, 1994, p. 295.

Shaked, Gershon. *Ha-Sipporet ha-'Ivrit 1880-1980*, Vol. 5, Hakibbutz Hameuchad and Keter Publishing House, 1998.

Vered, Danny. "Adam Lo Adam," in *Ha-'Ir*, Tel-Aviv, Oct. 19, 1987.

Bedside Manners. *The Jerusalem Post Magazine*, Oct. 23, 1987.

Ma'ariv, Oct. 2, 1987.

Yedioit Aharonot, Oct. 2, 1987.

Ma'ariv, Oct. 10, 1987.

Chapter 7

THREE DAYS AND A CHILD
BY A.B. YEHOSHUA

LIFE OF THE AUTHOR AND HIS WORK
IN ENGLISH

A.B. Yehoshua was born in 1936 in Jerusalem as a fifth generation to a Sephardi family. He served in the Israeli Defense Force (1954-1957), studied Hebrew literature and philosophy at the Hebrew University of Jerusalem (1957-1961), absorbed western culture when he lived in France (1957-1961) and for short periods in the United States. He taught at high schools and universities in Paris (1963-1967) and in Israel. He lives in Haifa and has been a Professor of Hebrew literature at Haifa University since 1972. Yehoshua published short stories, novellas, novels, essays, plays and radio plays. His first story later titled "Mot Ha-Zaken" ("The Death of the Old Man") was published in 1957 and his first book (the same title) in 1962.

Yehoshua is one of the most important Israeli authors of the generation that began writing after the State of Israel came into being in 1948. In many ways his literary works did not embrace the Zionist establishment norms but questioned them.

S. Yizhar, S.Y. Agnon and Franz Kafka influenced his work. His first characters were detached from Israeli reality, and they faced surreal situations. He mixed reality with fantasy, marked by destruction and deterioration (see Shaked, *Ha-Sipporet*, 158-162).

Yehoshua's early works, writings of a symbolic-allegorical nature, were particularly influenced by the nonrealistic writing of the Israeli

Nobel Prize winner, Agnon (*The Book of Deeds*), which ignored and negated the limits of time and place to allow for the creation of meaningful metaphorical situations. Beginning with *The Lover*, a novel influenced by William Faulkner's work, Yehoshuas work was influenced by English literature. Yehoshuas work encountered Israeli reality, and presented life, reality and plot through various characters' points of views.

In his literary work, Yehoshua deals with Israeli reality and the Jewish existence in a larger sense. In addition, he confronts such universal conditions and problems as the loneliness and alienation of modern life. Yehoshua wrote about the desire to live, the war between one generation and another, love and jealousy and destructiveness (*Mot Ha-Zaken*, "The Death of the Old Man," 1962). The Israeli-Arab conflict, the young Israeli's search for meaning and the wandering Israeli (see "Mul Hyye'arot," "Facing the Forests," 1968) were also among Yehoshuas topics. Yehoshua explored all of these themes: the impact of the Six Days War (see *Layla beMay*, "A Night in May," 1974); the sacrifice of the young Israelis (see *Early in the Summer of 1970*, 1972); the Israeli family; the Arab-Israeli conflict, the Yom Kippur War; the Ashkenazi-Sephardi relations; the relations between secular and religious Jews; emigration — "the illness of Diaspora" (see *The Lover*, 1977, *A Late Divorce, 198; A Five Seasons, 1987*); the roots of the Sephardim; the Lebanon War; the city and the Kibbutz; the relations between German and Jews (*Mr. Mani*, 1990); the trips of the Israelis to India; Israeli physicians and the medical establishment (see *Open Heart*, 1994); Sephardi Jews and Ashkenazi Jews; the cultural dialogue between them a thousand years ago; man and woman; judges and judgment (see *A Journey to the End of the Millennium*, 1997)

In Yehoshua's literary works, the war syndrome produces situations that make social decay apparent. Often, the troubles of individuals who are rooted in their society are the mirror of the troubles of many (Hakak, 1993). Yehoshuas work relates to the Six Days war (*Layla beMay*), The War of Attrition (*Early in the Summer of 1970*), The Yom Kippur War (*The Lover*), The Second World War and the Lebanon War (*Mr. Mani*).

Yehoshua's pessimistic view of the Zionist dream was voiced in the 1960s through symbols but, in the 1970s, the author expressed this view much more directly. Perhaps both readers and critics were better prepared for his direct social and political criticism, especially after the 1973 war.

The characters in the fiction of Yehoshuas generation of writers relate in an individualistic and ambivalent way to the constantly changing reality described in their worlds (Hakak, 1993). The prose of Yehoshuas generation differs from the realistic-naturalistic prose of the preceding literary generation whose writing centered on the Israeli War of Independence. The prose written during the years of struggle for the establishment of the State of Israel and during the years of the State (see Shaked, *Gal*; Gertz, *Hirbet*; Sadan-Lovenshtein, *A.B.*), focused on the collective problems and experiences of that tempestuous generation and on problems of the "here" and "now." This literature presented characters with a clearly defined system of values, characters that identified with the basic social values of the State of Israel and of Israeli society.

The shift from this stage of Israeli literature to the later stage, which concentrated on the individual, conveyed a sense of rapture concerning the individual's identification with his society; the writers depicted the individual as lacking values and faith and portrayed his life as restless and undermined. The individual was described as wandering aimlessly, as lonely and desperate and also as rebelling futilely against his feeling of estrangement and detachment. The firm ideological orientation, which was common to the characters and authors of the period of the War of Independence and the years immediately following, does not exist for writers like Yehoshua or Amos Oz.

In the earlier stage of Yehoshuas work, Yehoshua had to struggle with a norm, common to some Israeli authors and critics, according to which the writer avoids social and political criticism in his work. Consequently Yehoshua utilized symbols in order to comment on Israeli social-political reality. In 1975, Yehoshua felt that surrealistic writing led to a deadlock and decided to listen closer to reality instead of imposing his will on it (see Yehoshua, "Likhtov"). It is possible that the Israeli-Arab conflict and its casualties caused Yehoshua to closely encounter political and social reality in his literary work.

Yehoshua's literary work, particularly since 1968 ("Mul Hyye'arot," "Facing the Forests"), constantly relates to Israeli social-political life. The stories in *Facing the Forests*, where "Three Days and a Child" is included, have individualistic or social situations through which the author creates the meanings and messages.

Three Days and a Child was published in 1965. (The movie was produced in 1967). In *Three Days and a Child*, we see Yehoshuas tendency both to relate to reality and to search for the general, the symbolic and the intellectual. As in many of Yehoshuas works, the implied author neither detests nor judges his characters but simply attempts to understand them.

Dov, as many other characters in Yehoshuas literary work, is frustrated and deprived, distressed, restless, aimless, lonely and yearning for love. Already in Yehoshuas early stories, Israel is depicted as a problematic and complicated nation rather than Israelis being a "chosen people" with an exemplary, model society — a light to the world.

The pre-existing perversions of Dov are exposed through the distressful and complicated situation described in the story, when he possibly loves a woman who does not love him, and he is looking for both revenge and attachment.

Yehoshua is widely recognized internationally. His books in English translation include: *Three Days and A Child* (Doubleday, Peter Owen), *Early in the Summer of 1970* (Doubleday), *The Lover* (Doubleday, Heinmann, Dutton), *A Late Divorce* (Doubleday, Harvill, Dutton), *The Five Seasons* (Collins, Flamingo Fontana), *The Continuing Silence of a Poet* (stories, Peter Halban, Penguin), *Between Right and Right* (Doubleday), *Mr. Mani* (Doubleday and Peter Halban), *Open Heart* (Harvest Books) and *A Journey to the End of the Millennium* (Doubleday).

THE PLOT

The plot of this story is dramatic; it includes unfulfilled love, jealousy, toying with murder, snake biting and other climactic events and situations. In contrast to the dramatic events, the narrator's tone and narrative rhythm are low-key. Within the story, the author provides us with a good summary of the plot under his subtitle "Reflection" (p. 71):

> It is a simple case. A woman and a man have left a kibbutz (a common affair, that) and have come to Jerusalem. They have a small son, and there is nothing wrong with that. Since they were required to pass an examination, and since they have not touched a book for a long time, they shut themselves up in libraries and left their little boy in my care. I am no friend of theirs, but I know that they have no one else in Jerusalem to turn to.
>
> I fell in love with a woman years ago, fell hard, painfully, silently. Since she is a heedless woman, pensive, losing herself in reveries, she forgot my love, and sent her husband

at dawn to wake me and hand her child, her only son, her image, over to me. And it was hot, and end-of-summer heat wave, and it was Jerusalem, a harsh town.

First I kissed the child, then I listened to his pointless stories. Finally I took him to the Jerusalem Zoo, because he was beginning to get bored, because I was getting bored myself. I dozed off on a bench in a corner, and meanwhile the child slipped away and climbed onto a battered fence that rose and became a wall.

His life had been in a balance.

Amazing that I stayed calm, that I could still have wished to sleep.

The protagonist was lonely in the kibbutz where he fell in love with Haya. He left the kibbutz and moved to Jerusalem where he became a student and a teacher. In Jerusalem, he lived with his girlfriend Yael, who was courted by Zvi. At the end of the summer he cared for Yahli, the son of Haya and Zeev. Due to his emotional confusion, he, on the one hand, loved Yahli and, on the other hand, he attempted several times to stage Yahli's "accidental" death.

Dov found himself neither in the kibbutz, a place he perceived as close to nature, with idealism and labor, nor in Jerusalem, a place characterized by intellect and individualism. The little boy was brought to him during the last days of summer vacation, while he was lonely, having problematic relationships and dealing with his non-completion of his undergraduate studies. He lived comfortably in his own country, had an education, a position and a girlfriend, but did not seem to be happy. He seemed to unconsciously avoid his graduation: "I have been stuck…with a self-made labyrinth…I need inspiration…" (p. 54). His graduation will end his somehow sheltered life and will increase his restlessness and counter his quest for goals and meaning in life.

The reader, reading descriptive paragraphs, dreams, reflections and other elements in the course of the story, must follow the plot, keeping in mind the motives and the consequences of the characters' actions. Its reliable protagonist, who is not following the chronological order of the related events, tells the story.

JERUSALEM AND THE
KIBBUTZ

The dichotomy Jerusalem-kibbutz is central to the story and was acknowledged in other analytical works about this story (see Gertz, Shoham and Shalev). For a long time Dov held that these two entities contradict each other in their characteristics and population, he idealized and romanticized the Kibbutz and faulted Jerusalem.

Dov perceived each one of these two places, Jerusalem and the kibbutz and their respective people, as opposites. The Kibbutz in Dov's imagination was a place of communal life, love, harmony, beloved but unattained woman, fertility, nature, moisture, life and fulfillment of national ideology. While Jerusalem was a loveless place, a place of selfish individualism, disharmony, slow construction, dryness and withering in which he has an attained but unloved woman. The treatment of Jerusalem is not nostalgic and not romantic; it is not a city of mystery and holiness. If Dov can only realize that faulting the Jerusalem days and nights, its people and institutions is the result of his confused view, he will become a dynamic character in the story and better his life.

In some ways the dichotomy of kibbutz-city reminds us of the similar dichotomy of forest-city in the literary work of S.Y. Agnon, the Israeli Nobel Prize winner who influenced Yehoshua (Hakak, 1993, pp. 56-78).

Jerusalem "is a quiet town" (p. 53), "stewing in its silence," "a hard town. A harsh town, sometimes," a town of "empty nights" (p. 66), "a city of the dead," "its calm is feigned" (p. 67). The narrator does not idealize or beautify Jerusalem, and he points out its neglected and sealed spirit. He sees in it a forlorn alley; with cracked pavement, shuttered houses, "some of them are in ruins...the border... a section of the belt of menace encircling Jerusalem" (p. 81) is close. Jerusalem is "odd. Such a scholarly town" (p. 97).

Jerusalem is a city of extremes; its darkness at night and light during the day are both harsh. Day and night in Jerusalem are troublesome. From the scaffolding of the Jerusalem museum, the narrator sees "pencils of light at the university, the National Convention center in gloom. The urge of the heavy blocks of government offices... Jerusalem...All its houses are dark" (p. 98). Jerusalem is "odd. Such a scholarly town" (p. 97), and it does not radiate life and joy even though it embodies the past (the

Jerusalem Museum), present (the National Convention Center) and future (the Hebrew University of Jerusalem with its students and scholars).

Both nature and people weigh down the life of Jerusalem. Jerusalem's daylight is destructive. The narrator cannot find in it the "special kind of light" (p. 54) he needs that will inspire him to complete his thesis in mathematics. When he taught, the sun entered through the window, "the light would glare into my eyes. It was pure torment" (p. 79). Jerusalem is a city of "a mighty sun and a world of blaze...stewing in its silence" (p. 66). The summer light is connected with the blaze, even animals in the Jerusalem Zoo hide from the searing heat" (p. 68), "the women and children hiding from the heat" (p. 108), Jerusalem is a city of "dry heat" (p. 69) in it "the sun is burning overhead" (p. 70), "the dry air parching the nostrils" (p. 104), the desert wind "blows steadily over Jerusalem" (p. 54), "the sky is reduced to a turbid haze" (p. 108), the summer day is "fierce yellow day, its incandescent air dancing" (p. 108) before the narrator's face.

The people of Jerusalem are also depicted in an unfavorable manner. "Its people are always tense, always anxious," they have worried eyes and caustic humor, "frenzied greed for mail, devouring newspapers" and they are immersed in "the endless pursuit of endless honors" (p. 67).

The social communication of the people in Jerusalem is self-serving, when the "little professors" spot someone more important than the person they approached in order to boast about their innovations, they drop the person they are talking to and go to the more important one. The Jerusalemites are busier with words than with life itself, fussing with neologisms constantly.

The human contact is not direct, "everyone is bent upon symbols" (Ibid.), they consider themselves; their language, walk and meetings; the Jerusalemite sun, wind and sky as symbolic. Not much is left for a real, simple, well-rooted, practical earthy life and direct unpretentious, non-intellectual human contact. It is no wonder that the frustrated ironic narrator, observing the child imitating all of his movements including urinating, ironically "feels" that he can consider himself a symbol, too (p. 68).

In Jerusalem Dov is distanced from the people, including his girlfriend and his students. With his students he "was over the river and out of reach," "alone, lonely" (p. 80). At home, he also feels lonely (p. 89).

The kibbutz and its people are portrayed in contrast to Jerusalem. In the kibbutz, one finds the blessing of the rain. Already on his way to the kibbutz "all day the rain beat down upon the roads," "gray dripping sky ahead" (p. 61); it was "a rain-drenched mountain kibbutz" (p. 62). The fertility of the kibbutz is striking:

> The world — awash and teeming with growth. Sprouts were shooting out of the spongy soil, climbing in the dark. Trees branching out over roofs, casting roots into the moist depths. Lawns were bursting forth tumultuously. Fillers sprouting far and wide.
> The smell of wind and rain swept my face (p. 63).

The "huge, fearful belly" (p. 62) of Haya also represents fertility. Fertility is illustrated in Dov's dreams also. In his dream he saw "a field in dazzling light, and tiny drops of rain like a vapor moving upon my face" (p. 100). He was walking along the open furrows when he met Arieh, a member of the kibbutz, whose damp coat was "glistening in the radiant light" (ibid.). The sun was helpful, "this full sun bathing the whole field in light. A sun is facing us, directing our progress" (ibid.). The moist was so abundant that he felt "the tractor rises and descent like a ship over waves" (ibid.). "Thorns sprout...juicy thorns soaring and blooming" (ibid.) contrary to Jerusalem's dry thorns. The kibbutz grew thorns because the townsfolk are getting interested in them. The city life affected the kibbutz and its use of nature, the kibbutz, due to economical considerations, catered to the inclinations and whims of the townspeople, and it served them.

Dov looked at the broken leaves of one thorn and saw that "yellowish sap is oozing from the cuts" (p. 102). The thorn may remind us of the cactus, a very popular symbol for the Israeli-born, emphasizing its sweetness inside and its prickles outside. In the kibbutz there is practicality: "Arieh smashed the snake's head with a single blow" (ibid.) — contrary to the helpless way the city snake was handled in the story.

The dream revealed to Dov that he should not be quick to judge Jerusalem, Yael and their thorns. In Jerusalem we find "thorns and briers. Along history of thorns" (p. 69) and "Yael...was taken up with thorns" (p. 82) — now Dov learns that thorns are not all bad and that the kibbutz makes efforts to have them by growing them.

THE CHARACTERS AND
THEIR NAMES

The names of the characters are of animals, and they are analogous to the characters to a certain extent. The symbolism of any animal depends on its symbolic pattern and the literary context. I will relate to the meanings of the characters names and suggest their implications.

Haya (Hebrew — an animal) is close to nature, as if she is part of it. "She used to go barefoot, in work clothes...as though she had been born in the fields...her feet...filthy and pure at the same time," these were "mud-covered feet" (p. 74). Dov's hands "were daubed with the sticky dark sap" of grapes near her. "Her belly was huge" when pregnant (p. 62), an expression of her fertility. Haya does not have any sexual inhibitions. Only one time did Dov sleep with her, when he came to the kibbutz unexpectedly. "On one path, between lawns, she met me and took hold of me suddenly; frightened, in need...We went and lay on a bed in a room whose door stood open, people passing to and fro continuously" (p. 121). Dov's one time sexual experience with Haya suffices to portray her as lacking sophistication, tenderness and sensitivity. No wonder that the sexual experience the narrator had with Haya is not the subject of his yearning and is not the evidence of his possible romantic fulfillment. Instead, it is the source of agony, shame and pain: "But I cannot speak of it. Tears are choking me" (p. 121). This was not an experience of harmony, mutual respect and love. The needy Haya used his body.

She is not thoughtful, "she is a heedless woman, pensive, losing herself in reveries, she forgot my love" (p. 71), Dov, who is familiar with Haya's "lack of courtesy and her carelessness," tells us (p. 55). She is close to nature, self-centered and insensitive.

Haya's husband, Zeev (Hebrew — wolf) represents valor in that he took Haya, a woman desired by many men ("like children we fell in love with her," p. 74). He can devour his competitors with his bright "strong teeth" (p. 59); Zeev is impolite (pp. 55, 57), he relates to Dov as though Dov owes him something (p. 54).

Three-year-old Yahli is probably 'Eyal or 'Eyali ('Ayil in Hebrew is a ram). He, too, is part of the animals of the story, "a pale little bundle" (p. 58, "cub" in the original Hebrew text was translated as a "bundle"), "like a puppy" (p. 58). Even though "the lions, bears, and wolves" (the names of these animals are also the names of characters in the story Arieh, Dov, Zeev) in the Jerusalem Zoo bored Yahli, he is part of the human-animal world himself and is connected to the Biblical-sacrifice story (as discussed below).

The name Dov (Hebrew: bear) is open to various interpretations; he is in a way cruel (he could kill Yahli) and crude (as evidenced by his attitude to Yael). Dov agreed to take care of Yahli for few days, and he traumatized the boy. This fact may, to a certain extent, illustrate the common idiom in Hebrew, "bear service," an act that was done with good intention but instead caused a harm — like the bear that threw a stone in order to chase away a fly sitting on his master's forehead and smashed the master's scalp. Dov is also in certain ways dormant, passive in many ways, like some bears in the winter.

Dov loves Haya, a woman of "rare beauty" (p.73) but sleeps with Yael (Yael in Hebrew is not only a female mountain goat, but also a graceful woman, a beauty). Dov calls Haya at the beginning of the story "a beloved woman" (p. 53). Even though he did not see her for three years, he believes he is in love with her (p. 54). But this unequivocal assertion is put in doubt: "It is out of laziness, no doubt, that I still consider myself in love" (p. 56).

The attraction to Haya is sensuous while Dov's relations with Yael are of understanding, not love (p. 84). But understanding suffices for the two to consider marriage (p. 53). Haya is a part of nature, "Yael belonged to the Nature Lovers, was one of them," they are "vegetarians, naïve prose poets" (p.82). Haya ("animal") is not. Haya, however, left the nature and went to the city; Yael lives in the city and is immersed in nature as a subject of her studies. Unlike Haya, Yael "isn't pretty. Tall, thin, brisk. Her hair is dry and straggly, her hands rough, her legs forever scratched" (p. 83), but the reader may find her beautiful on the basis of this description.

Zvi (in Hebrew: a deer), a student of zoology, was in love with Yael, a student of botany. Zvi, a deer, is often also the animal representing the lover in Medieval Hebrew poetry. Zvi and Yael were made for each other. Zvi's appearance may remind us of a deer: tall and lanky, "his slender limbs thrust forward" (p. 92), while Yael (a mountain goat) is "tall, thin, brisk" (p. 83). After the snake escaped from the box Zvi stood "white-faced...as one condemned to death" (p. 99) as if the escape was a forewarning of his sacrifice. Dov says that he is very fond of Zvi (p. 91) and can discuss with him many things. Zvi's pockets are full of vermin, he collects scorpions, spiders, grasshoppers and snakes, and he has love and compassion for every living thing. When it comes to people, however,

Zvi, another Jerusalemite, is a-personal, he can discuss the sun, light, time, insects etc., but nothing that relates to his love or Dov's condition.

Arieh (in Hebrew it means a lion) is a man of strength, decisiveness and apparent authority. He is a lion in a sheepskin coat, "big, bearded," even the Alsatian pup "sprawled at Arieh's feet and licked his boots" (p. 60). In another occasion, "Arieh smashed the snake's head with a single blow" (p. 82). He is the strong king of the animals.

Characters that play minor roles in the story also have the names of animals or resemble animals, to remind us that this is a world in which everyone fights everyone in accordance with his abilities. Yahli wanted to see Deborah (Hebrew: a bee), "a little girl his age whom he had left behind at the kibbutz. His little sweetheart, perhaps" (p. 81). The bee, like the cactus, has a sting and honey, and Deborah is the future Haya. Whoever depends like Dov so much on the honey (pp. 90, 93, 108, 114, 122) must accept also the sting of the bees. Yael's parents are "like two seedy old foxes in their burrow" (p. 84, see also p. 86). Dov's neighbor too is part of the animals — "in his striped pajamas, prowls like a panther in the passage" (p. 96), and later he twists about Dov "like an animal" (p. 98).

The use of animals hints to the fact that our human life, as sophisticated as it may look, is related to man's initial stages on earth and to his instincts. Academic studies, knowledge, physical beauty, love of nature, these and all the elements of our civilized life cannot change the fact that people in many basic ways are not different from animals.

SYMBOLS, MEANINGS AND MESSAGES

Dov's life in the kibbutz may seem completely fulfilling, his intellectual, ideological needs, and his emotional life were intense and satisfied. He went to live in a kibbutz in order to serve national security and national economical needs and goals, and he also fell in love. Contrary to his idealistic, altruistic life in the kibbutz, his life in Jerusalem centered on accomplishing a personal goal, receiving an academic degree. The hope for mutual love between Haya and him was replaced by the understanding between him and Yael. Instead of being emulated by fresh followers in the kibbutz life, he became a student; the campus and the classrooms took the place the kibbutz fields. Dov feels emptiness in his life and nostalgia for the kibbutz.

The cactus is widely used among Israelis as denoting roughness on the outside of the Israeli-born but sweetness inside them. The cactus symbolizes (p. 102) the Israeli-born, emphasizing the sweetness of the cactus inside and its prickles outside. Thorns exist in the city and in the kibbutz. The thorns, with their dryness and pricks, symbolize first the self-centered, somehow insensitive townspeople, including Yael who was immersed in her study of thorns. At a later stage in the story, Dov was reminded that thorns are not only a part of Jerusalem's scenery but also of the kibbutz. The kibbutz goes out of its way and grows thorns because they are sellable and profitable. In spite of their pricks outside they may be sweet and full of life inside ("yellowish sap is oozing from the cuts," ibid.). Dov should only take his time, have an open mind and explore the thorns in their totality rather than superficially judge them by their shell alone.

At the end of his story, Dov's hand struck a thorn and he tried to identify it. "It felt like a safflower, to wit:

> A honey plant, swarming with bees...its seeds are them far...the peripheral seeds...ensure the plant's propagation in its native soil (pp. 128-129).

If Dov is not prejudiced against a thorn, he may find in it many positive attributes, as it is in this case: Sweetness, being attractive to bees, the ability to be perpetuated far away and in the thorn-native soil. Dov learns that thorns exist in both Jerusalem and the kibbutz, and that they can be desired and laudable. It is not the fault of Jerusalem that he feels alone, "without soil or sky" (p. 54), without roots or faith, the only reason for these feelings is his perception and emotional configuration. All creatures face death, including the "animals" in the story, but the honey plant will exist in its native soil and afar. If the "animals" in the story are people in general including the Israeli-born, and the honey plant represents them specifically, the new generation of the Israeli is a generation of survivors; they will exist in the kibbutz and far away from it.

Dov himself, the narrator who faults the people of Jerusalem, is a big "thorn": In reality, a person who would confess to such intents and acts would find himself in prison for attempting time and again one of the most evil crimes, homicide. Dov attempted time and again by acts or omissions to inflict death on a little boy entrusted to him by letting the boy place himself in hazardous and sometimes attractive situations of which the boy was incapable of appreciating the danger. Dov owes a special duty to this boy due to the boy's age and the obligation he took on himself. In comparison with Dov's repetitive criminal attempts, the faults of the other characters are insignificant. The hypercritical "refined" narrator exposes himself as a criminal. His self-assessment that he is "not stubborn, nor...violent" (p. 56) contradicts his actions, which speak louder than his words. The dichotomy, kibbutz-Jerusalem, seems now more a product of Dov's perception than of reality.

This is true about the people and the life conditions in the kibbutz and in the city. People carrying names of animals live in both the city and in the kibbutz. Some soft sophisticated animals — Yael (mountain goat) and Zvi (deer) — live in Jerusalem, while some vigorous or less sophisticated animals live in the kibbutz — Haya (animal), Zeev (wolf), Arieh (Lion) and Deborah (bee). In the kibbutz, too, we can find darkness in the rooms, hard rain, hail, "everything deemed, drooped. Mist..." (p. 62), while in Dov's room we can find also light (pp. 59, 99, 109, 128). Dov has an understanding with Yael and only pain with Haya.

The kibbutz members are not portrayed as more personal and caring communicators than the city people. After not seeing Dov for two years, they do not show better communication abilities than that of the Jerusalemites; they slapped Dov's back and "uttered some trivialities" (p. 63). Zeev and Haya had very little to say to each other even at their most intimate moments (p. 64).

Being one of many young people in a kibbutz with ideals does not solve a major problem of modern man: the narrator was one of about hundred young people who went to work in a kibbutz, "we did not think ourselves lonely. Nevertheless, we were" (p. 74).

The story causes Dov to look within himself for happiness, for right and wrong, for the ability to find beauty and goodness. The person and not his place determine the person's happiness.

War and peace, destruction and construction are competing in the story. This is illustrated in the story by the tank v. the tractor. Zeev brings to Dov's apartment "typical kibbutz toys...clumsy wooden tractors, plows, mowers, tiny figures of agricultural laborers frozen in ridiculous attitude" (p. 59) for Yahli. The tractor later stands up for the agricultural machines as a symbol of peace. In the absence of a tank, Yahli started "plowing" (p. 60). Later Yahli tells Dov about "a tractor that went up a rock and down again" (p. 65). Dov promises to buy Yahli "a tank to defend his tractors" (p. 66) and indeed did so (p. 87).

The Israeli national and the personal situation merge in these toys. While war is glorified and many types of myths are connected with it, the notion of something silly and childish associated with it is not new to literature. Zionism made it clear that it is dedicated to both, work primarily and war when necessary. The name of the Israeli army is IDF — Israeli Defense Force, defense is its goal. Now the story posts a warning that once an entity possesses arms there is no assurance how, why and when the arms will be used. In a situation in which all people carry the names of animals, arms are a necessity, which carries with it a heavy price.

The existence of power tempts and leads to the use of power and, once a person or a nation has the implements of war, it is hard to predict if they are used for defense or attack. And Yahli indeed, at his first play with the tank, did not use it for defense; he rather began "shooting at everything in sight" (ibid.). The feelings of power and possibly anger tempted him to exercise his "power." Dov gave the tank to Yahli having in mind that Yahli will use it in his game to defend his tractors, but Yahli "arranged all his tractors in a line...the tank...gun aiming straight at it. Instead of defending it, threatens" (p. 102). Once power is given, there are no guarantees for carrying out the use intended by the giver. Weapons could also be used against the one who provided them. After Dov gave the tank to Yahli as a gift, Yahli "took the tank and, his face very pale, very grave, he aimed the gun straight between my eyes and fired. I dropped dead on the rug. But he did not laugh" (pp. 87-88). An entity can give weapons to another entity and later be executed by them.

Later in the story, Dov dumped all the kibbutz toys in a corner. But Yahli, sick, dashed the tank to the floor; the gun came off, and he kicked the tractors (p. 111); when people are ill, the arms cannot help. Dov gathered the tractors, picked up the little tank, and looked for the detached gun (p. 112), striving to keep the tank intact regardless of its necessity.

When Yahli felt better, he and Dov were "awakened by the roar of a tractor that had lurched down the hill and began nibbling at some nearby rocks" (p. 122), and Yahli, in his bed, pushed his tractor over the pillow. Outside Dov's apartment, the tractor driver explained to Dov that he came to gnaw at the hill because a natural science wing of the museum complex was going to be built there — presenting dried plants, fossils and stuffed beasts (p. 123). This is the victory of the tractor over the tank. The museum will present plants such as the ones Yael studies. Now Dov discovers a new fact about himself: "I am attached to this neighborhood" (p. 124).

When Yahli and Dov were at the old Moslem graveyard, they made believe that they were at the kibbutz. It must be that there was nothing so Jewish about the houses of the kibbutz to disrupt this make-believe. They gave names to tombs as though they were houses, dining halls, the nursery, the tractor shed and carpentry shop in the kibbutz (p. 77). The possibility that a Moslem graveyard can look like the kibbutz does not support the perception of its being flawless. Jerusalem is not the only place that can be a "town of the dead" (p. 119), but the kibbutz can be, too.

THE END

Dov tried kibbutz life with its ideals and left it; he then tried life in the city but his life was unhappy, full of confusions, yearning, reservations and a critical outlook toward the people around him. He can continue this lifestyle or open up for a more positive, well-balanced outlook on life.

If Dov continues in his present lifestyle, he will have to continue faulting Jerusalem and its people and going back to yearning for his love for Haya. Yael is "gray," "bruised, her dry hands scratched...Piles of thistles...are scattered on the floor" and "She will never be beautiful" (p. 128). He can continue being pitied: "So great is the pity we sometime bear each other" (p. 84). (The original Hebrew — "zo 'al zei" — speaks of Yael's pity for him only). He can continue believing in the unrealistic and unfounded dichotomy of Jerusalem versus the kibbutz, smelling illness in a nostalgic mood and turning away from himself. "The child's smell emanated from the pillow; vomit, blood and soap. I inhaled deeply like a father intoxicated with his first child" (ibid.).

Dov chooses the second possibility, that is, to open up for a more positive, well-balanced view of life. At the end of the story, after sending Zvi to the hospital, Dov's perception of Jerusalem is changed. On the hill by his house, Dov feels the dewdrops and the caressing flowers, which moisten his skin. He notices the thistle buds, the rustling insects, the joy of the delicate grass; he sees the sky thawing before his eyes and how "streaks of light rising and fusing its blackness into a soft gray. Jerusalem in its bareness, its rocks, its secret fertility" (p. 121).

The dramatic tension is dissipated at the end of the story. The narrator dreams, shops, tell stories. "Jerusalem changed moods like a snake shedding its skin" (p. 126). The simile reminds us that snakes can shed their skin, but that they remain the same, they still will have the poison, can bite and kill. Dov still did not make complete peace with Jerusalem, and he continued to treat it with suspicion. But Dov was not indifferent to the wind and clouds. Yahli's medical crisis had passed. Dov attempted to work on his thesis.

Dov tells Yahli a story about all of the beasts of the forest waging desperate battles. The majority died, those that survived did not deserve it. Every creature and plant was exterminated; only one little wolf cub was saved. Animals, like the people in the story, wage battles, but Yahli was saved.

In Dov's dream, he thought that his pupils were "lost in the alley-ways," but later he realized: "I have gone astray, apparently" (p. 116), and his students were trying to help him. With this he may be closer to the realization that he needs to find his way instead of thinking that everyone else is in the wrong place. The teacher who thought his students erred realized that indeed he himself erred. Had he immersed himself less in teaching others and more in working on a well-balanced perception, he would not have gone astray.

The Biblical story of Abraham's sacrifice is echoed in various ways in the story (see Shalev). Yahli reminds us of the ram in the story of Abraham sacrifice. The "ram caught in the thicket by his horns" (Genesis 22; 13) was used as a burnt offering in the stead of Isaac. Haya brought "her child, her only child" to Dov, the allusion to Abraham's sacrifice is clear: God said to Abraham: "take now the son, thine only son…and offer him there for a burnt-offering" (ibid. 1-2). Dov fantasized that if Yahli is sacrificed, Yahli will perpetuate the contact between Haya and Dov (pp. 110-111) because Haya and Zeev would never be able to separate from him if he was the man who was with their son before the son's "death." In Dov's imagination, his emotional life and regeneration depend upon Yahli's sacrificial death.

In the Biblical story the key word is "prove," meaning tested, tried: "God did prove Abraham" (Genesis 22; 1), tested Abraham to see if his faith was unconditional, absolute or not. Dov feels that being with Yahli "is a kind of a test," too (p. 97). In both stories, there is an innocent child who was close to death due to acts of an adult; the place in both stories is Jerusalem (Mount Moriah in Abraham's story is in Jerusalem). In

Abraham's story, instead of Isaac, a ram was sacrificed. In this story, instead of Yahli, perhaps Zvi (Hebrew: deer, reminds us of the ram) was the victim.

While the Biblical story of sacrifice was a trial of Abraham's unconditional faith in God, in this story the purpose of the sacrifice would be to initiate and perpetuate the contact of Haya with Dov, which is a selfish motive that would make the sacrifice mere murder.

But Dov, who has now made peace with Jerusalem, understands that the wolf cub, the innocent Yahli, should not die. Once he made peace with the nature of Jerusalem and with himself, Dov does not have the urge to inflict death. He accepts and understands that he should not use Yahli as a victim of his unfulfilled love, loneliness and jealousy and should not project his feelings towards Haya on Yahli. He does not need a grotesque act of sacrifice for his own revitalization. The existence of love and harmony or ennui in one's life depends on him and is not determined by the place where he lives.

The new Israeli cannot find meaning in his life. He tried living in a group and having the needs of the nation supersede his own needs; he later tried individualistic life and the pursuit of personal goals. He did not find satisfaction in either one of these options and he faults everyone and everything around him for his condition. Now he has possibly opened up to look into himself and to see the world around with new eyes.

THE MOVIE

Director: Uri Zohar. Producer: Amaz ya Hayyoni. Script: Uri Zohar, Dan Ben Amoz , Amazya Hiyyoni, David Gurfinkel (Literary adaptation. Based on A.B. Yehoshuas story). Photography: David Gurfinkel. Music: Dov Zeltzer. Editor: Jacques Erlikh. Cast: 'Oded Kotler, Yehudit Solei, Jarman Onikovski, Ili Gorlitski, Misha Osherov, Stella Avni, Nisan Yatir, Barukh David, Shoshana Do'ar, Shay Oshorov. 1967. Black and white. 90 minutes.

Three Days and a Child was produced at the time of the *Kayiz* ("summer") movement. (See in this book the discussion of the movie, *Black Box*.) *Kayiz* was a movement of the small-budget, young Israeli cinema of the 1960s and the 1970s, which presented the problems in Israeli existence (see Kronish, pp. 76-92; Shohat 180-197). The emphasis of Israeli movies was shifted in the *Kayiz* cinema from the heroic, ethnic-stereotypic, popular, vulgar and sentimental movies, to the artistic, psychological, individualistic, serious, socially aware and sensitive movies. Some filmmakers of the *Kayiz* movement are the makers of some of the movies discussed in this book: Dan Wolman, the director and the script co-author of *My Michael*, is known for his films *Floch, The Dreamer, My Michael, Hide and Seek, Soldier of the Night, Nana, Baby Love, Up Your Anchor, The Love Contract and The Distance*. He is also known for television films such as *Gimpel the Fool, The Story of Basha, Stempanyu* and *Scapegoat* We will also be acquainted with Mikhal Bat-Adam, a central Israeli cinema figure who is the director, script co-author and actress in *The Lover*. Bat-Adam appeared in many films including *I Love You Rosa, The House on Shelush Street, Daughters, Daughters* and *Atalia*. She starred in *Moments, The Lover, Aya* and *Imagined Autobiography*. She has made several feature films and is known as an actress, director and screenwriter (see Kronish, pp. 150-153).

Three Days and a Child of Uri Zohar as well as some of his other films (the 1965 *Hole in the Moon*, the 1970 *Take Off*), portraying characters with their painful detachments are examples of the *Kayiz* movement cinema and Zohar's new wave movies.

Jerusalem may seem to be a microcosm of Israel in Israeli cinema. The monastery in *Himmo King of Jerusalem* is in Jerusalem; it is the place of the residence of Eli in *Three Days and a Child* and of Hannah and Michael in *My Michael*. It is also the place where Adam finally found the lover in *The Lover*. In Jerusalem, we meet Jews and Christians, orthodox Jews and secular Jews, scienctific and religious beliefs, war and peace, Ashkenazi and Sephardi Jews. It is holy and secular.

'Oded Kotler, one of the most gifted Israeli actors, plays the role of Dov-Eli in this 90-minute black and white movie directed by Uri Zohar. For his lead role, Kotler won the "Best Actor" award at the Cannes Film Festival in 1967. Illi Gorlitski, another important Israeli actor, plays the role of Zvi. The movie includes various symbols. The camera often reflects special photography angles, pointing out various sharp contrasts.

Until the 1960s, Israeli cinema was not concerned with the social-political reality of Israel but with the collective Zionist ideology with its heroic and pioneering themes. Menahem Golan, Ephraim Kishon and Uri Zohar were three leading characters in 1960s filmmaking that gave expression to Israeli reality with its problems and individualistic values. Menahem Golan produced ethnic films; Ephraim Kishon produced comedies with ethnic and social settings. Uri Zohar, the 1936 Tel-Aviv born Israeli, who is the director and the script co-writer of *Three Days and a Child*, in his parodies, bravely questioned Israeli values that were unreasonably immune to criticism. In the 1960s and the 1970s, Uri Zohar was a celebrity in Israeli theater, film and radio; a comedian; director; actor; scriptwriter; and winner of the coveted "Israel Award." Uri Zohar, Menahem Golan and David Parlov received the "Israel Prize" for their achievements in Israeli cinema.

In the 1967 *Three Days and a Child*, Zohar shifted from the comic to the dramatic and psychological. The movie centers on the individual and his problems, not the collective and its needs and achievements. Eli (Dov) is an Israeli born young man, who is rough on the outside and sensitive on the inside. Throughout the movie the viewers sense the sensitive emotional tightness of the love-hate relationships.

In 1967, the year the story was made into a film, Israeli cinema was not independent of the political structure and of the political establishment and did not have a tradition of independence in expressing social and political views (Gertz). The movie, like the story, does not focus on national needs but on the existential problems of the individual. One may, however, draw conclusions about life in the city and in the kibbutz and about the emotional and ideological issues of the Israeli-born generation of that time.

Viewing the movie with its reflections, dreams and descriptions of nature, we must make connections between the various parts of the story and figure out the chain of causation, the motives and consequences of the actions. The structure of the movie plot is clear and easy to follow: An unfulfilled love causes anger, jealousy and yearning; these end up in vindictiveness and, as a result, repetitive temptations and attempts at murder and, perhaps, remorse. When an attempt at murder ends, loving memories come back again, with the recognition that it is an unfulfilled love, which causes anger, vengeance, a murder attempt and perhaps remorse. This is a deadlocked circle of events until the end of the story, which leads to a positive resolution. The lucidity of the movie plot required some changes to the story's sequence of events.

The events in the movie are the same as in the story. In the story the dramatic events are downplayed externally, the rhythm of the plot slows down by the reflections, repetitions, dreams, symbols. and descriptions. The movie, however, gives emphasis to thespian events, particularly to those events, which describe Yahli's possible imminent death. Zvi's struggle with the snake in his being bitten by it is also a dramatic happening embraced in the movie. The slow parts of the movie allow us to internalize the death perils and gradually build up to the next climactic, deadly situation. The frame of the plot and the variety of deadly perils expressed by the strong presence of the music prevent monotony.

Like in the story, the movie, too, presents the protagonist's point of view. The three days are described without a perspective. The flashbacks portray the emotional world of the narrator, and in many instances people, places and situations are evaluated to well suit the dichotomy of kibbutz and city Bells, flutes, lights, serenity, tender memories participate in illustrating some of the protagonist's kibbutz memories, especially most of Eli's (Dov's) romantic memories from No'ah (Haya). But, when the validity and impartiality of these memories is questioned, we pay attention to squeaking objects, the loud and inconsiderate conversations in the kibbutz restaurant, the repulsive sounds of food chewing, the lack of discreteness, the impoliteness, the darkness, the backs people turn on each other, the squeaking of an opened door while two people are making love in a in a room whose door stood open and other people passing to and fro continuously. Words, sights and sounds are used to build and to destroy the dream-like Shangri-La, which is the product of human needs and imagination.

Among the modifications of the story in the movie are the different names given to some of the characters. The reason is not clear. It is possible that it was the result of an attempt to use what seemed to be more popular names, such as Shai (Yahli, the little Shay Osherov acted as Shay in the movie), No'ah (Haya) and Eli (Dov).

The movie opens on the streets of Jerusalem. The dominating sights are crowded and inelegant streets. Human communication does not play a major role, but Eli and Yael seem to have a warm, friendly, intimate relationship; and Zvi, Yael and Eli (in his mid-twenties) too seem to have a friendly relationship. The camera follows Eli-Dov and Yael walking on the streets of Jerusalem, which provides an opportunity to show various street sights. In these first few minutes we do not hear the words of the characters.

Then we hear in the background, a voiceover with the opening paragraphs of the story, and we see and hear Yael and Eli in Eli's apartment. They both are naked. Their dialogue in this part of the movie is measured; it does not exist in the story. The scene was added due to its sexuality as an allurement to the movie. It also illustrates the essence of the relationship of Eli and Yael. Eli is evasive emotionally but interested in sex. Yael looks at him intimately, but he is indifferent and distanced. The memories of Eli from his love come between him and Yael. As long as he is under its influence, he does not give his relationship with Yael a fair chance. The romantic-nostalgic, possibly melancholic, music expresses his attachment to the past and detachment from the present. Finally they are facing each other, but he is told he has a phone call and this suffices for him to leave Yael, alone and offended, in his bed. The scene is a compact illustration, an addition to the story, showing the relationship described in the story by telling.

In general, the role of sex is broadened somewhat in the movie. Zeev, the husband of No'ah (Haya) was on the line, asking Eli to care for Shay for a few days. When No'ah got on the line, various pictures from the past flashed in Eli's mind — he visualized No'ah, as she was on various occasions, an attractive and cheerful woman in the kibbutz setting. The romance and its background, are in contrast with Eli's present life. The conversation with the neighbors whose phone Eli was using does not exist in the story. The addition intends to illustrate the non-enchanting life of the milieu. Even the little daughter of the neighbors treats her doll roughly.

Eli went back to his apartment and Zvi, Yael and Eli are now at the same place, the conversation between the three is another addition to the story, illustrating the complexity of this triangle. Eli is rough with Zvi, and the nostalgic romantic memories represented by the music distance him from Yael.

After Zvi and No'ah left Eli, in another flashback, Eli remembered his visit in the kibbutz after Noah's pregnancy three years ago. The memory was blended with tractors, fields, trees, plants and birds chirping. But when Zeev came into the picture, he was rough and did not even respond to Eli's greetings. The small, enclosed room, with Zeev's back to the door, is the opposite of the opened fields. Zeev's greetings, manners and voice are heard; in the background are the mooing cows. The kibbutz dining room is typified by loudness, inconsiderateness, vulgarity and the absence of personal communication. The salt and pepper implement is not enclosed and everyone's fingers are plunged into it. Zeev plays a major role in these scenes, with some vulgarity and indifference to the presence of other people near him. There is very little communication between the various characters.

Now we see at Eli's apartment, at night, the other triangle: Zvi, Yael and Eli. Eli was hurt in the past when Zeev, who had No'ah, did not demonstrate fine manners in front of the loving and heartbroken Eli in the kibbutz, now Eli plays the role that Zeev played in the triangle, No'ah-Zeev-Eli. Eli eats in a crude manner. The analogy of the two situations is clear — Eli who had Yael now mocks Zvi wittily, and Yael's smile reminds us of No'ah's smile, to the sound of Zeev's loud chewing manners in the kibbutz dinning room. Both males are mockingly demonstrating self-confidence, victory, possession and roughness in front of the impassioned, loving male, who dreams about the female they had. The humiliated heartbroken Eli wants to rid himself from his hurt by hurting another man in his situation. Like Zeev, who invited Eli to stay overnight and went to sleep with No'ah, Eli invites Zvi to stay overnight and goes to sleep with Yael. The complete analogy between the two situations is the product of the movie, illustrating in a concise manner the hurts, the characters, the triangles, the deadlocked relationships, and how pain did not generate compassion in Eli but some masochism.

Once Shay (Yahli) was brought to his apartment in the morning, Eli becomes tender due to Yahli's resemblance to his mother. Without words Eli projects on Shay his love and yearning for No'ah, in a most tender, yet sensual and possibly perverse manner. There is little talking between Shay and Eli.

An energetic, joyful music, distinguished from the tender, nostalgic music that we heard when Shay was with Eli in Eli's apartment, accompanies Eli and Shay's constant activities outside the apartment. The time at the zoo is brief in the movie, unlike the time at the graveyard. Here the drama includes hide-and-seek, a desperate and scared little boy and the possibility of his being killed by a car. The background noise of the street reinforces the danger. The tranquility at the graveyard with its trees, plants, light breeze and birds chirping; the innocence of Shay; and his constant calling Eli "friend" ("haver") are in contrast to the cold-blooded, plotting Eli. In this scene, Eli and Shay appear separated most of the time.

A mix of soft and alarming music marks the visit at Yael's parents' home. Few words are said, without acts of human tenderness for the little child. The squeaking of the swing is dominating for a long while. Did Yael grow up as a thorn, having everything materialistically, except warmth, understanding and communication at home? Yael's parents look "like two seedy old foxes in their burrow" (see the story, p. 84, see also p. 86). The latest part on the swing reflects the view of the dizzy Shay. Yael's mother strikes the main issue: "You don't love Yael," she wonders why Eli does not leave her alone. This triggers a flashback to the first meeting between Eli and Yael, in which we see that attraction, humor, wit and good communication drew Yael and Eli to each other and made them joyful together. It is no wonder that after this flashback Eli does not validate Yael's mother's belief that he does not love Yael.

Shay's dangerous situation near the balcony rail is brief, avoiding a repetitious scene in its motives and character.

When Eli is on the phone with No'ah, he attempts time and again to be personal with her, but she avoids it, which hurts him. Afterwards, we see him opening the box in which Zvi put the snake. In his nightmare, Eli recalls various rough, cautioning, or indifferent reactions, including those of Zeev (wild laughter) and No'ah (indifference), to his decision to leave the kibbutz. None of these reactions was a personal attempt to find out why he wanted to leave and none of them was compassionate or tender. The nightmare and the telephone conversation with No'ah, who suddenly with her husband remembered him when they needed him, provide an explanation to setting the snake free.

Eli woke up from his nightmare into the arms of his love-starved married neighbor. The difference between the aging, neglected woman, missing the passion and romance in her dreary life, to Eli who happened to want her that morning, is sad. Eli wants to hurt Shay by making love to her in front of Shay, but once she discovered the little boy she demanded that they stop.

Near the pool, many female students surround Eli. Many loud words are said but we cannot understand anything. It all amounts to noise, not to communication. The abundance of the giggling girls only makes Eli feel lonely, and he remembers the day he worked with No'ah in the kibbutz. Contrary to the noise, now we hear a romantic, nostalgic, sentimental tender melody, the chirping of birds; we see fruitful fields, space, brightness and human beauty. Eli and No'ah are at the center, and Eli is so captivated by No'ah that he does not need words with her. The silence between the two speaks more than thousands of words while all the words of the students do not amount to one word.

In contrast to the romantic music in the flashback background, we hear thereafter a squeaking of a swing, and we see Shay dangerously climbing on a high wall, while Eli desires Shay's death.

On the bus, Shay avoids Eli, and finally Eli forced him to sit next to him. It was possibly remorse that motivated Eli to treat Shay now with compassion.

In the story, Zvi clearly takes the blame upon himself for the snake's escape (p. 100). In the movie, Zvi states that he did not open the box in which he left the snake, supporting our understanding that it was the malicious act of Eli. After a violent, self-righteous outburst, Eli and Zvi are friendly. The search for the snake is tense, silent and slow, once it was found the rhythm is fast, nervous, alarming.

The military van, which took Zvi to the hospital, was changed to a scooter in the movie.

On his way back, Eli goes through a rich Jerusalem landscape of olive trees and shrubbery; the light is soft, and the birds are chirping, reminding us of the kibbutz fields.

On his way to his apartment, Eli remembered the one and only time he slept with No'ah. In this scene, the squeaking open door is dominant. We see No'ah's face looking sideways, her fingers that barely touch Eli, her lack of personal interest in Eli, the lack of emotional intimacy before, during and after the lovemaking and No'ah's turning to the side after the act of using Eli. There is no verbal communication between the two during this scene.

The neighbor's husband sees Eli coming back to his flat and laughingly expresses that he doesn't know if he should greet Eli "Good Morning" or "Good Night, hinting to Eli's adventurous sexual night. Ironically, the neighbor does not understand that his wife is needy and desperate. The sexual incident and the husband's mischievous question portray the milieu in which one may not know that he is the cause for a sad laughter. The gap between the neighbor's implications hinting to Eli's adventurous sexual night and what Eli went through is enormous. Through these additions, the movie portrays the ennui in marriage; when matrimony and life-sharing unity becomes real, this is what becomes of it.

Eli enters his apartment. Shay expresses his distrust of Eli by finding refuge with Yael. Yael asks what happened, but Eli did not explain.

No'ah and Zeev came to pick up Shay, but Eli who yearned so much for No'ah pretended he was asleep. He peeks through the window and sees Zeev, No'ah and Shay holding hands. Eli goes to bed; Yael sits at the foot of the bed. Eli turns his back to her and faces the wall. The nostalgic, romantic, melancholic music plays in the background. Can life out on the hill near Eli's house induce, however, a new beginning? The close of the movie, like the close of the story, is now open. Hope is not unfounded. The music may hint that Eli is in love with his unfulfilled love, nothing changed, and he refuses to accept life that is mirrored in his neighbors' apartment and at Yael's home.

BIBILIOGRAPHY

Gertz, Nurith. *Sippur me-Ha-Seratim: Sipporet Yisraelit ve-'Ibuddah le-Kolnoa'.* Ha-Oniversita ha-Petuha, 1993, 2nd edition, 1994.

_____. *Hirbet Hiz'ah ve-Ha-Boker she-le-Mohorat.* Hakkibbutz Hameuchad, Tel-Aviv, 1983.

Hakak, Lev. "Israeli Society as Depicted in the Novels of A.B. Yehoshua." *Equivocal dreams* Ktav Publishing House Inc., New Jersey, 1993, pp. 79-143.

_____. "Molkho in *Five Seasons*: A New Outlook." *Mahut*, Haberman Institute for Literary Research, A (6), summer 1989, pp. 254-264. Reprinted in *Hadoar*. November 17, 1989, pp. 19-22 and Nov. 24, 1989, pp. 19-22.

Sadan-Lovenstein, Nili. *A.B. Yehoshua: A Monograph.* Sifriyyat Po'alim, Tel-Aviv, 1981.

Schnitz er, Meir. *Ha-Kolnowa ha-Yisraeli.* Kinneret Publishing House, 1994, p. 85.

Shaked, Gershon. *Gal Hadash ba-Sipporet ha-'Ivrit*, pp. 11-70. Sifriyyat Po'alim, Tel-Aviv, 1971.

Shalev, Mordekhai. "Shelosha Yamim ve-Yeled." *Ha'arez*, Nov. 8, 1968 and Nov. 15, 1968.

Shoham, Uri. *Ha-Mashma'ut ha-Aheret: Min ha-Mashal ha-Alegori ve'ad ha-Sippur ha-Pararealisti.* Makhon Kaz Leheker ha-Sifrut, Oniversitat Tel-Aviv, 1982, pp. 283-305.

Shohat, Ella. *Israeli Cinema: East/West and the Politics of Representation.* University of Texas Press, 1989.

_____. *Ha-Sipporet ha-'Ivrit 1880-1980*, Vol. 5. Hakkibutz Hameuchad and Keter, 1998, pp. 158-180.

Yehoshua, A.B. *Three Days and a Child.* Peter Owen, London, 1970.

_____. "Likhtov Prosa." In *Ha-Kir ve-ha-Har: Mezi'uto ha-Lo Sifrutit shel ha-Sofer be-Yisrael.* Zemora-Bitan, 1989, pp. 86-105.

Yerushalmi, Joseph. A.B. Yehoshua: Bibliography: 1953-1979. Sifriyyat Po'alim, 1980.

Chapter 8

MY MICHAEL BY AMOS OZ

THE AUTHOR AND HIS WORKS
IN ENGLISH TRANSLATION

Amos Oz was born in Jerusalem, Israel, in 1939. In 1954, when Oz was 15, he went to live in the kibbutz (a collective settlement) Hulda, where he graduated from high school. The Kibbutz later became an important theme in some of his literary works (such as *Where the Jackals Howl; Elsewhere, Perhaps;* and *A Perfect Peace*). He served in the Israeli Army (1957-1960). In 1960, when he was 21, he went back to work in the cotton fields of the kibbutz and also got married. In 1961 he published his first short story. He studied Hebrew literature and philosophy at the Hebrew University of Jerusalem (1962-1964), and was also a Visiting Fellow at Oxford University. He taught at various institutes, was an author-in-residence at the Hebrew University of Jerusalem and a writer-in-residence at Colorado College. Amos Oz has been named Officer of Arts and Letters of France. He is an author of novels and short stories, and is also an essayist. Oz's first story was published in 1961 ("Sedek Mefulash la-Ruah") and his first book, a collection of short stories (*Where the Jackals Howl*), was published in 1965.

The literary works of Amos Oz have been widely translated and internationally acclaimed. In 1998 there were 272 of Oz's books in translation in various languages. In 1999, *My Michael* was included in Bertelsmann's one-hundred greatest novels of our century. Oz received various awards and much recognition in and out of Israel, including honors from France (French Prix Femina) and Germany (1992 Frankfurt Peace Prize) and the Wingait Award in England. In Israel he received the Brener award in 1978, then the Bialik Award and the highly prestigious Israel Award in 1998. Amos Oz has been involved in Israeli political life since the 1960s. Oz was one of the founders of the "Peace Now" movement. He lives in 'Arad, a town in Southern Israel, and teaches in various institutions, particularly at Ben-Grunion University of the Negev.

Oz is known for his fiction but he also published well-received non-fiction books. One of his books, a political reportage (*In the Land of Israel*) published in 1983, is based on a journey in Israel in 1982 and blends a journalistic, documentary, ideological and publicist's elements. Another book is a protest of the 1982 Lebanon War (*The Slopes of Lebanon*) published in 1988. Oz published books about social and literary issues in 1979 (*Under This Blazing Light*) and 1993 (*Shetikat ha-Shamayim*). The essays in *Under This Blazing Light* follow the author's interviews and lectures from the beginning of the 1960s until the end of the 1970s. Oz clearly does not consider himself a systematic philosopher but rather a person who is easily excited and reacts emotionally to various matters.

The literary works of Hebrew authors such as M.Y. Berdichevski, Hayyim Yosef Brener and S. Y. Agnon influenced the fiction of Oz. He was also influenced by Russian authors, particularly Anton Chekhov, and is also well familiar with English literature.

In his literary works, Oz strives to understand and reflect the people of Israel. Oz's writing was poetic, allegorical and symbolic but, later, it shifted to the realistic and actual. Oz's expressionistic full-of-pathos style represents his revolt against realism. There is a fusion of the fantastic and the realistic in his literary works. The messages, the characters and the plot, or simply one of those elements is intensified. This reveals the problems that generate divisions in the life of the Israelis. Conflicts mark many of Oz's themes. For example, the descendants of the founding settlers disagree with many of the values of their fathers. The weakness of Zionist fathers conflicts with their strength. The urge of the human flesh conflicts with tradition. Reality conflicts with fantasy. Zionism conflicts with emigration from Israel. The perceptions of the skeptical youngsters conflict with the values of the elderly. The dream of peaceful Jewish life in a little country conflicts with heroic dreams. The well-protected traditional life conflicts with attraction to the unknown. The search for forbearance conflicts with the cruel outcome and the struggle to build conflicts with the destruction.

Oz gives unique and constant expression to Israeli reality by touching upon the painful and the ferment. Oz's writing is rooted in Israel and centers on its people, their trials, their nature and sensitivities, their need for faith and dialogue and their need for decency. The author is determined to expose and tell the truth.

Shaked (*Ha-Sipporet* , pp. 223-227) finds three stages in Oz's literary work. In the 1960s, Oz's work strove to expose the hidden psychological life of his characters, their suffocation in the petite bourgeois life, their futile attempt to defeat the social norms and the illogical aspects of the masses (*Where the Jackals Howl, Elsewhere, Perhaps, My Michael, Unto Death*). In the 1970s and the 1980s, his work confronts the Israeli social context. The characters explored the strong forces that shape society (*Touch the Water, Touch the Wind; The Hill of Evil Counsel, A Perfect Peace, Black Box*). In the third period, Oz was inclined to write about adventurers- and about representatives of Israel with a melodramatic past, who retired, and about aging warriors. The characters attempt to escape from the public and from history into some hidden limited shelters (*To Know a Woman, The Third Condition, Don't Call It Night*). These stages do not represent stylistic or other artistic changes, and the subjects are often not easily dividable.

After publishing short stories, Oz began publishing novels (see Shaked, *Ha-Sipporet*, pp. 205-229). Oz's fiction is well rooted in Israeli social and political reality. The short stories compiled in *Where the Jackals Howl* (1965) and the novel *Elsewhere, Perhaps* (1966) illustrate the destructive factors in Kibbutz life in particular and in the Israeli society in general. *Elsewhere, Perhaps* tells the story of the events of one summer mainly in a kibbutz in the north of Israel, a story of love, hatred, jealousy, friendship, pain, repulsion, pity and joy, with the declared intent of the author to evoke in the reader mixed feelings toward the characters. While in *My Michael* (1968) we hear the echoes of the 1956 Sinai War, the novella *A Late Love* (*Ahava Me'uheret* in the book *'Ad Mavet,* 1971) relates to some of the impacts of the 1967 Six Days War. *The Hill of Evil Counsel* (1976) takes us back to the pre-state days, the days of the underground movements and the beginning of the War of Independence. *Black Box* (1987) presents the conditions in which the social political changes took place when the Ashkenazi-Sephardi conflicts led to the first time defeat in Israeli election of the Labor party ("left") by the Likkud party ("right"). The characters cannot evade history and cannot avoid political and social debates (*To Know a Woman,* 1989, *Don't Call It Night,* 1994, *Ha-Maz av ha-Shelishi, (The Third Condition,* 1991). The attempts to have a territory of his own within Israeli existence and to solve the enigma of life are typical to the ex-secret agent in to *Know a Woman.* The protagonist in *Pinter ba-Martef* ("Panther in the Basement"), 1995), as a boy befriended a British soldier and was accused by his friends of being a traitor, an accusation that caused him to look at his relationships with his parents, his friends and enemies.

Oz's literary work does not reflect an optimistic outlook of the land and the people of Israel. Ideological skepticism and the feeling of collapse of values do not support an optimistic view of Israel. The view of Israeli reality in Oz's work is often ironic. Israeli society is probed and explored. The narrator is unapologetic for his point of view and sometimes supports the ostracized, oppressed, unstable, unrecognized characters in a society that applies collective judgmental criteria.

The Israeli condition is not unfamiliar to the modern reader, and while the milieu is Israeli, the problems are universal.

My Michael (1972) explicates the dullness of the petite bourgeois class and the loneliness of the troubled individual who strives for an exciting life.

Oz, like other Israeli authors who wrote in the 1960s, shifted the literary focus from Israeli society and its needs to individualistic, human needs. The political aspects and actual national events do not dominate this novel. This is not a social-political novel that focuses on the fate of the nation, but on that of individuals.

In 1952, Oz's mother, Fania, committed suicide at the age of 39. She was a sad, depressed woman, who suffered from pain and used to stare out the window regularly. His father, the brother of Professor Joseph Klausner, a well-known historian of Modern Hebrew literature, was busy writing the history of world literature. The impact of this fact was felt by some critics in the novel *My Michael* , specifically by the character of Hannah Gonen. In this novel Oz portrays the psyche of the characters living petite bourgeois life. Some find in these lives full satisfaction while others rebel and suffocate.

Thousand of articles were published about Oz's literary works (See Yerushalmi).

Oz's books in English translation are: *Where the Jackals Howl* (Harcourt Brace) ; *Elsewhere, Perhaps* (Harcourt Brace) ; *My Michael;*

Touch the Water, Touch the Wind (Harcourt Brace) ; *The Hill of Evil Counsel* (Harcourt Brace); *A Perfect Peace* (Harcourt Brace); *In the Land of Israel* (Harvest books); *Black Box* (Vintage International); *The Slopes of Lebanon* (Harcourt Brace) ; *To Know a Woman* (Harcourt Brace); *Don't Call It Night* (Harcourt Brace); *Fima* (Harvest Books); *Israel, Palestine and Peace: Essays* (Vintage); *Panther in the Basement* (Harvest Books); *Soumchi* (Harcourt Brace); *The Story Begins: Essays on Literature (Harcourt Brace);   Under This Blazing Light: Essays* (Cambridge University Press).

THE PLOT

The relationship of Hannah and Michael are central in the novel. Hannah, born in 1930 (p. 92. NB: All the references are to the Bantam book edition), met Michael, who was four years older than she (p. 154), in 1950. They dated, met each other's families, got married, progressed economically and moved from their rented apartment to an apartment they purchased. In 1951, they brought a son into the world. Michael is too "square" for Hannah and is a plain figure for this woman, who fantasizes about relations with various romantic, heroic, courageous and adventurous characters. Hannah suffered emotionally; she became more and more disillusioned, detached and ill. Michael kept progressing in his academic career, but the marriage was troubled. Through the structure of the actions in the novel, i.e. the plot, we learn about Hannah and Michael's childhood and adult life, and a little about their life between these two stages. In 1960, when Hannah began writing her novel, she was a 30-year-old woman and pregnant again. She remembered her relationships with her husband and described them in a non-chronological order. She began writing in January 1960, and ended in May 1967.

The main plot is not in the actions and it is not the static external plot, but in the quite static internal life of Hannah, who is a static character, whose feelings and frustration are unchanging, and whose desires are unfulfilled.

Hannah's ties to the people around her were loose, including her family friends (pp. 147-150), and her ties with her own family, including her mother, son and husband were not strong. She escaped from actuality and daily life to a fantasized world that was adventurous, heroic, violent, sensual and erotic. It included the submarines Dragon and Tigress, Nautilus and various romantic, heroic, courageous and adventurous characters such as Michael Strogoff; Captain Nemo; the Arab twins, Halil and Aziz; the modern Hebrew poet Shaul Tchernichovski; and Yvonne Azulai, the driver Rahamim Rahamimov. Various characters in Hannah's real life appear in her dreams, such as Michael, Jenia and Kadishman. The confused mixture of reality and dreams does not build a bridge between Hannah and her husband Michael.

As a spouse of a young scholar, Hannah enjoyed some security and status in her desolate life. At the same time she was appalled by the lifestyle of the Israeli upper-middle class of the 1950s, because she perceived that lifestyle as meaningless and distorted. Within time she became indifferent to the events around her. The differences between Hannah's internal wild fantasies and reality were incompatible.

In her dreams and fantasies, Hannah escaped to a wild, heroic and destructive life. "To be quiet and wise: how dull" (p. 157) — she thought. One of the advantages of the dreams, according to Hannah, is the absence of the decision-making process: "One of the reasons why I enjoy being asleep is that I hate making decisions... in dreams... some force... makes decisions for you..." (p. 16). Her fantasies culminate in hallucinations and insane acts and, at the end of the novel, she fails establishing good contacts in reality and dreams, and she fantasizes a final destructive revenge.

THE NARRATED MONOLOGUE AS A CENTRAL TECHNIQUE

A represented speech or narrated monologue (German: erlebte Rede) is a speech from a character that is presented through an author's discourse. It is a subtle way of expressing and presenting the relationship of a speaker to a character. The reader recognizes the represented speech by the language and the content. The represented speech has various functions and effects. The device of the narrated monologue is used often in *My Michael* ; it mainly expresses the ironic tension between the narrator Hannah and another character. Hannah appears as the explicit speaker, and she represents the speech of various characters, while she is participating and present in the speech. Her values and concepts are at the background of the speech. In this way Hannah expresses her attitude toward and criticism of the character and the character's ideas, style and values. While in her narrated monologue Hannah is often ironic, the reader may be affected in a different way and not identify with her irony.

It is necessary that the reader recognize the narrated monologue in the novel and its effects on him (Hakak, 1977). The following paragraph (p. 34), in which Hannah's mother talks to Michael a short time before the wedding, demonstrates the complexity of the narrated monologue:

> And finally, Mother.
>
> My mother cried when she spoke to Michael. She told him in broken Hebrew about my father's death, and her words were lost in her tears. She asked if she could measure Michael. Measure? Yes, measure. She wanted to knit him a white sweater. She would do everything she could to have it ready in time for the wedding. Had he got a dark suit? Would he like to wear poor, dear Yosef's suit for the ceremony? She could easily alter it to fit him. There wouldn't be much to do. It wasn't much too big and it wasn't much too small. She begged him. For sentimental reasons. It was the only present she could give him.

The narrator, Hannah, calls the reader's attention to her presence at the outset of the paragraph: "And finally, Mother" — she is a present witness. She is the only speaker at the beginning of the paragraph, and then she goes on to use indirect speech and direct speech ("measure"? — seems to be Michael's question). A close reading of the balance of this paragraph must take into account the phenomenon of the narrated monologue and its effects.

Hannah's mother talked about physically measuring Michael, so that she could knit a sweater for him. The narrator, Hannah, is present, criticizing her mother for not measuring what he is as a person and for decreasing the meaning of the word in such a context to its least important meaning without connoting anything.

The color of the sweater Hannah's mother wanted to knit was white, which is a color that appears in the novel several times (for example, pp. 14, 44, 85, 170). Sometimes white unexpectedly connects to danger, violence, poison, dirt, death, terror, madness and fear. Hannah's mother, Malka, lives in a simplistic world of black and white. White represents purity and joy and it is the color of the sweater she will knit for Michael. Through the use of white in the novel, Hannah implies color, like life, has complexity and may carry negative qualities.

The Arab twins, "alert and white-fanged" (p. 23), "their teeth were very white" (p. 40) were prepared to murder her (p. 172) and, at the end of the novel, are connected to terrorism, death and destruction: "White teeth bared to bite out the pin of a grenade" (p. 246). "White-coated attendants" propelled Mrs. Glick to the ambulance (p. 145) when she became dangerously insane. The narrator speaks of destructive "crowds of white toothed urchins" (p. 93), thinks about "Moby Dick, the noble white whale" (p. 89) who also can be destructive; white face expresses fear (p. 122); the white dress highlighted the color of the charcoal on it (p. 85). In her dream, Hannah spoiled her white wedding dress (p.53), too. White may be associated even with poison and death: "How pure, by comparison, is chemical poison: clear white crystals" (p. 175); "…solitary dead tree stands on the white slope" (p. 16) which Hannah dreams about. "I prefer the darkness… The white light terrorizes Jerusalem," Hannah tells us (p. 16).

Like Michael's father, who talks to Hannah at his first meeting with her about the death of his wife, Michael's mother ("One day he would tell me a very sad story," p. 31), Hannah's mother talks to Michael at her first meeting with him about the death of her husband, Hannah's father ("poor, dear Yosef," p. 34, the translator omitted the words "of blessed memory" which appear in the original). Michael wore Hannah's father's wedding suit for his own wedding and for his father's funeral (p. 132). One evening in the week following the funeral, Hannah came to Michael's study "and saw Yehezkel Gonen" in her husband, "Michael seemed to be acting his father" (p. 135).

When both Michael and his father dressed in black suits at the wedding, Michael resembled his father to the degree Hannah addressed Michael as Yehezkel (p. 42). Michael thus continues his father and Hannah's father. The fact that people are nothing but a version of previous generations seems horrible to Hannah: "It's not the fact that you're your father's son that's horrible, it's that you have started talking like your father… And my father… And after us Yair. All of us. As if one human being after another after another is a nothing but a reject" (p. 228). This general observation of human life is now applied to Michael's specific look. Hannah's mother promises Michael that "there wouldn't be much to do" in order for her to alter her husband's suit to fit Michael. This is another symbolic hint about Michael's "size" and absence of individuality.

Hannah's mother wants to do the alterations "for sentimental reasons." The term "sentiments" is carefully selected here. The Gonen family does not like the word "feeling." Instead, the word "sentiment" is used. "Sentiment is only painful," (p. 179) said Michael in another context. Michael is therefore careful and fearful about feeling. "When people are contented and have nothing to do, emotion spreads like a malignant tumor," (p. 20) said Michael in another context. Can he feel at all the "sentiment" of Hannah's mother? Michael's father has a "sentiment" to give his grandchild the name of his father, Zalman (p. 66), ignoring the fact that the unpopular antiquated non-Israeli name would leave his grandson open to ridicule. Michael and his father use the word "sentiment," meaning feeling (pp. 103, 109, 111, 121, 126, 139, 140, 179). The word "sentiment" is used in the original Hebrew text; the use of the non-Hebrew word helps to create a distance between the speakers and the discussed feelings. The Gonen family approaches feelings through the screen of logic and propriety.

The narrator, with her values, concepts and criticism is present throughout this paragraph. She tends to find symbols and meanings in everything around her. Therefore, her understanding of "measuring" a groom would be far different from her mother's limited scope of the term. The mother does not see the problem with Michael's fitting into Hannah's father suit, the man who treasured "the remarks of every good-for-nothing" (p. 24), while Hannah dwells on the fact that there were minor differences in the measurements of Michael and Hannah's father. Also, Hannah's mother is not aware of the mourning and death associated by her daughter with the wedding and the black suit. Emanuel, Hannah's brother, is spontaneous and direct: "The girl's going to get married and you'd think from her face she'd just been widowed" (p. 34).

The mother-daughter communication is therefore very limited, and the narrator is presenting her mother as a mother who wishes well, but is incapable of seeing and understanding her daughter's pain and fear. The distance between mother and daughter contributes to the daughter's feeling of loneliness and isolation; she is near people, but not with them.

The narrator treats her mother in this paragraph with irony. The language in this narrated monologue represents the mother's rhythm of speech and manners, her style and concepts. She does not "elevate" to the painful, poetic, detached world of her daughter, she cannot see the meaning beyond the basic and tangible. The reader however has to ask how is he affected by the irony of the narrator. There is warmth, care and tenderness in the mother's words; the reader may find the narrator's attempt of ironic presentation of her own mother and the mother's norms as unjustified, and he treats the narrator — not her mother! — with irony. In this case, the implied author and the reader may enrich the understanding that the mother is human and compassionate, while the narrator is judgmental and cold. Similar situations are encountered in the descriptions of various characters, including Michael, his father and his aunts; all of them have human warmth, care, practicality and giving hearts.

The technique of the narrated monologue is used extensively in the novel, and its many subjective effects on the reader enrich the enjoyment of his reading.

THE UNRELIABLE
NARRATOR

Hannah has a coercive, aggressive, ill personality both physically and verbally. For example, she tells us the following story about her:

> One evening... [Michael and I] went down to the sea...
> Michael refused and I tried to explain. I didn't listen to him.
> With a strength which surprised me I tore his shirt of him.
> Threw him down in the sand. There was a bite. A sob. I bore
> him down with every part of my body as if I was heavier than
> he was...
>   ... There were fine lashes of rough pleasure, piercing and
> searing. Michael was frightened. He didn't recognize me, he
> mumbled, I was unfamiliar again, and he didn't like me. I was
> glad I was unfamiliar. I didn't want him to like me.
>   ... I went on laughing silently till dawn. (pp. 233-234).

Hannah can be not only physically but also verbally imposing and coercive. Hannah thinks that determination, forcefulness and aggression may adapt and shape facts to an interpreter's will:

> Like most humanities students, I had always imagined that all
> facts are susceptible of different interpretations, and that a
> sharp-witted and determined interpreter could always adapt
> them and shape them to his will. Provided he was forceful and
> aggressive enough (p. 230).

A key to understanding the novel is the fact that the novel's narrator is an unreliable one (See Band). The protagonist Hannah, who is presenting her memories, tells *My Michael.* There is disparity between her perceptions of the events and that of the reader. The narrator, motivated by revenge and having a neurotic demeanor, presents everything exclusively from her own point of view. She selects the events that she writes about, presents them from her subjective point of view and evaluates them. The narrator majored in Hebrew literature, and she is aware of the power of words. She "attended lectures on Hebrew litera-ture" as a first-year student (p.8, see also p. 31); she read modern and Medieval Hebrew literature and world literature (p. 180, 98-99) and seemed to be a poetess, even though she did not write poetry (p. 213, p. 228).

The narrator, Hannah, is therefore unreliable because she describes everyone and everything from her subjective point of view while she is ill and, at times, she acts insane. Her understanding of events and people is affected by her delusions, fantasies and infantile attitude toward various aspects of reality. In her writing, she strives for revenge; she even imagines sending the Arab twins to commit terrorist acts in Israel (pp. 245-247). She is attracted to the twins, to their exotic world and to their destructive power more than she is attracted to Michael. Due to the narrator's revenge motive, to her ability to coerce the facts and to her distorted psyche, the reader should constantly question what she writes. And the reader should sometimes doubt the "truthfulness" of the description, in spite of the sympathy he may feel for the narrator who is on the edge of insanity among people whose desires possibly call for mockery.

In light of her problematic personality, the reader must be cautioned about the "truthfulness" of the portrayed world when he reads Hannah's accounting of people and events. At the beginning of the novel, Hannah is a young, neurotic woman, with heroic dreams, but later she is exposed as ill, detached from reality, swinging back and forth between madness and a stable life and fascination with physical and emotional illness. Hannah's contact with reality bordered with illness since childhood. "I was a queen...When I recovered...I experienced a feeling of exile" (pp. 15-16) she says about her childhood illness. At a later stage she returned to her "old childhood yearning, to be very ill" (p. 60). She "remembered fondly" (p. 167) her childhood illness, and she is drawn to illness (p. 167-170). The implied author treats the emotionally ill Hannah with both compassion and reservations and cautions the reader not to believe everything she tells him.

Already the first paragraph of the novel may reveal, in a second reading, that we have an unreliable narrator in the novel:

> I am writing this because people I loved died. I am
> writing this because when I was young I was full of the
> power of loving. I do no want to die (p. 1).

Reading this paragraph (see Band), the reader may ask various questions, such as: Who are the people she loved who died? Did she love any of the people who died in the course of the novel — Mrs. Tarnapoler, Hannah's landlady before Hanna's marriage (p. 232); the neighbor, Mr. Glick (who died ten days before Passover, perhaps the coming holiday of redemption was marked by redeeming him from his insane wife, p. 236); Dr. Urbach (p. 243); the old kindergarten teacher, Sarah Zelda, (p. 221); and other characters whose death is mentioned in the novel? Did Hannah's feelings for her father elevate to the feeling of love? Doesn't her passion for death and violence and her fascination with illness contradict her claim that she does not want to die?

The unreliable narrator is also revealed through her distorted relationships with the people around her.

THE NARRATOR'S
RELATIONSHIPS

Hannah's relationships with her father, mother, husband, son and the Arab twins, Yoram and with fictional characters are central to understanding her. Hannah rejects the people around her for many reasons, one of which is their inability to appreciate love, spiritual growth and happiness while they are committed to insignificant, materialistic goals. Hannah herself, however, though critical of others, is unknowingly full of emotional distortions like those whom she despises. Neither her distorted disappointing reality nor her disappointing dream worlds give her peace (Gertz, 1976; 1982, pp. 1-63. Gertz is the first to point out a long detailed, well-founded list of distortions, some of which are mentioned here as well).

While Hannah considers herself a loving woman, the reader may not concur with her. It is difficult to find love in the way she acts as a wife, mother, daughter and friend. Hannah claims: "I loved my late father more than any other man in the world" (p. 2). Her recognition of his faults is only more convincing than her love for him. She remembers his "treasuring the remarks of every good-for-nothing" (p. 24). "He did not regard it as beneath his dignity to spend his whole life kowtowing to powerful forces whose nature remained hidden from him. I loved him more than I have ever loved anyone else in the world" (p. 209).

Hannah's attitude toward her mother is different: "What a small place my mother occupied in my thoughts. She was father's wife. That was all... I made no room for her in my heart" (p. 241). The reader does not find justification for this attitude, the same way he cannot accept the frequent sarcasm and lack of compassion for Michael's father.

Hannah thinks of herself as being better than those scholars and famous people whom her father so admired; she concludes they were born and died as an "utter nonentity. Period" (p. 224). Simcha, the maid, has wisdom: "...most of my friends, they marry men like their pas...It's a rule...the husband is always like the father" (p. 188). Hannah married the kind of a man her father admired.

Hannah claims she loved Michael (p.1), in one situation she says: "I love you. I loved you when we met in Terra Sancta" (p. 86), but the words are not backed up by works, deeds or actions.

At the inception of their relationship, she liked the thought that she was "stronger than this young man" (p. 6); she "enjoyed his discomfiture," the "embarrassment of the student Michael Gonen" (p. 8, she liked the fact he was "trying too hard" to please her (p. 9); she "enjoyed his efforts" and was glad that she "was causing him some exertion. It was because of me that he was coming out of his cocoon and trying to be amused and amusing" (p. 5), excited (p.11) and embarrassed in her company (p. 21), behaving like a child near a teacher (p. 20, 21), but these are not expressions of love.

Hannah is occupied with her assessment that Michael is not a witty man (i.e. pp. 3, 5, 26) while she wanted "to meet a strong, sensible man some day" (p. 209), not an "utter nonentity" (p. 224) like Michael. Michael understands that his wife wanted "a prince-poet-boxer-pilot husband" (p. 217) instead of him.

Numerous times in the novel she thinks of her Michael as a child (i.e. pp.11, 13, 20, 21, 46, 56, 62, 63, 133, 223) or as her own child (i.e.

p. 79); and at the end of the novel, when Michael goes to Yardena, Hannah says: "You couldn't go on being my thoughtful elder son" (p. 244). Relating to Michael as a child may give Hannah a feeling of maturity and control, not love.

One of the strongest obstacles to Hannah's love and acceptance of people is her perception of the absence of their individuality; she fears that all people are rejects, drafts thrown into the wastebasket (p. 228). Therefore, one should not be surprised reading that Hannah relates to her second pregnancy in 1959 as "a sordid, grotesque travesty" (p. 243).

Michael is just another "crumpled draft thrown in a wastebasket" (p. 228); he is not free to chose and decide his way of life: "I was the hope of the family...they all bet on me as if I was their racehorse" (p. 22). It is not a surprise that the Gonens talk about Michael in a collective possessive way. The father speaks about "my Michael" (p. 30); Aunt Jenia and Aunt Leah talk about "our Micha" (pp. 67, 128). Hannah also speaks of "My Michael" (p. 66, 194), sometimes clearly with compassion (pp. 37, 38). But her husband's name — Michael — only highlights her attraction to the other Michael, Michael Strogoff, with whom she is enchanted (i.e., pp. 22, 164, 171, 172). Hannah's position that "a family isn't a relay race, with a profession as a torch" (p. 7) did not change Michael's family position.

Michael is a copy of the old professors — they had a certain status, some security; their lives were well organized — but they all represent an endless repetition; they go forward in time but their future is known at the present, because they do not attain anything that Hannah deems as progress. Michael's voice will be like that of the old professor, "slow and resonant" (pp. 3-4). Five years later, listening to her husband's lecture, Hannah will say: "I suddenly recalled the old geology lecturer...Where will I be, what will I be, on the day when Michael catches up with the shadow of the old lecturer from Terra Sancta" (p. 120). Michael will fulfill his father's wish and become a professor in Jerusalem and continue the scholarly chain of his father's grandfather (p. 7); he is a mere copy of previous generations, including the old people connected to him — Glick, Kadishman, his aunts and his father.

Hannah claims she has very high standards of family bond and intimacy: "Touching. Merging... Melting. Fusing..." (p. 223); but at the same time, she is capable of different relationships based on neurotic lust: "I made contact only with his body... in my heart I knew that I deceived him again and again (Ibid.). She does not make efforts to peruse true family intimacy and close relationships, not even with her mother, husband, son and father-in-law.

Michael and Hannah's wedding takes place at about the same time as Michael completes his seminar paper (p. 36); Hannah gets pregnant before Michael's final examinations (p. 55); the birth of their first born takes place at about the same time as his final, graduation exams (see Shaked, *Gal*). When in the spring before Passover of 1959 Michael finally reaches the completion of his doctoral dissertation (p. 188), the strong marital tear takes place. Passover, therefore, was not a celebration of new "freedom," spring and family togetherness for him, but a contrast to all these traditional feelings. The climactic point of the progress in Michael's academic career marks the opposite results in his family life.

The stability of Hannah's life was insufficient for a good marital bond because she considered her husband a shallow ordinary man, while she was yearning for characters that brought fantasized orgies and violence into her life.

It is also hard to find an expression of Hannah's motherly love. "I was an indifferent mother during the early months of my son's life," "yes, Yair was wicked" (p. 78) Hannah tells us. She did not like Yair's look "when he was so bursting with joy" playing with his father, and she expressed her unfounded fear that Yair "would not turn out to be particularly bright" (p. 82). She abused her son: "I beat Yair whenever he displayed this sullen insolence…I would thrash him…until, panting, I succeeded in wringing the sobs from his throat" (p. 101). While the dentists were amazed at Yair, his mother concludes: "a child of five who was fascinated by tooth-rot would grow up to be a disgusting person" (p. 202). She clasped her son in an affectionate embrace only when she played with him and he seemed to her "like a real sea captain" (p. 211) — the affection was the fruit of an error. Michael encourages her to try to love their son (p. 139), but can Hannah love?

The protagonist Hannah claims she loved the Arab twins (p. 23), nonetheless, in her games with them she was "Princess" and they were her "submissive subjects" (pp. 13-14); she "ruled over the twins. It was a cold pleasure…" (pp. 5-6). She was the twins' superior in all the games, but was she in love with them?

Hannah had similar relations with Yoram Kamnitzer, The Gonens' neighbors' son. His feelings and suffering are not of a great interest to her, her control of him is. She wanted him to love her so that she could monopolize him, enjoying his embarrassment, humiliation and despair (page 199). She "deliberately" tormented him (p. 200), and enjoyed her possessiveness and control ("He was mine. All mine. He was at my mercy"), his suffering and astonishment (Ibid.); she wanted to "achieve the mastery" she "longed for" (Ibid.). When she failed in extracting his confession of love for her (p. 202), she feels that "time would be ever-present... hostile to Yoram and her" (pp. 203-204).

Hannah claims she only intended to offer Yoram "a handful of friendly words...because... I had not discovered in him the magical power of flexibility or the floods of deep-flowing energy" (p. 203). What would this mother and wife have offered the minor Yoram had he had the "magical power" or the "energy" she related to?

Hannah has similar attitude toward fictional characters. Abraham Mapu (1767-1807) in his novel *Love of Zion* described love between Tamar and Amnon and, when the narrator reads the novel, she again converts love into control: "If I were Tamar I would make Amnon crawl to me on his knees for seven nights... I would order him to transport me in a sailing ship" (p. 17). As to Michael Strogoff of *Moby Dick* she plans to "subjugate a last Michael Strogoff for the last time to the will, to the mission, of a deposed princess" (p. 203).   It appears therefore that, when Hannah talks about love, she thinks of conquering, ruling and controlling. In short: "The Princess has spoken...Down, rebellious subjects, down...you shall all be white for I am a white princess" (p. 170, see also p. 111). Even when Hannah does not speak about such a deep emotion as love but about friendship, the reader may remain perplexed. Hannah speaks time and again about her "best friend Hadassah" (i.e. pp. 166, 180, 218, 235), but we don't see any act on her part substantiating her friendly feelings for Hadassah.

Hannah's need for a position of power and supremacy is manifested not only in her attitude toward people, in her dreams and in the way she relates to fictional characters, it is extended also to transportation objects or to her being in them; ship, trains, airplanes, cars, carriages (p. 113). In her dreams she "was a general on the train" (p. 15). She wanted to be "the princess of the train" (p. 89), to order the airplane "to flash green and red" (p. 112-113). In these vehicles she was a general, emperor and princess. Hannah feels that "time is slipping away" (p. 109) and therefore she wants to travel within time to distant places, using and controlling any available vehicle; but she is unsuccessful. Time does not grant her wishes and does not take her anywhere. Therefore she did not "come to terms with time" (p. 236), she felt that her life is static while time is dynamic, which caused her to futilely fight it, "ignore it deliberately so as to confound it..." (p. 212). Knowing Hannah's expectations and her attitude toward time, one understands why she repeats time and again the following words, as if they were a refrain: "The dreary sameness of the days" (i.e. pp. 151, 152, 157, 219).

Michael understands that fulfillment of all the "dreams," including acquisition of a new apartment, a small car and travel to Europe requires time (p. 212), but such a trip and a car were not much for a woman who commanded airplanes, ships, submarines and trains.

One would wonder why Hannah has such a strong urge to govern, decree, regulate and dominate. She cannot control her own life but desires to control everyone. Hannah fears that life is accidental, and that it does not allow for individuality and free choice. She is reminded that even her choice of Michael for a husband happened by chance (pp. 50-51, see also p. 41). "Who is he? What do you know about him?" (p. 27) wonders Hannah about Michael even after he proposed to her, and she asks the same question in the course of her marriage (p. 103). Hannah's need to govern may be a reaction to her submissive parents — to her father who annulled and effaced himself, and to her meek, docile mother. Her snobbish, high-hat attitude toward people may be the result of the people's non-recognition of her "uniqueness."

Oz mentioned famous scholars who lived in Jerusalem and says: "I am from Jerusalem... I almost did not know that they existed, except that my father sometimes said to me: 'Here is a world famous person walking on the street.'" (See Oz, "Me-'Ever"). The autobiographical memory found a clear expression in Hannah's memories in *My Michael*: "My father was extremely fond of the phrase 'world-famous.' He would whisper excitedly that some professor who had just vanished into a florist's shop was world-famous, or that some man out shopping was of international fame."

When Hannah did not procure or lost the control and authority she wanted over people, she looked for ways to compensate herself; she found some comfort in shopping. She "stormed feverishly from shop to shop" (p. 90) and "Hysterically bought more and more things" (p. 160). Hannah's shopping urge is of special interest because she treats the people around her with irony for their materialism. The way Yehezkel, Michael's father, described his Michael, reminded Hannah of the way her father sold "a second-hand radio" (p. 30); learning about the thousand pounds Hannah inherited made Aunt Jenia accept the timing of the marriage (p.33). Hannah herself feels she was treated as merchandise: "I was carefully made and beautifully wrapped, tied with a pretty red ribbon and put on display, bought and unwrapped, used and set aside" (p. 87). But in fact, notwithstanding her resentment of the materialistic character of the people around her, Hannah is materialistic herself and shopping is part of her emotional life, an attempt to overcome her loneliness and detachment and to achieve. In light of the above, one may conclude that Hannah's concepts of love, friendship, family and achievements are as deformed as those of the people around her (see Gertz).

Each one of the three — Aunt Jenia, Mrs. Glick and the City of Jerusalem — are analogous to Hannah and illuminate her. Hannah perceives Jerusalem in a way that reminds the reader of Hannah herself (see Shaked, *Gal*). She sees "an ancient grove...clutching at the outermost houses of Rehavia is about to enfold and smother them in its luxuriant vegetation" (p. 93). Jerusalem may be attacked, "brooding hills waiting for darkness to fall on the shuttered city" (p. 94). Jerusalem is a "city of enclosed courtyards, her soul sealed up behind bleak walls...Villages and suburbs surround Jerusalem in a close circle, like curious bystanders surrounding a wounded woman lying in the road...(pp. 95-96). Inside Jerusalem, Hannah finds "a landscape pregnant with suppressed violence" (p. 14). Jerusalem "was shuttered" (p. 210); it can be "conquered...by enemy who hemmed her in on three sides" (p. 242); it is a city of darkness and mist (p. 163). One can see "ghostly shapes in the darkness" (p. 164); it is a city with "a blind alley...shuttered houses...iron shutters and iron doors secured with rusting bolts" (p.181). Hannah thinks that Jerusalem is not a city but "an illusion...insubstantial" (p. 21). The quarter where Hannah and Michael lived was built "of stone and iron...Iron hand-rails...Dirty iron gates...Battered fences...Rusty shutters hanging on a single hinge, threatening to hurl themselves down into the street..." (p. 102).

Jerusalem is described through the subjective eyes of Hannah who projects her feelings on her city. Like Jerusalem, Hannah maybe attacked; she too is isolated and lonely. Jerusalem is under attack; it is surrounded, enclosed, shut, cold, scary, unclear, dangerous and flimsy. Jerusalem is a mere extension of Hannah, who portrayed herself when she portrayed Jerusalem. Jerusalem, like the people and the routine of life, becomes another cause of Hannah's feeling of suffocation.

Aunt Jenia fulfilled the kind of dreams Hannah had, but her life is evidence that when the dreams come true they do not have the same results one may have in mind. Michael's aunt, Aunt Jenia, lived an adventurous, somehow heroic life, summarized in the novel (p. 67-68): Her first husband, a gynecologist, ran off to Cairo after a Czech woman athlete and hung himself in a hotel. Her second husband, an actor, had a nervous breakdown and then became apathetic. Aunt Jenia supported him in a boarding house.

Undoubtedly, Jenia's life has excitement, adventure and drama. She was engaged for six years to a man before he became her husband (p. 33). He was an ill professional who was charged with curing people. He first was interested in a woman of high professional education (Jenia) and then in a woman of bodily abilities; his adventures ended up with his committing suicide in a foreign glamorous hotel. Jenia's second husband was in the performing arts and became one of the living-dead. With her "downy mustache" (p.67) and her "short fingered, masculine hand" (Ibid.), "her face...like the face of a bad-tempered old man" (p. 222). Her male aspects are strong, but she claimed she was "forced... to follow the cruel path of fighting a man's fight in a man's world" (p. 129). All these adventures, struggles, glamour, control, did not lead to satisfying life.

Being jealous of Hannah's newly acquired status of motherhood, Jenia, in a state of denial, occupied herself with believing she was being protective of Hannah (pp. 67-68). Career cannot substitute for emotional life.

One may find analogies between Hannah and Jenia (see Gertz, "Iyyun"), the one who dreamed of adventures and the one who lived them: The names (Jenia — Hebrew, Hannah); Jenia worked with children (pediatric department) and so did Hanna (kindergarten teacher, p. 8), and both left — Jenia to work with old people (p. 222) and Hannah to be a homemaker, and then to work in the Ministry of Trade (pp. 221, 226); Hannah is ill and needs a doctor; Jenia is a doctor and is ill.

The world of adventures, when it becomes real, has no luster, and the life story of Aunt Jenia is evidence of that. No wonder that within time "an expression like an ugly sob had set on her [Jenia's] face" (p. 153). She began to understand that adventures, struggles and status may draw someone in, too late she realized that "time flies...time flies...Time waits for no man" (p. 154).

Aunt Jenia was in charge of healing other people, and she constantly gave advice to others, all on the basis of age and a diploma. She, too, lived her life dreaming, refusing to acknowledge errors, failures and feelings. But in a distorted society, Jenia, who cannot admit that her life is not evidence of wise choices and decisions, has leading, guiding, healing roles.

Mrs. Glick represents a progressive, probable future condition of Hannah. Hannah describes Mrs. Glick as a woman who "suffered from fits of hysteria" (p. 101). Dr. Urbach gave instructions on how to deal with Hannah "if there is signs of hysterics" after he leaves (p. 174). "...One of these days I shall go mad just like Duba Glick and it'll be your fault, Doctor Goofy Ganz" (p. 225) — said Hannah to Michael. Back from the institution, Duba "displayed silent resignation" (p. 221). She finally was accommodated in a home for elderly people suffering from chronic diseases where Jenia acted as a doctor for the sick and needy (p. 237).

GRANDIOSE SOCIETAL DREAMS

People around Hannah Gonen have many hopeful thoughts expressed by names, which only reveal the ironic discrepancy between the wish and the real world. Like Hannah, the people also have personal dreams. Some of their dreams are national in scope. The gap between dream and reality may elicit pain, mercy, mockery and ridicule. Its effects depend on the reader. Some of these dreams are expressed through giving names and are also expressed in wartime and personal choices (see Gertz).

For many years, Israeli literature developed the positive stereotypic character of the new Jewish man, the Israeli born, but *My Michael* does not nurture the myth of the Israeli-born hero; Michael is limited and dull; he is not a hero. His wife, Hannah, is a woman-girl; she is not a patriot; her life is not the fulfillment of the Zionist norms. She is attracted to the Arab twins and dreams about orgies.

The protagonist's name, Hannah, may remind us of the Biblical Hannah, who prayed and "the Lord remembered Hannah, and she conceived" (*First Samuel* , 2, 21), but Hannah Gonen's prayers are not answered. The kind librarian noticed a change in Hannah and, using the Hebrew meaning of her name and a pun, he says: "Bright joy illuminates Hannah in a most amazing manner" (p. 18) — but it did not happen; only his death saddened Hannah (p. 197). Hannah also drew a heart pierced by an arrow on the steam of the window and used hers and Michael's initials: HG, MG, HM. None of the meanings of these words, created in Hebrew by the various combinations of the initials of Michael and Hannah, came true — their marriage was not a holiday ("HG," Hebrew — hag). Michael was not a magus, magician ("MG," Hebrew — mag). And the marriage was not warm ("HM," Hebrew — ham).

Hannah relates to herself as a princess. Her mother's name is Malka (in Hebrew it means "Queen"), but the queen does not have a kingdom or a king.

Hannah remembers her father, the "king" of the house, doing chores and dressed in clothes which are not so royal: "Standing doing the washing-up with my mother's apron round him. Dusting. Beating bedspreads" (p.24). The father's name is Joseph but, unlike the Biblical Joseph, he did not become a viceroy.

Yair (in Hebrew it means "he will light"), the first-born son of Hannah and Michael, does not bring light; his birth does not take his parents' relationship from the darkness it is in. Yair asks: "Mummy, is it true that if Daddy was a king I'd be a duke?" (p. 177) — not a surprising question, considering that it is asked by the boy whose mother imagined she was a princess and his grandmother was called Malka. The "queen" is not a queen; the "princess" is not a princess; and the duke is not a duke.

Michael is a name of an angel and a leader (*Danie* l 10,13; 10, 21; 12,1), a prince (2nd *Chronicles* 21,2). "Gonen" in Hebrew it means "protector;" Michael is neither an angel nor a defender-protector; he also does not have the spirit of Michael Strogoff of *Moby Dick* He is not a prince, in spite of some gestures: "Like a duke in an English film Michael kissed my hand through his gloves" (p.14). Michael knows: "...I'm not cut out to be a dream-prince or a knight on horseback" (p. 139). In the army Michael's function was wireless communication (operator, see "Corporal Goofy Ganz, Signal Corps," p. 179), which makes his failure in communication in his personal life conspicuous and ironic. He gives a "message transmitted in code" (p. 12) to his wife, but she "didn't have the key" (p. 37). He was a geologist in his academic specialty; before he understood the closest people on earth to him he dedicated his life to delving down into the depth of the earth (see p. 45). Michael's communication to his wife about his expertise was not clear to her (p.153). The professor of Hebrew literature found symbolic conjunction of subjects in the marriage of Hannah and Michael: "Both geology, on the one hand, and the study of literature, on the other, delve down into the depths, as it were, in quest of buried treasures" (p. 45). This banal analogy, of course, did not help in Hannah and Michael's communication.

Michael's father name is Yeheskel but, unlike the Biblical Ezekiel, he is not a prophet and does not prophesy resurrection. Like other people and places who carry names of prophets, he is not one. "When we read the Books of Prophets at school, I imagined the Prophets as being like the writers and scholars my father had pointed out to me" (p. 9), but scholars are not prophets, and "the Street of the Prophets" (p. 13) in Jerusalem has no prophets in it. Jewish sages said: "Since the day the Temple was destroyed, the power of prophecy has been granted to the fools" (*Baba Batra* 12:). Michael changed this statement, stating that the "power of prophecy has been granted to men like you or me" (p. 163), to fools instead of prophets. In another context Michael wondered: "Is Hannah also among the prophets?" (p. 50), which is a paraphrase of the biblical "Is Saul also among the prophets?" (*First Samuel* 10,11; 10,12; 19, 24), a question expressing a baffling surprise. Like everyone around them Michael, Hannah and Kadishman are not equipped to predict the future, but all the three do that anyway — Hannah as to "know" what will happen at the end of time, and the two men as to the places that will be the target of the next war.

The name of the greengrocer is nothing less than Eliahu Mossiah (p. 164), but he is neither the prophet Elijah nor a savior (Hebrew: "moshiya"). Of a special interest is the name of his daughter, Levana (white) — her name is well suited to her personality — her face was white, her voice soft; she was a bashful, pleasing girl (p. 164).

Hannah's brother's name is Emanuel (in Hebrew it means: "The Lord is with us"), but we do not see unique blessings in his parents' life or his. Hannah waits for joy and fortune, but all she finally gets is two maids - Simcha (Hebrew: "joy." pp. 175, 177, 191), and Fortuna ("fortune," p. 228-229). Simcha is referred to, anyway, as Hadassah's Simcha — Hadassah's joy (p. 178, 180, even this joy is not the Gonens').

The world is not logical, and grandiose hopes will never cease. The line between the wishful and the real is thin. When a person is born, he is given a name — and the name often represents an error and is ironic.

The Sinai War provides grandiose dreams in the national arena. The novel was published after the Six Days War (1967) but relates to the Sinai War (1956). The novel describes the excitement and involvement of various characters in the war, their feeling that they are amidst a heroic national drama of winning and conquering. They talk about survival, justice, redemption, but the victory carries them out, and they feel powerful and vigorous. The narrative presents a gap between the characters' lofty, festive, dramatic, apocalyptic style on the one hand and their banal acts and reality on the other. This gap becomes comic, and the narrator, Hannah, who does not share any patriotic feelings, treats it ironically (see Gertz, "Iyyun"). Hannah acts as an outsider observer who detests the people around her. "Wallowed in the icy water" (p. 169) she strives to die and becomes a major participant in a fantasized orgy (Ibid.).

Simcha, the maid, was part of the national consensus, "they [the Arabs] certainly deserved it"(p. 187), she said while she was warming milk and ironing. Dr. Urbach resorted to lofty style: "These are important days, fateful days...it is difficult to refrain from scriptural thoughts ... almost apocalyptic..." (pp. 186-187) he said these words while he was concerned about Hannah's health, her throat, sleep and monthly cycle. Mr. Kadishman talked about "the message of these historic days," "this hand which wields the ax... is ours," "we are no longer a ewe among seventy wolves," "our army is pursuing the routed forces of Paraoh" (p. 193-194) while he wrapped "a thick scarf around his neck." Mr. Glick discussed his "poor, dear Duba," his wife, who was treated by electric shock, something that may be waiting for Hannah sometime along the road. A flowery style was used also in the announcements on the radio, including words such as "...the moral justification...Enlightened public opinion...From Dan to Beersheba we'll never forget...The Sinai Desert, historic cradle of the Israelite nation" (p. 181). "...Tiran...had returned to the possession of the Third kingdom of Israel" (p. 196). "New horizons were opened up to us" (p. 198).

When Kadishman offered Hannah his help when Michael was drafted, she mocked his high style: "'Pray do call, Mr. Kadishman,' I said mockingly. My Michael's choice of friends amazed me" (p. 194). The response lacked compassion and politeness.

Even during the war Hannah looked down on the people around her who longed for their grandiose dreams. The Arab coffee pot that Michael promised to bring (p. 178) and Hannah's period are representatives of what will be left of the societal war dreams about "important," "fateful," "apocalyptic" days. The thrill people get out of the pompous dreams is short-lived. The narrator may have, at times, distorted reality, characters and situations.

THE NOVEL CLOSURE

At the end of the novel, Hannah feels that time, the crews of her ship, the twins and her subjects, her friends and husband betrayed her and did not grant her any of her wishes in reality and in her dreams, therefore, she dreams of revenge.

Time, as a powerful entity, does not offer her relief, support, or resolution, only defeat and dissolution. Therefore, her anticipation of holidays, which do not bring changes, comes to an end when she feels defeated, witnessing "the first sparks of a celebration which was not in her honor" (p. 172).

While Hannah became uninvolved and passive, her friend Hadassah prepared to go to Switzerland (p. 236). Michael began wooing his blond friend, Yardena (p. 243), which reminded Hannah of their kitten, Snowy, "who once struggled with pathetic leaps to catch a moth fluttering just below the ceiling" (p. 244). In the past she saw herself — not Yardena — as the catch (p.153). In the past she saw how Snowy "would jump a few inches off the floor, opening and closing his little jaws as if he has already reached the moth" (p. 106), she sees the inapplicable symbolic potential in this scene — Michael's futile efforts, in her opinion, to capture Yardena's heart, but Hannah does not apply the scene to her own desires and dreams. She previously begged Michael to drive away with her (p. 190), but now she realizes that "For some years now Michael has been resting with his arms on the steering wheel... I bid him farewell. I am not involved. I have given in" (p. 244). Now Hannah is not part of the trip.

Hannah feels that new beautiful young women captured her place. Now it is Yair's teacher, not she, who is "...young...attractive, like a princess in a children's picture book" (p. 231). "Jerusalem was suddenly full of lovely girls" and Hannah is not one of them anymore (Ibid.). She is no longer the princess and the center: "A far-off band played...Young people marching... A princess. A ceremony. Far away" (p. 231). The feeling that she is not part of a procession and that her days as a "princess" are over is not new: "A procession is passing beyond the wood...There our your march and chant...military band and gleaming white uniforms..." (p. 156).

The feeling of aging, of decay, of being left behind relates also to Hannah's neighborhood: "The older inhabitants gradually left the district... We were left behind to keep watch over dying streets. It was a continuous, insensible decay" (p. 220).

Hannah conceived again, and sometimes she forgot "where I had put some object or article of clothing" (p. 243). This as a blow to the narrator who prides herself time and again on her memory, declaring repeatedly: "I cannot forget a thing" (p. 151). In the past, Hannah remembered every gift she received and every purchase she made. Now she did not mention the death of friends "...because forgetfulness managed to pierce my defense" (p. 221). Her memory is, again, selective, without priorities.

"... *Dragon* was far, far away...I am lost" (p. 114) she told us earlier, but now her "subjects," the crews of her dream's ship also abandoned her, they are "roaming the valleys in search of new girls...I am at rest" (p. 236). She became the victim of a secret plot by her "subjects" and "officers;" guns were pointed at her window and the assassins smiled (p. 170-172).

Dreams and reality became mixed up, i.e., Aunt Jenia became an old, threatening merchant in her dream, and Kadishman became "Michael Strogoff's cunning interrogator" (p. 193).

At the end of the novel, Hannah sent the twins to commit acts of terrorism, death and destruction against the society that she unfoundedly accused of being the cause of her condition.

While Hannah's criticism of the people around her has merit, she is unable to exercise self-criticism. She lacks the strength and wisdom that will make it possible for her to make good use of the gift of life she was given. It is insufficient to point out the weak spots around her; Hannah needs strength and discipline to build an alternative and to make the best of the gift of life.

THE MOVIE

Director: Dan Wolman. Producers: Alfred Flein, David Lipkind, Shlomi Cohen. Script: Dan Wolman, Esther Mor (Literary adaptation. Based on the novel of Amos Oz). Photography: Adam Grinberg. Music: Alex Kagan. Editorial: Dany Shick. Cast: 'Oded Kotler, Efrat Lavi, Irit Mohar-Alter, Moti Mizrahi, Rafael Z vi, Arnon Zafrir, Yisrael Segal, Irit Hamme'iri, Devora Halter-Kedar, Rivka Bekhar, Shimon Dotan. 1975 color movie. 80 minutes.

This is an award winning 80-minute, color movie produced in 1975, with the well-known Israeli actor, 'Oded Kotler, as Michael and the gifted actress, Efrat Lavi, as Hannah. It generated the largest number of viewers

of any of the *Kayiz* films. Kronish presents the achievements of the
movie in these words:

> Although there is a little plot development, the film's achieve-
> ment lies in its beauty and gentleness, and in the striking
> performance by Efrat Lavi...She is married to Michael...a
> reticent, sympathetic, hard-working scientist...
>
> A reflection of the divided city in which she lives,
> Hannah becomes melancholic, isolated and full of loneliness
> and tension... (See Kronish, p. 80).

The movie scenes take place in various sites in Jerusalem — such as
a kindergarten, a lecture hall, a construction site, a produce market, the
mountains, a grove, a wedding place, a mental institution, an apartment
and much more. All of them are often seen through the eyes of the
abnormal, divergent Hannah.

Jerusalem provided the setting for many Israeli movies produced
after the Six Day War of 1967. A significant part of the world population
relates to Jerusalem and its beauty, mysticism, history, religious beliefs,
culture and symbolism. Some of the movies that set Jerusalem as at the
background are: The 1967 *Three Days and a Child* ; Menahem Golan's
1969 movie *My Love in Jerusalem* ; the 1971 *I Was Born in Jerusalem*
about the highly acclaimed Israeli singer and actor, Yehoram Gaon (who
acts the role of Adam in *The Lover*); *I Love You Rosa* in 1972; the 1979
Moments ; and the 1989 *A Thousand and One Wives* , the latter two
directed by Mikhal Bat-Adam. Significant parts of the 1993 *Black Box*
and some parts of *The Lover* — both novels that are part of our study —
were also set in Jerusalem.

In 1978, Dan Wolman, the director of *My Michael*, presented
images, appearances and representations of Jerusalem in his short *To
Touch a City*. *My Michael* (1975) and *Hide and Seek* (1980) were both
directed by Wolman and, in both, the setting in Jerusalem is material to
the spirit of the movies.

The acting sensitively depicts important characteristics of many
characters, including Hannah, with her loneliness, illness and frustration;
Michael, with his non-spontaneous reactions; Michael's father, with his
tenderness and naiveté ; Hannah's mother, with her simplicity and
worries; Hannah's brother, with his spontaneity; the intrusive, self-
confident Aunt Jenia; the judgmental Ms. Tarnpoler; the mad Mrs. Glick;

the helpless and boring Mr. Glick; the distanced and limited Mr. Kadishman; Yoram, the young and enamored; and others.

The movie presents the differences between Michael and Hannah well. They are both young and intelligent but, while Michael is comfortable in his petite-bourgeois life, immersed in his step-by-step achievements, Hannah is unfulfilled and does not find meaning in the concepts and goals that comfort and motivate the people around her.

Most of the characters are self-centered and contribute to Hannah's loneliness and ill condition, and Hannah's life is like a stage on which they act. For example, in the hospital, after Hannah gives birth, Michael's father is most concerned about the baby's name, and Aunt Jenia about showing off her medical "authority." Hannah and the baby only provide a situation that may serve some needs of the father and the aunt.

Hannah's search for fulfillment, her imagination, creativity and sensitivity, her suffering, her monotonous marriage to her quiet and conventional husband, and the societal pettiness and tedious dreams make the viewer ponder about Hannah's role as a victim of her society.

People and Jerusalem contribute to Hannah's need a word here. While the setting is 1950s Jerusalem, Hannah's memories go back to prior to 1948 when Jerusalem was not divided into a Jewish and Arab section, and she could play with her Arab friends. Hannah lives at the west side of Jerusalem and is sexually attracted to the "other" side of the city, where the twins are.

The movie reproduces the connection between Hannah's spirit and Jerusalem; we witness Hannah's loneliness, sadness and alienation in the enclosed walls and alleys, iron bars and windows frames of the city. Other people, too, appear as lonely in the gloomy, big city — surrounded by mountains, crowded old buildings and with very little personal communication. As in the novel, Jerusalem in the movie, too, is a metaphor for Hannah (see Zertal).

The city offers a wide range of people, including professors. Hannah is more attracted to the more basic, down-to-earth, full-of-passion, spontaneous and expressive people, such as semi-naked merchants and construction workers, than to the pretentious and self-restrained ones. However, she avoids contact with down-to-earth people.

The landscape, the characters' silence and words, their facial expressions, style and gestures, the photography and music are all coordinated to depict sadness, loneliness and estrangement. The silence in the movie is not the outcome of agreement, happiness and understanding that makes words unnecessary, but the result of frustration, anger, estrangement and loneliness. The communication is often non-personal, informative, shallow and utilitarian; its common subjects are not the central emotions of a human existence, such as love and suffering.

While in this small-budget movie it is possible to demonstrate Hannah's fantasies about the twins, it would be far more expensive to illustrate her more alluring fantasies about Moby Dick, Nautilus, Dragon and Tigress. In their eight appearances — at times of Hannah's distress — the twins change from obedient, loving children to romantic exotic horse-riders and to violent rapists. In their childhood, the twins wrestled at Hannah's command, but they gain power in the movie. Typical eastern musical instruments, a flute or bells, accompany the appearances of the twins.

Shohat makes the argument that "serve little narrative function beyond mirroring and metaphorizing the repressed Dionysian inner self of Madam Bovary-like protagonist and her romantic frustration with her humdrum and unimaginative existence (Shohat, p. 205).

Other fantasies are far more theatrical but cannot be demonstrated in a small-budget movie. And the viewers are left without the submarines, Dragon and Tigress, Nautilus and various romantic, heroic, courageous and adventurous characters such as Michael Strogoff, Captain Nemo, the trains, the airplanes, the rebelling "subjects" of the princess and Moby Dick.

The movie, like the book, focuses on the individualistic and not on the national, social and political condition. The political condition merely provides the background for the personal family drama of a slowly suffocating marriage. In the movie, too, Hannah's family life reaches an impasse. Even at their own home, the Gonens are photographed in their isolation and separateness. In emphasizing the individualistic and not the national aspects, the movie follows the spirit of the novel, and also avoids possible conflict with the political establishment in Israel at a time that Israeli cinema still depended totally on the political establishment (about this issue as well as the placement of the movie within Israeli cinema and European cinema see Gertz, 1993). Short dialogues or the background narrative voice of Hannah taken from the novel accompany the plot.

The relatively inconsequential periods of life are fast and short in the movie, and typical episodes denote the general lifestyle. The movie rearranges episodes in order to make it easier for the viewer to follow them; it makes the cause-result connection between events and feelings clear and unequivocal. The scenes follow each other in an easy-to-follow order; each scene is a result of a previous one and may be the cause of the next one. By rearranging episodes that were dispersed in the text, the movie makes the viewer focus on a certain sub-plot in its entirety. Illness and madness are among the elements that generate many new situations. This may change the significance of a sub-plot. For example, Hannah's attempts to rule Yoram are more coherently presented in the movie, the episodes which are spread out in the novel appear in the movie as a clear sub-plot, making it more powerful in Hannah's family life and loveless drama. In the movie, Yoram's attempt to touch Hannah's breast (this erotic episode is an addition to the novel), her seductive and elusive conduct, her mad and teasing laughter dramatize Hannah's madness and the deterioration of the family unit. The proportionate time dedicated in the movie to the Yoram-Hannah sub-plot far exceeds the role of this relationship in the structure of the novel. The dramatic nature of an episode and the extent to which it fits into the movie plot determine the episodic role in the structure of the movie plot.

In the movie, a strong emphasis is put on the characters' diction and motions. For example, Michael's father is soft-spoken and his intonation is often even, depicting a gentle, somehow boring and detached person. Aunt Jenia's domineering, intrusive, pompous and bitter personality is depicted through her motions, voice and smoking mannerisms no less than through her words. Her attitude is tolerated in a society that does not differentiate between formal education and wisdom. The professor's even, non-emotional voice when discussing highly emotional themes in a novel may be an expression of the victory of the analytical over the emotional, it may also demonstrate the suffocation of feelings in an academic environment.

The music and the photography are a substitute for words in many instances in the movie. For example, the loud, jolly music, which accompanies the group-dance on the wedding night, is in contrast with the sudden silence of Michael and Hannah in their apartment on their wedding night. We hear the music of the song sung by a group; the words of the song illustrate that until the night the dancers will sing their song, which is "cleaving to the sky." But the dancers do not sing to the sound of music; Hannah and Michael are out of the dancers' celebrating circle, possibly hinting that they do not feel very festive.

The couple's first lovemaking lacks emotions. The somehow clumsy Michael is more aware of the proper folding of his clothes than of

Hannah's loneliness while she is staring and looking more as a non-participating victim than an eager virgin at her first lovemaking night with her husband. This continues the darkness, cold, non-emotional moment of Michael's marriage proposal. The morning after the wedding, at the kindergarten, Hannah is telling the story of the little girl Hannah, whose white Shabbat dress became dirty; this time, unlike the first time she told it, she is detailed and emotional. Hannah identifies with the little girl in the story, Hannah. While in the Israeli children's story, there is a miracle that happens to the little kind and helpful Hannah and her dress is restored; the miracle is not available for the narrator, Hannah, who lost her virginity in a lovemaking session during which she was passive. In general, physical contacts are ineffectual in the movie.

Darkness is also used to portray Hannah's disposition at the first visit at Michael's father, a visit in which the intrusive, pompous, bitter and unwise Aunt Jenia becomes dominant. Contrary to this darkness, we see years later at the same apartment, one of the very few happy and solidly bright pictures of Hannah and Michael while visiting there with their son. But this picture is changed later in the same apartment when Hannah, after making love to her husband, tried to share with him some of her memories. The apartment is dark and the sexually satisfied Michael is simply sound asleep facing the wall. Hannah's hunger for sharing psychological intimacy with her sleeping husband only makes the difference between their needs more noticeable and painful.

The Gonens, and particularly Hannah, look out through windows, doors, rails and bars and the picture of Hannah enfolding Michael at the window after renting an apartment is replaced time and again by Hannah alone. Hannah's watching Mrs. Glick's expressions of madness is a foreshadowing of Hannah's condition of madness. Mr. Glick asks Michael for help regarding his insane wife, while ironically Michael is helpless with his own unsound wife. Mrs. Glick's madness attacks are forceful; two of the possible effects are horror and pity.

The main device that portrays Hannah's unreliability is her madness. It is not hard in the movie to savor the stress, melancholy, disillusionment, loneliness, anxiety, yearning and contempt of Hannah. When the music and pictures are wanting, the voiceover of the narrator, quoting the most essential narrative, completes the illustrated situation. By portraying the limited nature of the people around the characters, including the well-educated ones, the movie implies the questions about who is sane and who is insane, who is the cause and who is the victim, what is meaningful, and what is meaningless in life.

Life can be empty even when it has all the strongholds of career, education and possessions. The movie well represents the possibility that the facade may be whole in its formal components — it includes family, extended family, position and career, security etc., but all these are nothing but a vacuous casing, an empty shell with in a meaningless life.

While in the movie the traditional, national and personal values and concepts of the old generation are questioned, the new generation does not present a sound alternative.

The setting of the movie is Israeli, but the themes of old and young generations, secure and superficial versus insecure and colorful life, the question if there is not something ill in one's spending his life in meaningless accomplishments, what is "sick" and what is "fit," are few of the universal issues of the movie.

The movie begins and ends with an ambiance of loneliness — the individual is Lilliputian in the spacious Jerusalem. At both the beginning and the end there is very little human voice while music and photography control the scenes, mood.

My Michael is an intricate, memorable, artful film. The characters' lives are intensely unveiled through poetic words and solitariness. The movie presents the question of the meaning in life and human relationships in a haunting manner.

The movie's screenplay (by Ester Mor) received an award from the Israeli Council for Culture and Art, and the movie received the 1974 Best Movie Award of Israel.

BIBLIOGRAPHY

Band, Avraham. "Ha-Mesapper ha-Bilti Meheman be- *Michael Shelli* u-ve- *Bidmi Yameha.*" *Hasifrut* , June 1971, Vol. 3, No. 1, pp. 30-34.

Gertz, Nurit. "Iyyun be- *Michael Shelli* le-Amos Oz." In *Hasifrut* , April 1976, No. 22, pp. 1-17.

_____. *"Michael Shelli."* In: *Amos Oz: Monografia.* Sifriyyat Po'alim, Tel-Aviv, 1980, pp. 122-138.

_____. *"Michael Shelli*: Amos Oz." In *Ha-Siporet ha-Yisraelit bi-Shnot ha-Shishim,* ha-Oniversita ha-Petuha, 1982, pp. 1-63.

_____. "Mirushalayim le-Hollywood Derekh ha-Midbar he-Adom: *Michael Shelli.*" In *Sippur me-ha-Seratim: Sipporet Yisraelit ve- 'Ibudeha le-Kolnoa'* Ha-Oniversita ha-Petuha, 1993, pp. 143-158.

Hakak, Lev. "Golem Ganz O Ga'on Madda'i." In *Bizaron,* June 1976, pp. 242-252. Republished in *Shedemot,* Winter, 1977, pp. 82-85.

Oz, Amos. *My Michael.* Bantam books, 1972.

_____. *My Michael.* Vintage International, 1992.

_____. "Me-'Ever le-Har Hoshekh, Hayyim Beli Heshbon (Otobiographia Sifrutit)." *Ha-Sofer* , No.1, Nov. 1994, p. 13.

Schnitz er, Meir.   *"Michael Sheli."* In *Ha-Kolnoa' ha-Yisraeli.* Kinneret Publishing House, Tel-Aviv, 1994, p. 161.

Shaked, Gershon. "Ha-Orev Yoshev ba-Heder." In *Gal Hadash ba-Siporet ha-'Ivrit.* Sifriyyat Po'alim, Tel-Aviv, 1973, pp. 180-203.

_____. *Ha-Sipporet Ha-'Ivrit 1880-1980, Vol. 5, Be-Harbei Eshnabbim bi-Khnisot Zedadiyyot.* Hakibutz Hameuchad and Keter Publishing House Ltd., 1998, pp. 158-180.

Yerushalmi, Joseph. *Amos Oz — Bibliography 1953-1981.* With selective supplement until summer, 1983. Am Oved, Tel-Aviv, 1984.

Zertal, Edith. "The Films of Dan Volman." *Ariel* , No. 44, 1977, p. 88.

Chapter 9

THE LOVER BY A.B. YEHOSHUA

THE PLOT

This is the story of an Israeli Ashkenazi family up until and following the October 1973 Yom Kippur war. Through the events in the life of
this one family, the reader views the story of Zionism and of the people
in Israel over the period beginning in 1881 (when the first Bilu settlers
arrived in the land of Israel). In this story the Ashkenanzi Israelis, who
dominated Israeli society, are disintegrating, which gives rise to the
Sephardi Jews in Israel and to the Arabs.

The story describes the crisis of Adam who, after dedicating his life
to his family, is witnessing its disintegration and even participating in its
devastation. Adam brings home an Arab boy who captures his daughter's
heart and a Sephardi man who emigrated from Israel. During his visit in
Israel, the Sephardi captures Adam's wife's heart.

The Lover focuses on the period of a few months before and after
the Yom Kippur War. It is the story of the ordinary Israeli family of Asya,
her husband Adam, and their children. Adam and Asya knew one another
before the War of Independence, while they attended the same schools,
the same youth-movements and youth-camps. They got married and, in
1973, Adam turned 46. When married, they first met with economic
difficulties but later, due to hard work, they attained substantial economic
success; their family, however, met with failure. Each of the interrelated
characters, three men and three women, views the identical events in
monologues representative of that character's one way and style, so that
the reader comes to know each character as it perceives itself and the
other characters and as it is perceived by the others. Each character

reveals its own wounds and by doing so it reveals its most sensitive side. Adam, his daughter Dafna (or Dafi), his employee Na'im and his wife's lover, Gabriel Arditi, chat about their experiences; Asya, Adam's wife reports her dreams when they occur; a stream of consciousness marks the monologues of Veducha when she loses consciousness.

THE STORY AND ITS
IMPLICATIONS

Unlike Yehoshuas early works that have a symbolic-allegorical nature, *The Lover* displays a strong contact with specific reality. The book is written in the spirit of Faulkner's *As I Lay Dying*, and it is told from a constantly changing viewpoint.

In his earlier works, Yehoshua had to struggle with a norm, common to some Israeli authors and critics, according to which the writer avoids social and political materials in his work. Consequently, Yehoshua utilized symbols in order to comment on Israeli social-political reality. *The Lover* displays a more realistic trend in his writing. The shift from his earlier symbolic-allegorical writing to writing realistically about specific and well-defined reality was a difficult one. The time and place of Yehoshuas novels are familiar to us. The characters are occupied not only with general intellectual issues, but also with daily problems such as money and sex. The style is accordingly suited to the individual character.

The Lover does not deal with Israeli reality alone. In addition to issues typical of Israeli existence, such as the relationship between secular and religious Jews or Between Sephardi and Ashkenazi Jews, the reader also encounters issues that relate to Jewish existence in a larger sense, such as the relationship between Israel and the Diaspora. Yehoshua, in addition, confronts in this novel such universal conditions and problems as the loneliness and alienation of modern life. Our focus, however, will be on those issues that specifically relate to the Israeli situation. The wars of 1967, 1973 and 1984 and the political situation in Israel caused various Israeli authors to become involved through their literary work with Israeli reality and its ideological crisis.

The Lover reflects Yehoshuas tendency both to relate to reality and to search for the general, the symbolic and the intellectual. Searching for the components that shape Israeli society in his novel, one has to remember that the implied author neither detests nor judges his characters but simply attempts to understand them.

The Lover examines some major aspects of Israeli life and contains harsh messages directed at Israeli society with little consolation. The author portrays the social, political and economic reality of Israel through astonishing situations that express disastrous and destructive elements in the souls of his characters. The reader witnesses the disintegration of stable middle-class families. Most of the characters appear as frustrated and deprived people, distressed, restless, lonely and yearning for love. In a condition of perpetual conflict both with themselves and with their environment, they are neurotic people attracted to sickness and living a disturbed way of life in the shadow of wars, an absurd existence marked by death, fatigue and aimlessness. The Israelis in this novel compose a problematic and complicated nation rather than a "chosen people" with an exemplary, model society, a light to the world.

The pre-existing perversions of these characters are exposed through the distressful and complicated events described in the novels. The characters formulate their various opinions concerning the distressful events, opinions that, by themselves are neither right nor wrong. An ambivalent attitude toward their reality lacks any unequivocal criteria to judge reality.

Yehoshua's pessimistic view of the Zionist dream is not new in Hebrew literature. While in the 1960s this view was, however, voiced more through symbols, in the 1970s the author expressed this view much more directly. Perhaps both readers and critics were better prepared for his direct social and political criticism, especially after the 1973 war.

Yizhak Barzilai (1984), describing the bitter social criticism in the books of some major contemporary Israeli authors, concludes (p.537):

> ... The fact that prophets of wrath ... appeared, among us, is not all negative. On the contrary, it is in the spirit of our old prophetic tradition ... it is good, hence, and encouraging that now, too, we have among us people who are zealots for the truth, and even if the truth is bitter and depressing, it may be assumed that the bearers of this truth will not allow us to rest while they see us failing and falling, but that they will elicit in us positive and creative powers.

In *The Lover*, Yehoshua was influenced by the technique associated with Faulkner: the author allowed the characters to speak in monologues without interference from the narrator or other characters. Yehoshua explained his choosing this technique (see Carmel-Flumin, 1986):

> ... When I started writing *The Lover* I felt that the center [of Israeli society - L.H.] is disintegrating, that there is a definite gap between people, and were I to write a novel in third person or in first person as an authoritative narrator, I would then be judging that reality and speaking in its name, speaking in the name of a non-existent center... The feeling of the disintegration of the center showed that the most correct way to write is to allow every character to talk with the total point-of-view accumulating from all the points-of-view together. This was both an aesthetic consideration and my own outlook as to the correct way to respond to the Israeli situation.

The novel presents the events from the points-of-view of various characters. In the frame of this presentation, our focus will be on certain facets of Israeli life as they are described in *The Lover*: family life, and conflicts between Arabs and Jews, between Sephardi and Ashkenazi Jews, between secular and religious Jews and between Israel and the Diaspora.

The six characters in the story are developed simultaneously both as individuals and as representatives of social groups. They are both speakers themselves and objects in the reflections of other characters and witnesses in the novel.

In this novel, Yehoshua, who was influenced by the symbolic, surrealistic fiction of Agnon, also distanced his approach from that of Agnon in various ways, including his use of spoken Israeli Hebrew.

IS IT THE STORY OF
INDIVIDUALS OR THE STORY OF
ISRAELI SOCIETY?

Does this novel portray Israeli society or is this simply a story of individual characters? It would seem that the author's ambition went beyond describing the lives of various individual members of Israeli society and that he strove in this work to depict Israeli society as such.

Yehoshua has himself related to the question wherever he intended to portray a whole society or just individuals. While an author's statement of intent is not necessarily the basis for judging his actual intent in writing, some of his statements concerning this question are certainly worthy of consideration. Indeed, the message of the novel compels Israeli society to recognize its dark and self-destructive aspects (Shaked, 1977).

This is a story not about individuals but about the Israeli psyche. The very names Adam and Asya might even allude to this. Asya bears the name of a continent, while Adam can mean "every man." The author addressed himself to the novel's pessimistic point-of-view in one of his interviews (with Aharoni, 1978):

> It was said that *The Lover* is a harsh book about the State of Israel. I do not wholly agree with this opinion. Literature, usually, is not optimistic; it is interested in the dark, problematic sides of life and also exaggerates them. And one must remember that *The Lover* is about Israel in the period after the Yom Kippur War, not the Israel of today when we saw the light again. There is also an optimistic thread in *The Lover*: here we have a group of people, which had lost its identity, especially Na'im. At the end there is some degree of order and everyone resumes his place.

Yael Feldman (1987) offers a psychoanalytical interpretation of this novel: the return of Arditi to Israel brings back to life two mother figures in the novel — Veducha and Asya, who are presented initially through their dreams. Veducha represents Zionism and Asya represents the State of Israel. The dreams of Veducha and Asya represent the loss of reality principle. Arditi, unlike the classical model of Oedipus, does not have to fight his way to his "mother." Adam brings him to Asya. All this distorts the Zionist metaphor of the sons coming to redeem their motherland.

In still another interview (Beser), the author defined this novel as "partially political." In his interview with Carmel-Flumin (1986), Yehoshua stated:

> Undoubtedly, there are in my texts some kinds of allusions to the larger structure. The question is the measure of its significance in the work... a good critic is one who stands before the living text and finds in it what there is in it, unlike those who approach a literary work and use it as a way of organizing their own ideas.

In *The Lover*, Yehoshua attempts to depart from the allegorical-symbolic style of his earlier works and to employ a well-defined and specific historical reality. Yehoshua uses spoken Hebrew in order to evoke specific aspects of Israeli social reality. In his earlier works he suggested this reality by depicting one aspect or another in a symbolic-allegorical illustrative manner; in this realistic-psychological novel, the author directly portrays various aspects of Israeli society. True, symbolic-allegorical aspects are present in *The Lover*, but the principle achievement of the novel lies in its openness to the diverse nature of Israeli reality.

The Lover is not the story of individuals but the story of Israeli society for social reasons.

Gertz (1983) investigated the relations between literature and politics in Yehoshuas work up through 1978 and the literary devices used in order to accomplish the connection between the two. I will draw upon and apply some of her ideas as to why *The Lover* is not only the story of individuals but also the story of Israeli society. The fact that national events are so strongly connected with the lives of the characters in these novels leads us to think that these are not only stories of individuals but also stories which depict Israeli life as such. In *The Lover*, the Yom Kippur War exposes more sharply the selfish individualistic deserter-nature of Ariditi for example. Arditi's life with the ultra-orthodox Jews is the result of the war. Also, the characters themselves connect and combine the individual and the national-political-historical dimensions. In addition, the relationships between the characters in these novels are sometimes representative of some aspects of Israeli society-at-large. In *The Lover*, the relationship between Veducha and Arditi represents the differences between the generation of the founders and many of the younger Israelis. Another fact supporting the opinion that *The Lover* represents Israeli society and not only individuals is that often a character's personal situation or attitude is clad in a national or political argument. The seriocomic officer in *The Lover* thinks that he seeks Arditi because of issues of national character but, in truth, he does so because he is personally a troubled, honor-seeking man who uses war and national-historical terminology for purposes of self-glorification. The officer has a kind of will, "written in elevated tones and poetic style, something about himself and the people of Israel. It was a strong mixture — destiny, mission, history, fate and endurance. A bloated anthology of righteousness and self-pity." The officer connects the national and the individual, and the reader, like Arditi himself, looks at his attempt with irony, because, after all, "he hadn't seemed really involved in this war." (p. 309)

The recurring appearance of a national situation in the work conveys the feeling that this situation is static and dominates the novel. In *The*

Lover, the Yom Kippur War both opens and closes the novel and is mentioned repeatedly in the monologues of various characters.

THE ISRAELI FAMILY

In the novel, *The Lover*, Yehoshua characterizes the life of the Israeli family as one of routine and boredom. Destructive elements dominate the disintegrating families: death, loneliness, anomaly, fights and the husband and wife's relationship.

The major failure of Israeli society is that of family life as depicted in *The Lover* through the family of Adam and Asya. Adam and Asya represent the generation of the War of Independence along with a society, which has lost the clues to the goals of its existence. Loneliness, rapid aging and disloyalty typify their family life. Adam, Asya, and their daughter, Dafi, live next to each other but not with one another. They are loveless, sensitive and lonely, lacking affection and drifting apart. Adam, a wealthy garage owner, is a tired father and husband surrounded by Arab employees; he is bored and lacks social and spiritual outlets. Asya is a secondary-school history teacher, intelligent and responsible as a working person, but frustrated, a woman with neither warmth nor a sense of beauty. Adam is not attracted to his wife.

Adam gave the key to his house to Na'im who became his daughter's lover, and he brought home Gabriel who became his wife's lover — acts of self-destruction on the part of a man who is both a father and a husband. His search for Gabriel is indicative of some sort of mental collapse. It is hardly normal for a husband to seek to bring back his wife's lover. In Adam's quest for Gabriel, Asya's lover, furthermore, he is seeking the deathblow, the *coup de grace* of his disintegrating family life, which has reached a dead end. On the surface, Adam appears an influential character both at home (the successful bread winner) and at his garage (he is the owner); however, he has no control over his life. He brought the lovers together at his own home and at work he depends upon other people to do his work: he neither manages his garage nor works in it. Nor does he act as a husband but rather brings another to substitute for him; he is, in addition, a passive father and he does not participate in the war.

Money is Adam's substitute for love, while for Asya (who likes old women), books substitute for love. Dafi's awareness of the lack of love in her family and the anxiety it inflicts upon her is the possible cause for her insomnia. The weary Adam loses his authority as a father vis-à-vis his daughter, Dafi.

Eros does not lead anywhere in the novel. It is distorted and cannot be long lasting and fulfilling as in the examples of Adam-Asya, Asya-Gabriel and Adam-Tali, or obstructed by strong powers, as in the case of Na'im and Dafi. And while Na'im and Dafi are able and willing to overcome the tension between Arabs and Jews, it would probably be significantly more difficult if they were older (Shaked, 1977). The working and personal relationships that develop are sometimes in conflict with the prevalent estrangement on a national level.

In the framework of these relationships, Adam's belief that he and Asya spared their daughter the impact of destroyed family life — "broken homes, families splitting up" (p.251) — sounds naïve or self-deceptive and may evoke an ironic smile, because Dafna is the product of a "broken home" that has the facade of a stable family.

The monologues of the lonely, unhappy and lost characters in *The Lover* reveal the misunderstandings of the characters on both an individual and national level and their flight to money (Adam, Dafi and Gabriel), to sex (Dafi, Asya, Gabriel and Tali, his fifteen-year-old daughter's friend) and to learning (Asya). The monologues interrelate, make for continuity in the plot, and stress certain meanings and characteristics of the characters. Gertz (1979) is correct in stating that the fact that we do not have one subjective opinion about the events results in a multiplicity of points-of-view, which brings the reader closer to reality.

The confines of social and sexual taboos are destructively threatened in the novel in the arenas of family (Gabriel-Asya, Adam-Tali), of nation (Dafi-Na'im, Adam's daughter and his young Arab employee) of state (Gabriel is an emigrant, *yored*) and of age (Adam-Tali). The disruption of family taboos (Asya-Arditi, Adam-Tali, Dafi-Na'im) and the national taboos (Arditi's deserting the army) neither brings vitality to the lives of the characters nor resolves problems (Barzel, 1977). Adam and Asya do not become young; Dafi and Arditi remain restless. War produces only death and wounds.

Yitzhak ("will laugh" in Hebrew), the orphan immigrant from Teheran who joined Asya's class, was killed in a war; Yigal, ("will redeem" in Hebrew, see Shamir, "Arba'a") the first-born of Asya and Adam, was deaf and, not sensing danger, was killed in an accident. Yitzhak did not laugh; he sacrificed his life as a victim of war; Yigal did not redeem. Tali ("my dew" in Hebrew) did not refresh Adam's life.

Dafna ("laurel" in Hebrew) does not possess the qualities required in order to triumph over life. These issues represent the national condition and not only that of the particular individuals portrayed in the novel.

In *The Lover*, the generation of the strong laboring settlers whose ideology matched their lifestyle is no more; the present is in the hands of a tired generation, that of Adam who has lost his values and much of his feelings, and that of Asya who invests very little in her family. The future is in the hands of a declining generation, as represented by Dafi. The affluence of the generation of the settlers' children (Adam and Asya) does not bring them happiness.

The novel presents the generation in a condition of entropy: Veducha, Gabriel's grandmother, is a survivor; Gabriel's mother died; Gabriel, Adam and Asya lead restless, aimless desperate lives; Dafi has neither the self-reliance and working drive of her parents nor the intellectual drive of her mother; the Jewish characters are all troubled, while at the end of the novel, it is Na'im, the Arab boy, who is full of hope. Terrorism, troubled relations between Arabs and Jews, war and tension — these will persist.

Fuchs thinks, "Gender-conscious analysis of Yehoshuas model of characterization reveals some important differences between male and female characters, most of which reflect traditional preoccupation of roles." According to Fuchs, the "blankness" and the "referentiality" of the women in Yehoshuas work "are necessary results of an inherently andocentric perspective that identifies humanity with masculinity and that essentially views women as supporting characters in the drama of life." (1984, p. 80). The arguments of Fuchs are sharp; however, due to the fact that nearly all of Yehoshuas characters are troubled, one could build a similar "case" as to Yehoshuas male characters. In this novel, Asya has a social and intellectual advantage over her husband Adam: she is better educated than he and her father was a public figure.

Viewing the families in this story as microcosms of Zionist society, the readers sense that this society is declining. Similarly, decline marks another aspect of the Israeli family: the relationship of husband and wife. *The Lover* deals with the husband-wife relationship and depicts it as empty of emotional, intellectual and physical bonds. The husband-wife relationship is not fulfilled either physically or emotionally. Taking into account the above relationships in the family, the reader is not surprised to discover that Adam sleeps with Tali, his daughter's friend.

THE ISRAELI-ARAB
CONFLICT

In *The Lover*, Yehoshua presents meaningful differences between Na'im, the Arab boy and some of the Israeli characters. The reader cannot but compare Na'im with Adam, Dafi and Gabriel. Unlike Adam, Na'im, who is Adam's employee, is full of life and vigor. He is an ambitious survivor, desirous of education and progress, emotional, bright, productive and diligent in a country in which physical labor has ceased being of value. Economically, he is dependent upon the Jewish economy. Na'im breaks into Veducha's apartment (which belonged to Arabs) through the window, but he becomes a legitimate tenant, essential to her life emotionally and physically. Na'im desires Dafi and sleeps with her; he reminds Adam of Dafi and Yigal, Asya and Adam's son who was killed; he reminds Veducha of her grandson, Gabriel. He thus has many aspects and might parallel different characters. He lives in Peki'in, the one place in the land of Israel continuously inhabited by Jews. He has no particular hostility toward Jews (pp. 185-186); he absorbs Israeli culture.

Na'im can recite Bialik's poem (p. 166) and uses the melody of "Jerusalem of Gold" as a whistling signal. At the same time one should not disregard the fact that of all Bialik's poems, he recites "Dead of the Desert" (p. 166), a poem in which the dead of the wilderness have risen "in spite of heaven and its wrath" to be "the last generation of bondage and the first of deliverance." The Arab, Na'im, identifies with heroes and heroism no less than the Jew and is capable of applying the expression of the Jews' rebellion against oppression to his own situation. Na'im captured Dafi's heart and body; he became indispensable for Veducha. Adam gave Na'im the key to his home, the "home" which is run by a tired and lonely family. This makes Na'im's work simple. Dafi has what Na'im wants: the opportunity to study, to progress, to live in comfort; however, she does not use her opportunities well, but rather she is negligent, not ambitious and materialistic. She considers using her parents' occupations as a means to survive at her secondary school. She is direct. In the future, the diligent, hardworking, life-thirsty, hopeful Na'im will prevail and consequently the Jewish future in Israel will be in danger.

Adam's garage is a site of power, energy, mobility, repair, living, human interaction and money that depends upon Arab labor. Adam owns the garage but he does not even know his employees; he is tired as an employer and as a businessman, while the Arabs provide the energy, labor and expertise required to maintain the garage as a going enterprise. The garage's income depends upon the labor of the Arabs and their Arab garage leaders.

Arab-Jewish relations bear a promise of healing only when both people know one another up close on an individual basis. Adam knows the Arabs better than do many other Jews, who speculate concerning them. Veducha is suspicious and unappreciative of Arabs; Dafi simply does not know them. But they all like Na'im once they know him and stop thinking about him as a stereotype. Adnan, Na'im's brother ends his life as a terrorist, but Na'im learns that "It's possible to love them and to hurt them too" (p352). The power to hurt someone who seems very strong makes the hurt person more human and even closer.

Morally, Jews claim a right to their land because they need a home, but this home, in which Arabs once lived, is enriching those who left it and who returned only in order to claim that home as an inheritance and to leave once more (Gabriel). In this context Veducha's home is a synecdoche for the State of Israel, the one home is put for the whole country: the Jews made a claim for their homeland, but once they had this home many of them did not maintain it. They left it and viewed it as a mere source of materialistic claims.

The war-syndrome in Israel, with its victims, corpses, people missing in action, is described in a low key.

In a history lesson taught by her mother, Dafna had a question, which was posed at the end of a class session (p. 250) — whether war was the only way to establish a state: "All this suffering around us ... wars ... people getting killed ... generally ... why was that the only choice?" The question generated laughter in the classroom, perhaps because it seemed unwise because everyone "knows" the answer. The thoughtful question is indeed the basic question of Zionism and it remains unanswered in the novel. The question is why the very costly Zionist solution was the only choice for the Jews. Oren (1977) thinks that in this question Dafna provides the author with the clearest evidence for the end of Zionism.

Adam raises still another issue in the area of Israeli-Arab relations (p. 124). The Israelis speak about Arabs, but they do not know them. The pressure, tension and suspicion between Arabs and Jews explain why Adam sees the Israeli Arabs as leading a "double life" (p.150, in the original Hebrew version: "a double bottom").

The Israeli-Arab conflict becomes less and less a central issue in these works of Yehoshua. In *The Lover*, Israeli society is deeply troubled from within, as many internal issues threaten its destruction. It must confront the possibility that "Thy destroyers and they that made these waste shall go forth from thee" (*Isaiah* 59:17). The Yom Kippur War clearly affects the lives of the characters in *The Lover*. But the impact of the conflict depends to a large extent upon the Israelis themselves. Adam's family in *The Lover* lacks the vitality needed for a secure survival. Under the circumstances, the Israeli-Arab conflict becomes less prominent: murder, ailments, madness, deviation, emigration, fatigue, ennui, loneliness, social tension, disregard of tradition — all these suffice to threaten the destruction of Israeli society even without the existence of an external enemy and a war situation.

THE SEPHARDIC-ASHKENAZI CONFLICT

Israeli society is composed of Sephardim and Ashkenazim. "Sephardim" are Jews of Spanish decent, and the term used by many as including Jews of Near-Eastern origin. Ashkenazim are Jews from central or Eastern Europe. Sephardi Jews in Israel for a long time expressed the feeling that they were discriminated against.

For a long time Yehoshua avoided the Sephardi-Ashkenazi conflict in his literary works. He also avoided the subject of the Sephardi-Ashkenazi issue. Both Sephardi and Ashkenazi authors who wrote about it were often trapped by such pitfalls as sentimentalism, stereotypes, or an extremist or apologetic approach (Hakak, 1981).

In *The Lover*, Yehoshua described two Sephardi characters, Arditi, and his grandmother, Veducha. Yehoshua commented about this (Carmel-Flumin, 1986).

> I also write about what is called the "old *Sephardim*" because they are part of me. Most of my identity as Sephardi consisted of an interaction with the Ashkenazi society, and this issue of uncovering one's identity more clearly was concealed with me in some drawer. This drawer was opened. This is not the Sephardi-Ashkenazi problem in general but the family myth … your blood and flesh, to seek roots in order to search for yourself. This is not particularly a response to a political or social problem. In general, everything is of one texture:

> politics, power struggles, family myth, psychological elements
> which appear to them political or social, for example, the
> Sephardi-Ashkenazi issue, but it does not occur to me to
> neutralize this element just because of this. I ask them:
> Gentlemen, please read my text carefully.

Yehoshua differentiates between the Sephardi Jews of the old settlement in the Land of Israel and Near Eastern Jews. In one interview (Levi, 1987), Yehoshua expressed his recognition that the Likkud party was successful in reducing the feeling of alienation of a large part of the population of Israel and made them feel that they became hosts rather than guests — they participated in the government and were accepted on the inside. The social restlessness was somewhat cured. According to Yehoshua, the struggle between Ashkenazi and Near Eastern Jews started with the mass-immigration following the establishment of the State of Israel. While Yehoshua himself belongs to the old Sephardi settlement in the Land of Israel who cannot speak about deprivation in the same sense as can Near Eastern Jews who attempted to assimilate into the Zionist mentality of Ashkenazi Jewry of Eastern European origins or roots. His own emphasis is on his being an Israeli. It was probably following his relating to the Sephardi-Ashkenazi issue in his novels that he felt personally less hard-pressed and threatened by those of the Near Eastern Jews, the later immigrants, who accused him of deserting and betraying them.

Gabriel Arditi, whose name is ironic (Gabriel — an angel; Arditi — vigor), is of a Sephardi family of the "Old Settlement." Gabriel had left Israel twelve years before he later returned to visit; he lives in Paris where he spent a few years in a mental institution. In order to desert the Israeli army, Gabriel changes both his appearance and his lifestyle, joining the ultra-traditional Ashkenazi fringe-society, which never accepted the values of the concept of the Zionist state. He abandoned his land, his army, his grandmother and his family together with his benefactors (Adam's family), but he feels neither guilt nor shame for having done that, because he is ruthless and spineless, committed only to what serves him best. He came to Israel to claim the legacy, which will be left by his grandmother — her car and her apartment (which belonged to Arabs). In this way, the value of a home, which had belonged to Arabs, will end up enhancing the life of an Israeli who has left Israel and does not make Israel his home. The basis of the argument that Jews returned to Israel, their home, and that there is a justified Jewish need for a home does not apply in this case.

Throughout most of the novel, our impression of Gabriel is based mainly on the way other characters view him. In his long monologue toward the end of the novel, however, we find him resourceful and perceptive, a person of style (Shenhar, 1977). Both Gabriel, the military deserter, and the seriocomic military officer, who wants to acquire heroic rank and status, are tainted.

The Sephardi 93-year-old Veducha, Gabriel's grandmother, belongs to the generation of founders and pioneers. Her story is really a story of Zionism, for she was born in 1881 when the first Bilu settlers arrived in the Land of Israel (p.139). When she is conscious, she is vital, wise and clear and exhibits a sense of humor; when she is unconscious, she resembles a stone or a plant. During the war she was unconscious, a state which represents the sleep or death of the old settlers in the 1973 war. Those who were left of Veducha's generation are facing the end of life and of the ability to impact it; they will at times be conscious and at times be unconscious. Gabriel's mother's death, which coincided with the founding of the State of Israel, may allude to the demise of the values of the older generation, the death of those who could carry on Zionist ideas and pioneers' abilities. Considering Arditi's human qualities and Veducha's present physical condition, the reader infers that the novel does not depict the Sephardi Jews as a redeeming element in Israel.

SECULAR AND RELIGIOUS
JEWS

In *The Lover*, Arditi joined the community of ultra-traditionalist Jews, not as a result of personality change, but as a result of sheer calculation. In association with that ultra-traditionalist element which never accepted the values of the State of Israel, he was best able to desert the army and disappear. For this purpose, he painted his grandmother's blue car (symbol of Israel) black (popular color of the clothing of such ultra-traditionalist Jews). Shwartz, Dafi's secondary school principal, does not forget to curse the "anti-Zionists" (p. 270) whose car collided with his own due to his own error. On a symbolic level, this collision may be understood as the confrontation between Shwart's Zionist values and the anti-Zionism of that sector of ultra-traditionalist Jews.

Students of *yeshivot*, talmudic academies, appear on the battlefield: "They came to cheer us up, to restore our faith, sent by their yeshiva to circulate among the troops, to give out prayer-books, to bind *tefillin* (phylacteries) on the young men" (p.300). But the soldiers knew: "These men are so free ... they come and go at will. They have no obligations" (p.301). Even in time of war there is a definite gulf, separating secular from religious Jews: "I could see that they were a little scared of us, a little wary" (p. 304). Arditi explains that he did not join the ultra-traditionalist Jews in Jerusalem out of choice: "Did I have an alternative? Where else could I go? Where could I hide...?" (p.311). He quickly perceived "how efficient they were, how well organized, how disciplined," unlike secular Israelis. He learned that "they lived a life apart in the land in their closed order" (p.316). He enjoys the shelter they provided for him while avoiding giving them "a clear sign ... that I linked my fate to theirs" (p.318).

The ultra-traditionalist Jews in *The Lover* are described through the sympathetic eyes of Arditi, who required their shelter and who, as an outsider, became an uncommitted insider. Arditi joined religious Jewry at a time of crisis, and he is an inside participant and an outside observer at the same time.

In his book *Bizkhut ha-Normaliyyut* (pp. 27-73, 105-140), Yehoshua maintains that life in the Diaspora avoids the conflict between religion and secularism, between state and religion, because there, the foreign state decides such matters. The strongest expression of the conflict between state and religion is found in *The Lover*, when Arditi avoids military service by joining the ranks of ultra-traditionalist Jews.

Rather than take a clear-cut stand, Yehoshua's novels depict the complexity of the issues involved in the relationship between religious and secular Jews in Israel. The issues are many and their resolution complicated. Yehoshua's contribution is evident in his relating to them in a moderate manner, depicting the characters on both sides as human beings with both virtues and faults, in his avoiding preconceived hostile attitudes and in his presenting complexities of some problems and conflicts related to some of these issues rather than seeking a simple one-sided solution.

EMIGRATION
"THE ILLNESS OF DIASPORA"

In his book, *Bizkhut ha-Hnormaliyyut* (pp. 27-73, 105-140), Yehoshua states that the Diaspora was not imposed upon the Jew but that the Jew desired it and still desires it. That desire, to his way of thinking, constitutes a kind of mental ailment.

In the context of discussing his book *Bizkhut ha-Normaliyyut*, Yehoshua explained (Carmel-Flumin, 1986):

> Living in Diaspora seems to be an abnormal situation, a distorted and dangerous one, and normality is to return to your country and to live in the full context of your national identity. The contents of this identity are a separate issue. This belongs to the struggles that every nation leads in relation to the contents of its identity, which continuously undergoes change, one connected with the history, the language and the character of the nation....

In an interview with Shwartz (1986), Yehoshua added:

> I am worried because of this illness that is called Diaspora; I am absolutely frightened in confronting the deep tie of the Arabs to the land and their large population in the area surrounding us.

In *Bizkhut ha-Normaliyyut* (p. 71), Yehoshua thinks that Israel should expose the pathology of the Diaspora and the fact that its existence is schizophrenic. The condemnation of those Israelis who emigrated from Israel ("yordim") will have a moral validity only when Israel condemns and rejects all of Jewish existence outside of Israel. Arditi in *The Lover* may serve as a literary example for Yehoshuas position (ibid. pp. 31-34) that the Diaspora was not something imposed upon the Jews but that they, in fact, desire it. Yehoshua points to the paradox in that while Jews detest the Diaspora, they nevertheless struggle constantly to continue their existence in it rather than fulfill the dream of returning to their own land.

In *The Lover*, Arditi returned to Israel only in order to claim his legacy and then leave again. In the Diaspora he earns his living by various kinds of work, from teaching Hebrew to translating materials for Zionist publications of the Jewish Agency (p.103). This, of course, is ironic.

Gabriel's living among that group of ultra-traditionalist Jews, which does not support the Zionist state, is only a variation of his leaving the country and deserting the army. Yehoshua recognized that after the 1973 war there were Jews who felt that Zionism had failed and who expressed doubts as to the justification of the existence of the Zionist state; he created Arditi in order to demonstrate an anti-Zionist possibility (according to Yehoshuas own testimony, Baretski, 1977).

Arditi in *The Lover* remains a problematic character. Leaving Israel does not help to rid himself of his neurotic existence in the country. The connection with the Diaspora is tempting, and emigration is viewed as a national danger. The Diaspora appears as a neurotic solution for a neurotic existence in Israel, one that does not resolve the real problems of the characters but nevertheless endangers Israeli existence by way of its temptations.

In a 1987 interview, Yehoshua anticipated that should Russia allow Jews to emigrate, they would either remain there, or go to America. This is "the eternal amusement of the Jews, their pseudo-masochistic games: when they leave Israel, they don't; and when they cannot they long for it" (Levi, p.23). In *The Lover*, only Arditi emigrated from Israel, but he is a detached man with a psychiatric history; he came to Israel to claim his legacy, to sell his grandmother's house and go back.

Emigration appears as a harsh reality of Israeli life. In the works of Yehoshua the harshness grew gradually. One has to accept Israel in order to adjust to it and constructively contribute to it. Physical presence is not a sufficient commitment — the heart and body should be committed in order to be an active participant in solving the country's problems in place of creating them or criticizing their existence.

CONCLUDING REMARKS
AND THE CRITICS
ON A.B. YEHOSHUA

In *The Lover*, the author relates the story of Israel through an object, a 1947 Morris car, which symbolizes the State of Israel. The automobile is a British product; this may remind the reader of the Balfour Declaration, a declaration of support for Jewish Zionist aspirations of the British mandate. (The Declaration was approved in 1920 and was incorporated in the Mandate on Palestine conferred upon in Great Britain in 1922). The light-blue color of the automobile suggests the two light-blue stripes of the Israeli flag. When the automobile was conscripted for military use its color was light blue, but the car was painted black, alluding to a coffin during the 1973 war, a time of crisis and death in Israel. It was "a very old model" (p.88). Gabriel thinks that "the engine won't start, there's a screw missing" (p.89). The condition of any "missing a screw" entity is commonly known. Metaphorically and practically, the one "missing screw" can cause the failure of the entire engine; the experienced eye in *The Lover*, however, perceives that not only a screw but the engine itself is "ruined and rusted" (p.90) and needs to be restored. Gabriel tells Adam that he "only came to pick up the inheritance;" he "wouldn't have come back for the load of junk," the Morris, but rather for the "old Arab house" (p. 92). The car is a very old model "painted bright blue;" it is a "little car" (p. 88). Veducha kept the interior of the car in good shape, but she required the help of an energetic grandson to take care of the engine; the grandson, however, sees the Morris as "junk" and as a source of money. Adam comments that 25 years ago, he had a "car exactly like it... but I don't feel any great nostalgia for it," and now only "some nut, some antique collector" (p. 90) would want it, even though "it's basically quite sound" (p. 92). 25 years ago, Israel was different and Adam's desires, values and problems were also different. During that interval of time, it is in his and Arditi's hands — the grandmother had left the 1947 model to Arditi, but he decided to leave and go elsewhere (Yiftah-El, 1977, *Shedemot*). At the end of the novel, Adam feels that "the car is going to fall apart under me" (p. 350) and, after he drops Na'im in Peki'in, he is "standing beside a dead old car from '47 and there is nobody to save me" (p.352). He is no longer the miracle repairman and it is Hamid, the Arab leader of his employees, who must come to his rescue. The disintegration of the car is analogous to the problems that threaten to destroy Israel.

The repair of the car, its restoration and "resurrection" allude to the restoration of the State of Israel. During the war it resembled a coffin. Given into the hands of Arditi, nothing is going to help it, and it is only bound to disintegrate by the end of the novel. Hamid, the Arab, is the only hope for saving Adam by repairing the "dead old car" (p. 351). In this context of emigration, the reader recalls that Gabriel could not afford to repair the car, which his grandmother had preserved. In order to evade his obligations to the Israeli army, he altered the color of the car, and he waited for his grandmother's death in order to sell it and leave. But even Adam, who is able to repair and maintain it, is tired and needs the Arab's help in order to repair the "dead" car (p.351), while he himself does not feel "any great nostalgia for it" (p. 90). The signals point to a clear danger to Israel's future.

Nurit Gertz (1976) contended that the fiction of the literary generation of the 1960s in Israel that includes Yehoshua, Oz and Kahana-Karmon, shares a common thematic structure which is composed of four stages: 1) the characters yearn for nature, people, Godlike authority, for a time beyond the present, and for a different space in which dramatic and exceptional events will occur; meanwhile they live routine lives in a desolate reality. 2) In the plot, the characters attempt to connect with the world of their yearnings through exceptional dramatic events in distant places. 3) The attempt connects instead with destruction or death. 4) Ultimately the characters return to the initial stage of detachment and to their desolate daily reality, and abandon their yearnings.

Gertz' model, even considering its rigidity and questionable aspects, is nevertheless applicable, to a significant but qualified extent, to the principal characters in *The Lover*. Adam, in *The Lover*, is lonely, isolated and bored. War took the lover away and provided Adam with a task: to search for the lover. Once he has found him, he resumes his state of isolation.

There is no question that in this novel, Israeli society is described in dark colors. One might view this in perspective by remembering that the characters are individuals, that the narrator intentionally chose to focus on particular sectors of Israeli society, that the tone of these works comes to warn of what may happen, and that only particular periods of the history of Israeli society are described in the novel. But even allowing for all these factors, the cumulative portrayal of Israeli society in the novel is harsh. A society characterized by such a degree of excitement and intensity, as a society with such characters, problems, heritage and struggles, pays the price for them.

Natan Zach (1983) attempted to address the question of why contemporary Israeli writers such as Tammuz, Shabtai, Be'er, Oz, Kenaz and Yehoshua deal to such an extent with madness, suicide, murder, alienation — in sum, with the dreadful aspects of life. The Holocaust, war and rapid changes in Israel, he suggested, may explain the frustration, the helplessness and the distress of the characters in contemporary Hebrew fiction. Zionism did not achieve the shaping of a new and healthy human being in Israel; instead, man as reflected in literature is quite ill. The strangeness; the distress and loneliness; the folly, death and alienation in contemporary Israeli prose might be explained also by the struggle between the generations and by the collapse of ideology and values, by the sobering reaction to hopes that were perhaps larger-than-life, by the lack of cultural identity on the part of the second and third generation of Israelis and perhaps by the fact that literature, in this case, precedes reality and serves as a mirror reflecting the moods, the fears and the yearnings of a new generation. According to Zach, many characters in the stories and novels of contemporary Israeli writers die because they are romantic characters that lack the ability to survive in an unromantic world. Their authors, he asserts, must instead allow their characters to live in a normal reality, which is neither hell nor paradise, one free of fictitious, unattainable models and abstract and absolute ideals.

Zach's contention is insightful and enlightening. But it does not provide a complete answer to the question. The problem of the characters in Yehoshuas novels does not lie in their being romantic characters unable to survive in a non-romantic world. Their difficulty is absolute, not simply relative to a non-existent, naïve and romantic model, to some abstract ideal or paradise. His characters do not suffer simply because they have discovered that the Israeli state, that Zionism, socialism, love, etc., are subject to compromise (see Zach, p.22), that they live in the shadow of some naïve and romantic model, but because their lives themselves are unbearably troubled.

The disintegration of the Israeli family is a microcosm, which mirrors the shattering of the Zionist dream. The family unit is composed of troubled individuals who suffer not only because of their own problems, but also because of the other members who compose the family — spouse, parents and offspring. Along with emigration, the Ashkenazi-Sephardi and the religious-secular conflicts weaken Israel. While the Israeli has attained a certain measure of economic satisfaction, he is crushed by his emotional problems. The Arabs, in contrast, are awake, potent and energetic. Consumed from inside, Israeli society will not endure unless it becomes aware of its ailments and determines to cure them.

The basic contribution of *The Lover* lies in the vivid portrayal of the internal destruction that is occurring, a destruction which Israeli society refuses to see as signs of a national disaster. One may emphasize Yehoshuas successful portrayal of characters in a way that is indicative of perspective, balance and sensitive perception and free of stereotypes — Arabs, Sephardi Jews of the old Israeli settlement, religious Jews, emigrants and others. One may emphasize Yehoshuas success in perceiving emigration from Israel as symptomatic of a larger problem, which he calls "the illness of Diaspora," or his success in illustrating the destruction that Israel will inflict on itself if it does not cure the illnesses involving family life, relations between Arabs and Jews, conflict between Ashkenazi and Sephardi Jews, between religious and secular Jews and emigrants and faithful citizens.

Israeli society accepts Yehoshua for his literary achievements. But it is also in need of a preacher who denounces it for its illnesses, who cares enough for it to diagnose these illnesses and to tie is destiny with its own. As someone concerned with curing the ill spots, Yehoshua would find as many ill parts or more in any other society. He is concerned, however, with the cure of Israeli society. The question is, "Will you still murder and commit adultery... and walk after other gods ... and come and stand before me in this house ... and say: 'We Are Delivered?'" (*Jeremiah*, 7:9-10). Posing the question is the first step toward betterment. Recalling that "Thy destroyers and they made thee waste shall go forth from thee" (*Isaiah* 49:17), is a summons to take the precautions necessary to assure the continuation and survival of a strong nation in a strong land.

THE MOVIE

Director: Mikhal Bat Adam. Producers: Menahem Golan, Yoram Globus. Script: Mikhal Bat Adam and Zvi Kretsner (Literary adaptation. Based on the novel of A.B. Yohoshua). Photography: David Gurfinkel. Music: Dov Zeltser. Editor: Tova Asher. Cast: Mikhal Bat Adam, Yehoram Ga'on, Roberto Polack, Fanny Lubich, Avigayil Ari'aeli, Eves Khativ, No'ah Isic, Mordekhai Ben Zeev, Ruth Geler, Rami Barukh. 1986. Color. 90 minutes.

This movie was produced with a budget of $300,000 in the summer of 1985 mostly in Haifa; there are also some scenes in Jerusalem. When the movie was produced, a Chuck Norris movie was also being produced in Israel with a cost of $300,000.00 a day (see Ohovski).

An Italian director (see Z imerman) planned another adaptation of the novel with a budget of $6 million, which in Italy is considered a low-budget movie. The producer liked the idea that a couple may come out of its crisis with the help of a lover (this idea is not in the novel - L.H.) and liked the relations between Arabs and Jews. As to making the novel into a film he said:

> A book is a book and a movie is a movie. These are two different languages. The book is only the base, on which I tell my story, which is different. The moment that I enter into the heart of the story as a director, I push it to other places.

The movie opens with Gabriel arriving at Adam's garage with the Morris and being asked to leave. Adam intervenes and keeps the Morris for repairs. The movie ends with Asya informing Adam that she asked Gabriel to leave and that Gabriel will not come back. With this full circle in the movie, peace comes back to the family.

From the novel, the movie draws erotic and the momentous situations and added sex to them. Here are few of the momentous situations: Adam is in bed with his naked wife, Asya; Gabriel faints in the garage out of hunger; Dafna screams when she is home alone and suddenly sees a stranger (Na'im); the principal announces to the high school students that their beloved teacher was killed in the war; calm citizens became alarmed by the 1973 war sirens.

The additions to the movie are either erotic or dramatic. Adam's pressing Asya's neck after he became sure that his wife was unfaithful is an addition of violence in the movie. We also see Asya attempting to seduce Gabriel at her own home during the first night of the war, thinking that Adam is asleep.

In the movie, Na'im does not recite Bialik's poem, "Dead of the Desert," implying that the Arab, Na'im, is capable of applying the expression of the Jews' rebellion against oppression to his own situation. But he recites some lines from Bialik's "On The Slaughter," a poem written by the national poet expressing his rage after the 1903 Kishinov pogrom against the Jews. This may make Na'im even a more moderate character that identifies with Jewish suffering.

The end of the movie is also different from the one in the novel. Adam does not drive the Morris in the movie, and all the symbolism of the dead old car near Na'im's village is lost. Other additions are Adam's crying on his way home after taking Na'im to his village, Asya's waiting for Adam at the house gate and the peace that seems to come between them. The reader-viewer may debate the reasons for the modifications.

The viewer is introduced from the outset to the loneliness in Adam's family. Adam, Asya and Dafna appear separately in their home. Asya is busy with her work and is not coordinated with Adam as to a sleeping time. Dafna is sleeping on the kitchen table and her mother, from a distance, is more concerned about Dafna's performing petite chores than Dafna's life. In bed, Adam's desire for his already naked wife suddenly stops; he cannot be intimate with her.

The romance of Asya and Gabriel is accompanied by guitar and romantic, Spanish music. Gabriel is portrayed in the movie as a lover with enthusiasm and initiative, and Asya is portrayed as attractive.

Humor is part of the movie. For example, Gabriel tells Adam that there is a problem: His grandmother did not die yet. He says so without pain or compassion. When Adam says to Veducha that he thought she lost consciousness, she responds that she has found it. The sequence of scenes points out the tragicomedy in the family drama. Adam is with the minor, Tali, while his daughter is with Na'im, and his wife with Gabriel.

In the movie, we see some authentic pictures from the 1973 war and wartime. For example, we see and hear Golda Meier, the Israeli prime minister at that time. The war and its national impact are not central to the movie.

When a journalist asked Yehoshua about the "multi-boobied epic that Bat Adam cooked," after the "small titied storm that became the movie sales promoter," Yehoshua said:

> One has to separate the book from the movie. The book is a
> separate organic entity. Whoever is looking for the material-
> ization of the book in the movie, will not find it. The book is
> a linguistic unit with its own rhythm...

The opinions of the movie reviewers and an interview with Bat Adam after the movie was made are thought provoking. The viewer may consider them while he is formulating his own opinion about the movie.

'Immanuel Bar-Kadma (1977), a well-known art reviewer in Israel, thinks that the main differences between the movie and the novel are in the point of convergence. Na'im's role in the novel was decreased in the movie and basic necessary information about him is missing from the film, as well. Bar Kadma felt that the movie failed in presenting the spirit of the people before and after the 1973 war. It dwells on the love triangle of Gabriel, Asya and Adam, while Asya is attracted to the unique freak, Gabriel, who represents our times; he is a mixture of decadence, restlessness and erotic attraction. Adam behaves as a masochist.

Another critic (see Mashiyah) thought that the movie introduces too much sex, and that the Yom Kippur War is displayed as though it appears in a popular action movie. It is an erotic movie with intellectual pretenses. This reviewer thinks that the sex in the movie is strangely aggressive, or often is not organic to the movie.

Ya'el Yisrael (1986) has various reservations about the movie:

> In the novel we found a portrayal of the condition of the disintegrating Israeli family. Yehoshua made a piercing statement about the hypocrite, sensitive Israeli society. He did so through the story of a typical Israeli family, that all of a sudden is penetrated by elements that agitate all of its well-covered layers: the sexuality, the madness and the tempest of desires. But what happened in the adaptation of the novel into another medium? Krezner and Bat Adam converted the book almost apiece by piece, but they lost the psychological depth and this is how the story became just another family melo-drama. Bat Adam did not include the past of Adam and Asya, which is necessary in order to understand the motive of the characters. Asya in her cinematic transfiguration played by Bat Adam is a beautiful woman, sensual and sexy while Yehoshuas Asya is a tough, hard, dry and sexless woman. All the wonderful associative paragraphs of grandmother Veducha... were cut out. The political background too, which is the time bomb of the Israeli-Palestinian problem, was lost on the way to the writing of the script. One could equally set the melodrama in Texas or in South Africa. So, what is left?
> — Many sexual scenes that exist or don't in the book, a lot of breasts, and external plot of a family that is disintegrating in a crisis, in which everyone is discovering his sexuality too late.

Several points are of interest in an interview (See Ohovski) with Mikhal Bat Adam who played Asya, directed the movie and was co-author of the script. Bat-Adam was the director of seven feature films, and she scripted all of them except The *Lover*, for which she shares the script writing credit with Zvi Krezner (see Kronish pp.151-152).

When she was asked about the amount of sex in the movie she said that "the sex quantity in the book and in the movie is identical" and that she is happy it is an erotic movie. She explains why, for example, she added the sexual scene between Gabriel and Asya:

> At my eyes, the most erotic scene in the movie is the one in
> which Gabriel is with Asya at his home and he asks her to take
> off her underwear and bra. It is a very erotic scene in spite of
> the fact that Asya is dressed and she takes them off through
> the clothes. One does not see in the scene a breast or another
> part.
> True, it is my scene. You cannot have a full movie, say that
> these two have a romance without demonstrating the feeling...
> I had to help the viewer to see that something is going on for
> sure... That is why this scene was important for me.

Asya in the movie looks younger than Asya in the novel. The movie
did not say that an attractive Asya in the movie may attract the viewer
more but said:

> It was not important for me to keep her original age. I thought
> that it is more essential to present the character from inside. At
> the beginning I experimented with various hairstyles... We
> tried to add silver hair. It looked artificial. It was not an
> attempt to flatter me.

When asked about hiding the political message in the movie, the
movie director said:

> Na'im's character makes it a political issue. I was interested
> in producing a placard... I should not be expected to come
> and make flags and slogans. It bores me. I could tell the entire
> story through Na'im and then the entire matter would have
> received a different weight, I chose another way.

Bat Adam rejected the argument that the movie could happen
anywhere and claimed that "the movie is absolutely Israeli," and "it is
simply made better than the previous movies" of Bat Adam.

The movie puts an emphasis on the ambiance. Mikhal Bat Adam
together with Zvi Kretsner wrote a realistic script, which is easy to follow.
Bat Adam is an experienced actress and director. The seven important
characters in the movie are the same is in the novel: Adam (Yehoram
Gaon, one of Israel most prominent singers, also an actor), Asya (Mikhal
Bat Adam, in her late thirties), Dafna (the 20-year-old Abigail Arieli),
Gabriel (Robert Polak), Tali (the 152-year-old No'ah Isic), Na'im (the 17-
year-old Khatib), Veducha (Penny Lovich, an experienced acting teacher).
Khatib is acting as Na'im with a great mastery of Na'im's character. In

1978, the Israeli Itsik Weingarten acted as Na'im in a play based on the novel (called *Na'im*). Yehoram Gaon as Adam is a likable, well-understood character. Roberto Polak as Gabriel and Mikhal Bat-Adam as Asya act their romantic scenes together in a convincing way.

The car also plays an important role. The romantic triangle is composed of Adam, Asya and Gabriel. Adam brings Gabriel to his home, and Gabriel, a Jew of South American origin, helps Asya by translating Spanish for her dissertation. Asya and Gabriel do not make substantial efforts to conceal the fact that they fell in love with each other, and Adam and the 15-year-old Dafna are affected by the situation. Adam pushed Gabriel to appear in his military unit and be drafted and, afterwards, he looked for Gabriel, Asya's lover. The movie like the book does not provide one clear reason as to why Adam tries so hard to locate Gabriel — is it guilt? Is it because of the love of Asya for Gabriel? Boredom?

Dov Zeltser, who received awards for best screen and stage composer in Israel, wrote the music for the movie. He wrote music for many movies, including *Kazablan, Eight Against One, The Highway Queen, I was born in Jerusalem, I Love You Roza, A Bit of Luck*.

The movie gives an expression to secondary plots: the story of Veducha; the short-lived romance of Na'im and Dafna; the "romance" of Adam and Tali, his daughter's friend.

BIBLIOGRAPHY

"A.B. u-Vat Adam. *Monitin*, March 1986.

Aharoni, Mikhal. "Na'ar 'Aravi be-Mishpaha Yehudit." *Be-Mahanei Gadna'*, No. 3 (449), Nov. 1978, pp. 10-11.

Bar-Kadma, 'Immanuel. "Hamme'ahev, mi-Keli el Keli." *Yediyot Aharonot*, Feb. 7, 1986.

Barezky, Nurit. "Nahuz Omez Lev Likhtov." *Ma'ariv*, Feb. 18, 1977, p. 6.

Barzilai, Yitshak. "Lashon, Sifrut ve-'Arakhim." *Hadoar*, Vol. 63, no. 33, Aug. 10, 1984, pp. 535-537.

Beser, Yacov. "Ha-Moah Hu ha-Miklat ha-Aharon shel ha-Herut." *Hotam*, June 11, 1982.

Carmel-Flumin, Nili. (Interview). "Min ha-Beged el ha-'Or." *Yediot Aharonot*, Aug. 15, 1986.

_____. "Bignut ha-Parshanut ha-Alegorit." *'Itton 77*, Sep. 1982.

Feldman, Yael S. "Z ionism on the Analyst's Couch in Contemporary Israeli Literature." *Tikkun*, Vol. 2, no. 5, Nov. 12, 1987, pp. 31-34, 91-96.

Fuchs, Esther. "The Sleepy Wife: A Feminist Consideration of A. B. Yehoshua Fiction." *Hebrew Annual Review*, Vol. 8, 1984, pp. 71-81.

Gertz, Nurit. "Me'ora' Deramati u-Zemannim Aherim'." *Siman Kri'a*, no. 6, May 1976, pp. 380-393.

_____. "Sifrut, Hevra, Historia." *Siman Kri'a,* no. 9, May 1979, 422-443, in p. 426.

_____. *Hirbet Hiz'ah ve-Habboker she-le-Mohorat.* Hakkibutz Hameuchad, Tel-Aviv, 1983, pp. 87-95.

Hakak, Lev. *Yerudim ve-Na'alim.* Kiryat Sefer, Jerusalem, 1981.

_____. "The Image of Sephardim in Modern Hebrew Short Story." In: *The Sephardi and Oriental Jewish Heritage,* The Magnes Press, The Hebrew university of Jerusalem, Isaachar Ben-Ami, Ed. pp. 297-310.

Levy, Gideon. "Ha-Hitpayyesut." *Ha'arez, Musaf,* May 15, 1987, pp. 21-24.

Mashiyah, Yig'al. "Ahava be-Zinnuk." *Davar, Devar ha-Shavua,* Feb. 7, 1986.

Ohovoski, Gal. "La Coquette." *Ha-Ir.* Jan. 31, 1986.

Oren, Yosef. "Hazono shel A.B. Yehoshua." *Ha-Arez ,* May 4, 1977, pp. 18-19.

Schnitz er, Meir. *"Ha-Me'ahev,"* In *Ha-Kolnoa' ha-Yisraeli.* Kinneret Publishing House, 1994.

Shaked, Gershon. "Hazel ha-Parus 'al Kullanu." *Yediot Aharonot,* Feb. 25, 1977. pp. 1-6.

Shamir, Ziva. "Arba'a Kenisot la-Pardes." *Yediot Aharonot,* April 29, 1977, pp. 2-3.

Shenhar, Aliza. "Ezem me-Az menuu-Vasar mi-Besarenu." *Al ha-Mishmar,* April 22, 1977, pp. 607.

Shwartz , Dror. (Interview). "Hassofer ke-Idiolog." *Hadoar,* Vol. 65, no. 60, 1986, pp. 16-18.

Zimerman, Dana. "Ha-Italki Roberto Pansa Yafik Co-Produkz ia 'al Besis Ha-Me'ahev shel A.B. Yehoshua." *Ha'arez ,* Oct. 21, 1997.

Yehoshua, A.B. *The Lover.* Translated by Philip Simpson. Doubleday & Co., Inc. Garden City, N.Y., 1978.

_____. *Bizkhut ha-Normaliyyut.* Schocken, Jerusalem and Tel-Aviv, 1984.

Yiftah-El, Ester. "Me'ahev ve-Aohev." *Shedemot,* No. 64, summer 1977, pp. 61-65.

Yisrael, Ya'ael. "Be-'Ikvot ha-Me'ahev." *Al ha-Mishmar,* Feb. 9, 1986.

Zach, Natan. *Kavei Avir.* Keter, Jerusalem, 1983.

Chapter 10

BLACK BOX BY AMOS OZ

THE NOVEL AND ITS PLOT

Black Box is composed of letters, telegrams, research notes and some book reviews. It follows the tradition of the epistolary novel — the entire narrative is conveyed by an exchange of fifty-one letters. The letters reveal the life and relationships of the characters and the changes they go through.

The correspondence of the characters takes place from February to October 1976, seven years after the divorce of Ilana and Alexander. Each of the characters writing letters (and sometimes telegrams) employs his own or her own style, and the letters express the characters' points of view and the way they perceive each other and themselves. In addition to the letters, the characters exchange telegrams between them. The novel also includes some of the research notes of Dr. Alexander and some reviews of his book.

On the individualistic level, the letters reveal the life and especially the troubled triangular relationship of Ilana, her ex-husband Alexander, and her present husband, Michael. On the national level, the letters reveal the social and political unrest of Israeli society, in which the new Israelis (represented by Michael Sommo) collide with the defeated old Israeli settlers or their offspring (Alexander Gideon).

In the novel, the old Askenazi settlers are emotionally or physically ill, or both. The vigorous and decisive Sephardim encounter them with their religious desires for territorial expansion. Through correspondence, the author strives to reveal the forces that caused the Ashkenazi Jews and the domination of the labor movement to collapse, and also to reveal the differences between the focus, orientation and concepts of the Ashkenazi old settlers and those of the Jews from the Middle East.

Many details of the characters' life are spread out in the novel in a non-chronological order. Re-organizing these details will help clarify the plot.

In the 1930s, Volodya Gudonski, a Jew who emigrated from Russia to Palestine, built a financial "empire" (p. 195). He had a wife and a son, Alexander, born in 1931 (p. 218). The wife died when Alexander was 5 (p. 99). In 1963, Gudonski decided to become a recluse (p. 98), and his estate deteriorated; he almost became a victim of various fundraisers and solicitors but, in 1966, while he became more and more melancholic, his attorney Zakheim managed to extract his money for his son Alexander.

Ilana and Alexander met when Alexander was 28 (p. 164). Ilana was about 20 years old, and both were serving in the Israeli Defense Force — Ilana in mandatory service and Alexander as part of his military career in the standing army. They got married in 1959 (p. 218) after she was introduced to his father. After a few months, Ilana became pregnant and, in 1960, had Boaz by her own decision. Alexander did not see himself "as cut out to be a father, and told her so from the start" (Ibid.). The marriage was troubled and, after nine years, they separated. They went through a vicious divorce in 1968, when Boaz was eight years old. Alexander's behavior "was dictated by hatred and vindictiveness" (Ibid. also p. 62). After the divorce, Ilana and Boaz went to live in a kibbutz where her sister and brother-in-law lived, because they had no money and no other shelter. After only six months, Ilana went back to Jerusalem, but Boaz stayed in the kibbutz for more than five years afterward (p.2). About two years after the divorce (p. 149), Ilana met Michael (Michel-Henri) Sommo.

Michael, who was born in Algeria in 1940, moved to Paris in 1954, studied at the Sorbonne for two years, and immigrated to Israel in 1960 (p. 31-32). Ilana and Michael got married in 1971 (p.33).

In 1974, the 13-year-old Boaz started studying in an agricultural high school (p. 3) and, during his two years there, the headmistress notified Ilana and Michael several times that Boaz was a violent boy. At the time of correspondence, Boaz was a 16-year-old boy, tall, with astonishing strength, bitter, wild and lonely, (p. 4) calling his mother a "whore" (p. 2) and her husband his mother's "pimp" (p.10). At that time, in 1976, Ilana and Michael's daughter was almost three years old (p. 9).

The situation of Boaz pushed Ilana to write to Alexander after about (p. 89) seven years of "total silence between them" (p.1).

During the correspondence Boaz changed locations and occupations several times, until he settled in his father's estate in Zikhron. Michael Sommo was affected by the money he received from Alexander and left his teaching position for real-estate transactions with nationalistic goals. Alexander's medical condition became terminal, and he came to die in Israel. He moved to the estate that his son Boaz now lived on. Boaz treated all the characters in his life in a well-balanced, fair and gracious manner and had begun repairing the estate. Ilana joined them, first with her daughter and then without her, when was returned to her father, Michael. The harsh way in which Ilana and Alexander described each other was replaced by tenderness and care. She comforted Alexander in a loving and caring way while Sommo filed for divorce, requesting that his wife be deprived of visitation rights for their daughter.

THE NOVEL TITLE

The black box of an airplane may lead to understanding the failure in the plane's communication and navigation systems when a disaster occurs. In the novel, we find few mentions of a black box. The author opens the Black Box, inside which is the story that may cast light on the cause of the crash of the relationship between Ilana and her husband, Alexander.

In his childhood Boaz used to sit at his father's desk and to draw "an airplane crashing in flames" (p. 76). Boaz was aware of his parents' bad relationship and "like a social worker" acted as intermediary between them (p. 77). Boaz's drawing is a sort of premonition, and the circumstances in which Boaz draws are part of the content of the "black box." Alexander, in a letter to Ilana, feels that their correspondence helped them understand what happened to their marriage: "As after a plane crash, we have sat down and analyzed, by correspondence, the contents of the black box" (p. 91), but Ilana disagrees: "We deciphered nothing, Alexander. We only exchanged poisoned arrows" (p. 144). One of Ilana's motives in writing to Alexander was to "decipher a black box" (p. 165); she feels that the "black box" which they opened after the crash did not provide the explanation of their family-life disaster. The novel does not decipher everything but, contrary to Ilana's harsh position, it does clarify the relationship to a significant extent.

In our first reading of the text we may think that we are deciphering the black box of Ilana and Alexander, however, in a second reading we find also the black box of the State of Israel. The various novel characters are the product of the Zionist dream, and the novel questions the qualities and abilities of the new Israeli. The individual characters represent different large social political groups in Israel, and they represent suffering and troubles in all the groups and the generations described in the novel. The information found in the black box shows the problems creeping down through the generations and their impact on Israeli society as a whole.

THE MOTTO-POEM

The poem "The Weeping" from Nathan Alterman's lyric poetry cycle *The Joy of the Poor* serves as a motto for the novel. In Alterman's poetry, the lovers' meeting is fatal; their love is eternal and is not wholly fulfilled. The poetic speaker is a living-dead, which represents a disintegrating society in a horrifying time of human existence.

When applied to the characters in the novel, selecting this motto-poem may imply that Alexander is incapable of separating himself from Ilana. They both are living-dead. Even in his death Alexander will feel "like a blind man" when Ilana will try to reach him, but she, too, is "entangled in the dark" until the end. There is care and attraction between the two, but no romantic fulfillment. He will always come back to her in her nightmares, in the gothic setting, and she will not be indifferent to him.

Alexander is no stranger to Alterman's *The Joy of the Poor* The day the court declared that Ilana and Alexander had no claims to each other, in the courthouse, Alexander wrote four lines from Alterman's *The Joy of the Poor* and sent them to Ilana via Zakheim: "You are the sadness of my balding head, / The melancholy of my aging claws:/ You'll hear me in the plaster of your walls, / and in the nightly creaking of your floors" (p. 169). In *The Joy of the Poor*, the lovers' house is gothic and horrifying. In these lines, Alterman describes the dead loving man coming back to his beloved who lives in a nightmarish house; she can hear him in the cracking plaster of the wall and in the creaking of the floor at night. When they separated, Alexander told Ilana through the poem that he would come back to her and even in death they would not part.

THE SOCIO-POLITICAL BACKGROUND

The time and place of the plot are essential to understanding it. The plot takes place in Israel and overseas. Ilana, Michael and their daughter live in a flat in Jerusalem. Boaz lives in various places and settles in the family estate between Binyamina and Zikhron Yaacov (p. 95). Alexander lives on the twenty-seventh floor of an office building, built of glass and steel, by the lakeside in Chicago (p. 92), and he moved to die in the estate.

The correspondence took place in 1976; it is a significant year because it presents the conditions in which social and political changes took place in Israel. In 1977, the Labor party ("left") in Israel was defeated in the election for the first time by the Likkud party ("right"), and the victory of the Likkud was the result of the vote of the Sephardim and Near Eastern Jews who felt for a long time that they were exploited like underdogs in Israel.

When the Jews from various Middle Eastern countries immigrated to Israel, they supported the labor movement (called "Mapai," The Israel Workers Party). In the elections of 1951 and 1955, more than 70 percent of the Jews of Near Eastern origin voted for that party, which lost in those years the support of some of its Ashkenazi voters. Within time, an intensifying rift between that party and the immigrants from the Middle East was identified. The Jews from the Middle East felt the Labor party neglected them because, after many years following their arrival in Israel, they still were discriminated against and in economical, cultural, political and social terms they lived at the margin of the Israeli society. They saw the Labor party as perpetuating the arrogance and brutality of the Ashkenazi rule and rejecting the values, cultures and abilities of the Jews from the Middle East. In 1977, the labor movement lost the elections for the first time in 29 years because the Sephardim voted for the Likkud party.

In *Black Box*, Oz portrays a new class of Israelis, the Sephardi middle class that is going to shape the future of Israel, as opposed to the "aristocratic" old settlers and their offspring.

Sommo recalls how much the Sephardim emulated Ashkenazim like Alexander, only to have more scorn later: "And how we admired you and those like you when we were young! How we looked up to you out of the depths! Such heroes! Such demigods!" (p. 211). Michael's bitterness is grave, and he speaks as a representative of a collective: "But we are as outlaws, our lives are unprotected, a disgrace to our neighbors and scorn to and derision to all those around us" (p. 209), "we are...doormats underneath your feet" (p. 211). Michael combines admonishing, contempt and tidings:

> ...And between wars, what did you do to the state? Defile it?
> Sell it for a mess of pottage? Feast on it?
>   That is why your time is up. Your bells are tolling... The
> kingship has passed, sir. Soon it will be given to your neigh-
> bor, who is better than you (p. 216).

The prophet Samuel said to King Saul: "The Lord hath rent the kingdom of Israel from thee this day and hath given it to a neighbor of thine, that is better than you" (*First Samuel* 15, 28). The allusion of Michael to the Bible implies that the Ashkenazim sinned: King Saul lost his status because of his sin according to the prophet, and Michael predicts the Ashkenazim lost their dominion for the same reason. In other words of Michael: "Professor Gideon may represent the achievements of the past, but it is my conviction that the future belongs to us" (p. 71). Gideon has no alternative but to admit: "...My time has indeed run out, Mr. Sommo. The bell really is tolling for me" (p. 220). The professor's political views are "more or less at the other end of the spectrum" (p. 24) relative to Michael.

Gideon also resorts to insults based on prejudice. In response to Michael's argument that he, Gideon, reduced Ilana to sin, Gideon writes to Ilana about her pious husband: "Such stories are apparently common currently in the background from which he comes."

THE CHARACTERS

Alexander's father, Volodya Gudonski, came from Russia to Palestine as a pioneer and became rich through real-estate transactions, iron importing and business with the British army. He was a shrewd, fun loving man who, in his heyday was "the great dealer in land and importer of iron...Tsar Vladimir the Terrible" (p. 95). Among many stories circulated about him was the story that in 1929 he killed three Arab brigands by himself, with a sledgehammer (p. 95-96).

Alexander, Gudonski's son, calls his father "Zeev-Benjamin Gudonski" (p. 96) — which may remind us of Benjamin-Zeev Herzel, the founder of political Zionism, who predicted the establishment of the

Jewish state. The family story of Herzel is marked with insanity and illness.

In 1694, one of Herzel's great-grandfathers punished his son for a religious sin, and the son died after one day. The father hung himself in the prison with his Tefillin (phylacteries). Herzel's grandfather's brothers were admitted to the Orthodox Serbia Church; Herzel's father was Austria-German in language and culture; Herzel's uncle was a Hungarian patriot. Within time, Herzel became distanced from his wife, who came from a manic-depressive family and regarded herself as the queen's mother. She was impulsive and unstable.

Herzel had three children who were born between 1890 and 1893. The fate of his children may provide the evidence of a family psychopathology and the fact that the genius is closer than the average person to madness. Herzel's children were educated as princes. They never studied in a school, and they expected their father to be a king. His eldest daughter, Pauline, was unstable, nymphomaniac, psychopathic and manic-depressive. She had heart problems. She took drugs and died at the age of 40 due to a heroin overdose. Herzel's son, Hans, was manic-depressive and was treated by Freud. He was circumcised, not when he was eight days old in accordance with the Jewish tradition, but after the death of his father when he was 16 years old. He converted to Christianity, was a Baptist, Catholic, Quaker, Unitarian and Lutheran. He shot himself the day his sister was buried. Herzel's daughter, Trudy-Margaret, was a psychopath; she was committed to mental institutions time and again. She inquired about the possibility of her becoming the Queen of England. She died of starvation in a concentration camp at the age of 40 during the Second World War. Her son was a British officer; he committed suicide in 1946 by jumping from a Bridge.

One may find powerful similarities between the families of Benjamin-Zeev and Zeev-Benjamin: Harsh punishment of children, extreme acts and then remorse, distance from fellow Jews, the absence of commitment to a woman, regal pomp and children with tragic destinies — these are some of the similarities between the fathers of Zionism and the pioneers. In both cases one may perceive the potential closeness of genius to madness. Gudonski, one of the foundering fathers, sets forth the relationships that encompass the illnesses of the forthcoming generations in his family.

Gudonski was attracted to Ilana when his son brought her to his estate for the first time in 1959. He tried to impress her and demanded her attention exclusively for himself, even kissing her lengthily on her mouth (p. 97). He planned an extravagant wedding for Ilana and Alexander without asking them if they wanted to get married, but forgot to go to their wedding because he was on a honeymoon in the Norwegian fjords with a new mistress (p. 98). At night, Gudonski gave parties to British officers, Greek and Egyptian merchants and real-estate agents from Lebanon, but "apart from Zakheim, hardly a Jew ever set foot" (p. 236) on his estate. His parties did not provide him with the friendship he needed.

Nothing in Gudonski's conduct attests to a commitment to his people or to Judaism. Ilana thinks of Gudonski's estate as "melancholy ogre's castle" (p. 133). Gudonski became ill with sclerosis (p. 19). Later he became insane and was committed by his son and his attorney to a sanitarium (p. 150). His son Alexander never visited him in the sanitarium, where Gudonski relates to Ilana as his "son's widow" (p. 155).

While Ilana remembers Gudonski behaving "like an overgrown dog...not very clever, baring his teeth to amuse...pleading for affectionate caress, dancing to make friends..." (p. 135), his son Alexander remembers his father "flashing rage like the Biblical Jehovah" hitting him over the head (p. 234, see also p. 226), and sees his father in the sanitarium as someone who changed "from a bear to a lamb" (p. 225).

Gudonski's character is key to understanding his son and his grandson. Gudonski made fortunes, but did not focus on his family. His violent nature, self-centeredness and madness, inattentive and unaffectionate attitude toward his son ended up in the three troubled generations in the novel. The generation of the old settlers in Palestine is presented as the primal cause for the condition of Israel in 1976. Gudonski had an estate but did not have love within his family. He had money but not happiness, guests but not friendship. He had a "grandiose library" but never opened a book (p. 28).

Gudonski's son, Professor Alexander A. Gideon, is an Israeli-born, sophisticated, analytical, highly capable professor. At times, his letters express intensity, and some of his acts are a sign of arrogance and a lack of sensitivity. His record is most impressive when it comes to formal achievements, such as military rank and academic publications, however, his record of human relations and wisdom is not commendable. He is strong when it comes to non-personal relationships and generalizations, but not when it comes to personal relationships and to emotional contacts; he is exposed as brutal, immature, weak and insensitive. He excelled in the arenas of battles, theory and intellect, but in the arenas of daily life, reality and compassion, he is deficient and inadequate. His concepts of human relationships led to his aloof life and to Boaz's troubles. After his divorce, he deserted his son and emigrated from Israel, but years later he came back to Israel to die there.

Alexander lived a non-intelligent life without emotional balance, and he died young of kidney cancer (p. 217). In Hebrew, the kidneys are the organs in which one feels pangs of conscience and remorse ("yissurei kelayot," see *Psalms* 16,7).

After the divorce Alexander could not and did not want to take custody of his son (p. 64). And Alexander did not commit himself to providing love and care for Boaz, after cruelly divorcing the woman he was enamored with all his life (p. 94). Too late he learned and he tried to teach Michael that Michael's daughter Yif'at (Madeleine Yifat, "yifa'a" in Hebrew is beauty) "is the only hidden glory. There is none other" (p. 232).

Various animals are used by various characters to illustrate Alexander. Ilana pictures his "wolfish jaws" (p. 7, see also pp. 159, 160, 165). The charismatic forceful, devouring wolf is beaten "like a puppy" (p. 252) by his caring worried wife at the end of the novel on his deathbed in order to make it clear to him that he does not have the strength to climb stairs. Alexander is characterized as other animals the most prominent being a dragon, which depicts cruelty, and a snake, which symbolizes venom. He is the dragon who slew the damsel (Ilana) and finally dispatched himself (p. 44. See also p. 82), but she loved Alexander, not despite his cruelty, but because of it (p. 165). As a dragon, Alexander cannot understand grace, kinship and tenderness (p. 84), but in 1976 Ilana wondered if the dragon became a shabby, floppy and sloppy dragon, a Vampire stuffed with rags (p. 85). Alexander feels that Ilana is the one who slew him, the dragon, while he was sinking into death (p. 90). Ilana also describes Alexander as a snake with fine slow poison that did not slay her at once but destroyed her over the years (p. 39). He also behaved as a lizard watching an insect or as a viper even in social settings (p.75). Ilana also views Alexander as a vampire (p. 74, see also pp. 84, 85). Alexander relates to both his images as a viper and a vampire with irony (pp. 65, 103, 239). If these were not enough, Michael relates to Alexander as a raven (p. 184) to emphasize Alexander's cruelty, in accordance with some Jewish folk tales. At the end of the novel, tender feelings replace Ilana's harsh metaphors describing Alex.

Indeed the perception of a brutal side of Alexander is corroborated by his violent acts. In his childhood, he would kill animals in a cruel way (pp. 226, 237); he blew up his electric train with gunpowder (p. 226), had fits of temper, and inflicted damage on his body and toys. Fantasies of war and bombardment were part of his childhood games (p. 233); he had outbursts of fury and rare bloody violence "and once, in a fit of rage, he picked up a chair and broke Monsieur's nose" (p. 238). Alexander uses battlefield terminology to illustrate human relations. For example, he viewed Ilana's letters to him as an attack of fresh troops without warning while his tanks had no fuel or ammunition (p. 90). Ilana's suicide attempts by swallowing foreign substances only evoked his dry snigger and his sarcastic remarks about "stomach-pump drill" (p. 125).

During his childhood, Alexander noticed the camels, "the softness of their necks," their sadness and "the delicate lines of their legs" (p. 236). But like the warriors in the stories Hirbet Hiz'ah and "The Prisoner" of the Israeli author S. Yizhar, Alexander's aesthetic appreciation of camels did not prevent him from becoming a "camel-slayer" (p. 230) for no reason (pp. 228-229). The most electric moments in his life were in the war (he is a hero of war), when, with his gunfire, he smashed whatever displayed signs of life, inhaling the stench of charred flesh (p. 93). He tossed three hand grenades into a bunker full of Egyptian soldiers, burst in and sprayed them with a submachine gun, and was splashed with blood and brains (pp. 221-222). On his deathbed in the silence of the night he said: "It was a slaughter, not a battle" (p. 247) — who was he thinking about?

At the age of 28, Alexander told Ilana that he planned to reassert the common denominator of violence in history. Then suddenly he shouted at the waiter and started killing the flies (p. 164). His obsession with violence came from his own psychological structure and from the symbolic fly killing episode may allude to the future impact of his research — it will not go beyond killing "flies."

As a scholar, Alexander received international recognition for his book *Between Fanaticism and Zealotry*. In a letter to Michael, Alexander summarizes the point he wanted to make throughout his scholarly life (pp. 233-234). He wanted to prove that people annihilate themselves "because of the theological disease" (p. 231) and because of their obsession for redemption, which is only a mask for an absence of talent for life.

In an interview about his novel (see Charney), Oz stated that in this novel we find "people who would not settle for anything less than the absolute," all of the characters have "a certain core of zealotry," except perhaps Boaz who has "tremendous respect for life itself." Oz defines a fanatic as a person who "regards anything at all as more important than life itself," while "fanaticism springs from... a shortage of gift for life, an enthusiasm for life."

It is noteworthy that while Alexander dedicated his life to the understanding of the fanatic, he, the internationally recognized scholar, is unknowingly a fanatic himself. His description of the emotional and ideological world of the fanatic suits his own world (pp. 126-128, 144-147, 175-177). His theories do not help him realize that he is typified by narrow-mindedness, unreasoning zeal, intolerance and hatred. Theoretically he wants justice and morality; he wants to understand zealotry. He recognizes the zealotry of Sommo, his antagonist, but cannot look into himself and see that he is an extremist, brutal and immersed in his ego.

In the novel we find Alexander's scattered intellectual reflective notes. From this speculative, non-abstruse introspection, one may conclude that the author strove for but unfortunately did not manage to produce the evidence justifying the academic prominence of Alexander, who does not come through as a profound original thinker of an international caliber.

The other characters' outlooks on Alexander in the novel are not complimentary. The reader must closely examine the validity of these opinions and insights because they may stem from misunderstanding, anger, jealousy, etc.

Michael considers Alexander "the King of Villains" (p. 48), whose son at one stage followed his tainted path of "arrogance, cruelty and wickedness. Causing suffering" (p. 49, see also p. 54). "...A confirmed evildoer and rogue imbued with the spirit of Belial" (p. 208. "Belial" - Biblical, wickedness). His acts are identified with the acts of Biblical characters such as those of Cain, who murdered his brother, and King David, who caused Uriah to be killed so that he, King David, could take Uriah's wife (p. 214) and the sons of Zeruiah (p. 216), who were used to their swords and the wicked king Ahab (Ibid.).

Ilana portrays Alexander in an emotional way. While Ilana thinks that Alexander does not know the meaning of the word "love," she thinks he is or was strong and clever (p. 4). She wondered if he found anyone who could offer him "a single crumb of gentleness" (p. 12). She sees him as "wicked, solitary" and impute to him "malicious glee" (p. 38), with a "mask of contempt and arrogance" (p. 39). In his military service he was noticed for his "icy malice," cruelty, terror and contempt (p. 158). He was "wedded to tanks" (p. 161). Ilana perceives Alexander as a helpless man who never did anything on his own and always relied on his checkbook (p. 40).

Zakheim remembers Alexander as a "strange, gloomy child" (p.195), "a large, pampered child, a decadent boy emperor," cruel (p. 199). Then, as a teenager, Alexander was "good-looking, sad, and a little violent" (p. 201-202). Zakheim looks at Alexander's relationships as an adult and finds a pattern: first Alexander tramples and then he apologizes (p. 197). He ponders on the enticing combination of ruthlessness and helplessness (p. 199) and the "fragile savagery" (p. 200) in the character of Alexander. From Zakheim, we also learn that Alexander was injured in a raid (p. 202). Numerous times Zakheim expresses his belief that Alexander is as insane as his father. Some of Alexander's actions, such as thrusting a stick into a beehive (p. 231), may make us wonder.

One may wonder why Alexander gives away so much of his money. Giving away money excites the reader of course and adds intensity to the plot. Ilana thinks that the money was given to the family maliciously in order to demolish and smash their way of life (p. 125). Zakheim, Alexander's lawyer, thinks that Alexander was acting as a madman (p. 19). Michael thinks that Alexander gave the money because he was riddled with remorse and because he, Michael, healed Ilana's shame and watched over Boaz's footsteps (p. 23). Alexander does not want to be questioned about his motives (p. 13), which reminds us that human motives are hard to define with certainty.

One can conclude from the life of Gudonski and his son that one can be rich and miserable, and that behind the fences of the envied Israelis there are only errors, loneliness and misery. The lonely, introvert, arrogant Alexander cannot be happy and cannot make other people happy.

The relationship between Ilana and Alexander also illustrates an aspect of gender war (See Balaban). "You have the womb — you have that advantage," wrote Alexander to Ilana (p. 101). Ilana wrote: "I was drawn to you as though bewitched from muddy depths of primeval female subservience, ancient servitude...the submission of a Neanderthal female whose survival instinct...make her through herself at the feet of the hunters, the hairy savage..." (p. 159). Ilana and her husband have a bond of lust and perhaps sadomasochism (see Charney) with each other, "in reinstating her connection with him she is asking for abasement...He responds by throwing money at the problem — along with insults aimed from on high at everyone's most vulnerable spots" (Charney).

Ilana is an educated woman, sensuous, romantic and "liberal." Her father died in a construction accident in Israel when she was about 12, and her mother died one year later. The family destruction originated accidentally from the construction efforts. Ilana arrived in Israel from Poland when she was a child with a Holocaust background. She was married first to an Ashkenazi from an old settler's family and then to a Sephardi. She is hurting and suffering, sentimental and practical. She relates to her ex-husband with love and hatred and with a venomous and submissive attitude. It is somehow enigmatic that a woman of her needs and experience married Sommo and remained faithful to him. Each one of the two men fulfills different needs for Ilana, and she wants them both simultaneously.

Boaz, Ilana and Alexander's son, is a handsome, tall, blonde hippie, both ignorant and sincere. Everyone wants to teach him, but he is everyone's teacher. He traces the main problems of the characters around him, articulates them and proposes solutions. He has the talent of understanding people's hearts. He is interested in the earth and the sky, desires life and not death. Boaz found the most important truths about life. We do not know how Boaz became so insightful and wise. It is possible to read Boaz's name as encompassing the name of the author: Bo oz, "bo" in Hebrew means in him, "oz" in Hebrew means vigor, might — he is vigorous. It may imply that the author, Oz, identifies with Boaz's biography and ideas.

We observe Gudonski giving his grandson Boaz old (gold) coins, but we do not observe him giving him love (p. 99). Ilana describes Boaz as a boy who imitated his father during his childhood, and who tried wisely to reconcile with his parents, playing in harmony with his father (pp. 76-77). At the age of eight, Boaz was a careful, disciplined, timid child but, in 1976, at 16, the six-foot-three-inch, handsome Boaz (p. 137) was a "bitter, wild boy whose hatred and loneliness have invested him with astonishing physical strength" (p. 4). Ilana feels there is a tragic similarity between Boaz and Alexander. "Boaz belongs only to himself, and perhaps he is a stranger to himself as well" (p. 62). "You are better and purer than any of us," (p. 190) Ilana wrote to her son.

Alexander remembers his son well; including the time Boaz threw a potted cactus at him when Alexander did not agree to stop punching Ilana (p. 65-66). Alexander received monthly reports about Boaz and Ilana and his conclusion was: "And everything I know, including his violence, I like a lot...we don't deserve him, either of us. Neither of us deserves anything, apart from a bullet in the brain" (p. 66). Ilana's sister, Rahel found in Boaz "decency and clear logic," different from the common logic (p. 52). Zakheim summarizes his impression of Boaz: "The Gulliver is evidently fashioned of passably good materials, albeit totally demented..." (p. 197).

The physical strength of Boaz is fanciful. He broke down a wall at the police station and escaped (p. 86). With a tire attached to a rope, he injured nine soldiers and five policemen before he was overpowered (p. 85), which brings the association of Samson (Judges 15, 16) to Alexander's mind (p. 90). Another time Boaz reminds Alexander of Atlas the Titan (p. 223). Alexander relates to the possibility that Boaz is bisexual: All the girls in the commune or the "hippie colony" (p. 197), which Boaz set up "seem to be his mistresses. Maybe the boys too" (p. 224).

Michael relates to Boaz as a horse (p. 3) and as an ass (p. 109), but Alexander remembers the way Boaz used to sleep at night, "like a cub dug into a hole" (p. 65).

Boaz will inherit the house from his father (p. 218). Meanwhile Boaz is repairing the estate. "...The pit that Volodia Gudonski dug and his grandson cleared and restored" (p. 255). Now the estate is full of rain water — the water and the pit are symbols of life, freshness and renovation, but Ilana thinks that all this is only temporary: "One day he will go off on his rambles and not come back...Not a living soul will remain. The lizard, the fox and the viper will inherit the house and the weeds will return" (p. 257). She thinks that he will do what his grandfather and father did. If Ilana is right, there is no question who is going to win "in the battle that will erupt one day between Boaz and Sommo" (p. 95) as Alexander expects. If Ilana is right, the Israeli-born Boaz cannot be relied upon for the regeneration of Zionism. When the destructive elements are so many, more than just Boaz is needed in order to reinvigorate the Zionist dream.

Boaz and Sommo are both Zionists. The Zionism is of few words and of meaningful action, which is positive for him and for the country - staying in Israel and not going to his father in America, and repairing the family estate. One's life, according to Boaz, should be constituted of life, not of words, politics, or spiritual heritage. The Zionism of Sommo is more sophisticated verbally; it includes longing for Jewish glory and involves the Jewish historical heritage — while Boaz lives in the present without historical perspective.

Of special interest are the views Boaz developed about life and people. Ilana articulates the ten commandments of Boaz (p. 158) and concludes that Boaz is the opposite of his father. Unlike the Biblical Ten Commandments that deal with Man's relationship with God and Man's relationship with Man, Boaz's commandments deal exclusively with man-to-man relations. They reflect compassion, tolerance, attention and a desire for a happy and sensible existence. His internationally recognized father devoted much of his life to tanks, but Boaz, the inarticulate, does not give a damn if he does not qualify to be drafted for the army (p. 142). He can teach his father wisdom: "the whole place is full of wise guys riding tanks" (p. 140) instead of living it up.

Michael Sommo, Ilana's husband, is of North African (Algeria) origin; he is Alexander's antagonist. He is a non-accredited teacher of French, a man of poor appearance. After living in Paris, he went to Israel where he is driven by nationalistic religious ideology. Michael has no inferiority complex amidst formally more educated Israeli-born people such as Alexander Gideon, because he views his own way as the correct, just and ethical way. Michael thinks that the messages of the Bible and the wisdom of the rabbis clearly outweigh Alexander's knowledge. He is devoted to a larger Israel and ready to utilize politics for his goals, specifically Jewish settlements in Hevron and Kiryat Arba' that are holy to the Jews. Sommo views the territorial expansion of Israel as a central element of his Zionism.

Sommo may be pleasant and moderate in many ways unless his ego and values are undermined, which may generate a zealous reaction from him. He is well connected and, with the help of his relatives in various public positions, he can pull many strings. Michael may be viewed as ungrateful, extrinsic and hypocritical with false piety. Some critics found the character of Michael in the novel offensive to the Sephardim (Weiss, 1987; Yeshua'ah-Light, 1987). Others objected to this view (Carmel-Flumin, 1987).

Three of Michael's letters are addressed to Alexander; the fourth one is addressed to Alexander, Boaz and Ilana. Alexander's terminal condition brings about changes in Michael's attitude in his third and fourth letters. At the end of the novel, Alexander is dying. Sommo thanks God for his mercy. Chapter 103 of *Psalm* was carefully selected: God's great mercy is "toward them that fear him" only. East (Sephardi Jews) and west (Ashkenazi Jews) met, and "as far as the east is from the west, so far hath he removed our transgression from us," and "the mercy of the Lord is from everlasting to everlasting upon them that fear him," and Sommo who fears him will prevail.

Both, Alex and Michael are unable to see that literary fiction reflects life, including their own: In his last days, Alexander began to have a faint "curiosity to hear about other folks' lives. Tales that he, like you, always used to regard with utter contempt: *Le Pere Goriot*, Dickens, Galsworthy, Somerset Maugham..." (p. 246) — both men fail to see how much "fiction" may touch their lives and help them understand it, because it is about them in so many ways.

Indeed, *Black Box* is about them, and it deals with the themes of the literary works that they treated with contempt. Because of the inability of the two men to see that nothing in their lives is new in literature, their lack of interest in other people's life is ironic. They are unable to see clearly the reflection of the major dilemmas of their lives in literature. The characters' lives are different from the way they perceive their lives.

Zakheim is Alexander's friend and attorney; he is witty, cynical, lustful and practical. Zakheim immigrated to Israel in 1925 when he was 10 (p. 107). In 1976, he was a 61-years-old. In 1941, Zakheim volunteered for the British army and for five years wandered in several countries (p. 201). In 1943, he was a second lieutenant in the British Army (p. 198). He was discharged in 1946 and got married in 1947 (p. 201). In 1949, he was the deputy military attorney in the Israel Defense Force (p. 194). He suffered a tragic loss in 1953 (p. 202).

Zakheim corresponds with Alexander through telegrams and letters, the third of which provides the reader with some expository information about Alexander's childhood.

With all of his self-righteousness and devotion to his family and clients, Zakheim would not miss an opportunity for pleasure, as we can learn from Ilana (pp. 82, 103), or a business opportunity. When he learns that his family can benefit from Michael's ventures, he does not miss the opportunity. His tone in his correspondence with Michael changes accordingly.

Even though Zakheim is Alexander's legal counsel, he often serves more as his business manager than as his lawyer. Indeed, Alexander wrote him: "You are a business manager and not a confession priest" (Hebrew p. 181, the sentence was omitted for no apparent reason from the English translation p. 203). He served the Gudonski family for 38 years (p. 193) and conducted 11 lawsuits in order to extricate Gudonski's property and put him away (p. 202).

Reading the novel may raise various legal questions in one's mind. Was it not Zakheim's legal duty to protect his incompetent client, Gudonski, by creating guardianship rather than transferring Gudonski's property to Alexander? If Alexander was the legal trustee would Zakheim, representing Gudonski's interest, act to transfer the property from Alexander as a trustee outright to Alexander as an owner (p. 100)? Was Zakeheim in compliance with the applicable rules of professional conduct when he persuaded another lawyer to transfer the legal files of a client to him against the instructions of the client (p. 147)? Would ethical lawyer breach confidentiality and inform someone about the general content of his client's will especially when there is the possibility of conflict of interest (p. 107)? Would a lawyer threaten someone who gives his client in a civil matter a hard time with incriminating information he has (p. 25, see also 69)? Due to ethical considerations, Zakheim refused to represent Michael's organization — is this enough to avoid issues of conflict of interest when he had his son-in-law doing business with Michael who wanted Alexander's property (p. 106)? Would Zakeheim advise his client, Alexander, that the client's allowing his minor son to stay and work on the client's estate in another country might be interpreted as kidnapping the client's son from the son's mother?

Rahel, Ilana's older sister, is well-balanced, reliable, stable and wise. Ilana, who lives on the edge, mocks her. Rahel expresses her philosophy of life in an articulate, poetic way in a letter to Ilana: "There is no point in your making fun of me: I didn't invent the fixed choice between fire and ashes - I have my own closed circle" (p. 173). Rahel recognizes the dullness and ennui in life, but one has to choose the least of the two ills. She knows the alternative, the temptations, the excitement in a theatrical drama as part of one's life, the dreams, but she is also realistic: "Who does not dream occasionally of taking off, flying away, and getting singed on some faraway flame?" (Ibid.). It is no wonder that Rahel, the only surviving relative of Ilana, avails herself of Ilana constantly. She responds in four letters to Ilana's two letters. Ilana sees her sister as "dear old clever, normal Rahel," whose "normality is an escape from life" (p. 17).

It is up to the reader to decide whether the choice we have is indeed only between extremes — fire or ashes — or if moderation is possible too. And it is up to the reader to decide whose life does he value more — Ilana's who lives on the edge in fire, or Rahel's who lives in ashes?

The main question in the novel is what the characters did with the gift of life. This question is applicable to all of the characters in the story and presents the main issue in their lives. The characters in the novel yearn for love and affection, but they are lonely and miserable. They question their ways but it is too late to change. While Alexander thinks that "all happiness is basically a trite Christian invention. Happiness...is kitsch" (p. 94), Ilana thinks "there is happiness in the world...indeed in your case it is beyond your reach...the merging of the I with another" (p. 118).

In his fascinating insane discourse with Ilana at the sanitarium, Gudonski asks: "And what do I do? Na, tell me what I do with the gift of life? What do I spend it on? Why do I sully it? I smash teeth, I cheat, I steal, and, above all, I hoist up skirts" (p. 153). The Hebrew text is written in the past tense, giving the sense of self-accountability as to what Gudonski did with his life. In his madness he can clearly see that he dissipated his life.

His son had a similar destiny. Alexander attained some academic stature, but he is alone, dreamless, passionless and lifeless: "men and women, money, power, and fame — they all leave me cold" (p. 61). Alexander's death due to kidney cancer (p. 217) is symbolic; in Hebrew, the kidneys are the organs in which one feels pangs of conscience and remorse (*Psalms* 16,7). It is no wonder that he wishes to cancel his presence retroactively (p. 227). Indeed, not even one single character in the novel gives us the feeling that he can appreciate fully the gift of life. We question even Rahel, who takes life for granted in the ashes, because, in her opinion, the only alternative is fire (p. 173). We doubt Boaz's stability and find his academic-intellectual investment shameful.

The failure of the individual characters is connected with their view of Israel. Again, it is the incompetent but mindful Gudonski who questions the role and qualities of Israel in Jewish life:

> What is Palestine? *Realia?* Palestine is dream. Palestine is *cauchemar*, but still is dream. Perhaps you have deigned to hear of a Lady Dulcinea? Well, Palestine is like her. In the dream, myrrh and frankincense, but in *realia* swinery! Misery of swines. And in the morning — 'behold it was Leah!' What Leah? Malaria. Ottoman Asia...(p. 152)

Palestine is cauchemar — a nightmare (French: cauchemare). If Palestine is Dulcinea, the Jewish pioneers are Don Quixotes. Only in dreams is Palestine "myrrh and frankincense" — perfect subjects of a romantic dream as the Biblical allusion implies: "Who is this that cometh up from the wilderness...perfumed with myrrh and frankincense" (*Song of Songs*, 3, 4). Gudonski thinks that when one wakes up in Palestine, he discovers his illusive situation. And the situation is not unlike that of Jacob who loved Rachel and served Rahel's father, Laban, for seven years in order to marry her. Instead Laban brought his daughter Leah to Jacob, "and it came to pass in the morning that, behold, it was Leah; and he said to Laban: '...wherefore then hast thou beguiled me?'" (*Genesis* 29, 25).

Gudonski came to Palestine not out of love and ideology, but rather his father smuggled him out in the middle of the night, so that he would not be hacked to death because he slept with a peasant girl. He had an image of Palestine: "...wilderness! Graveyard! Fear! Foxes! Prophets! Bedouins! And the air all blaze!" (p. 153) — there is nothing holy or romantic about this image; prophets and foxes are mixed, in this articulated, emotional image, composed by short exclamatory and definitive sentences.

Other characters make the connection between individual lives to the State of Israel as well. Michael, wondering about the unethical conduct of Alexander, wonders: "Perhaps...the ancient Jerusalem is not here, or the Biblical Land of Israel, but somewhere completely different? ...Perhaps that is why it befell that there is no G-d in this place?" (pp. 212-213). Ilana thinks of another option — that the fault is not with the country but with those people, who could not find it:

> When I was a little girl...I fell under the spell of the old pioneer songs, which you don't know because you came here late... To this day I tremble when they play 'In the land the fathers loved'... As if they are saying there is a land but we have not found it. Some jester in disguise has crept in and seduced us into loathing what we have found... (p. 257-258)

Ilana questions the people who possibly went awry; it is not the country that she blames.

THE CHARACTERS'
STYLE

The characters are characterized and distinguished by their different styles.

Ilana's style is emotional, poetic, lyric, nostalgic and romantic, with many metaphors and hyperbolas; it is an individualistic, gushy and imaginative style.

Alexander's style tends to be restrained and, often, it is informative, factual, even dry and curt at times. Other times it is articulate, sharp-witted and analytical. And yet at other times — particularly in his last letter — it is a poetic style with emotional eruptions. The notes he writes on his cards are written in the style of academic-reflective publications.

Boaz writes in slang with numerous spelling errors. The clever content and vision we find in some of his letters controverts his limited vocabulary and grossly faulty spelling. It reminds us that wisdom and education do not necessarily go hand in hand. Boaz does not have his mother's stylistic creative abilities, not his father's stylistic rhythm and firmness and not the spirit and knowledge that make it possible for Michael to make stylistic connections between old Jewish sources to daily reality.

Michael's style is correct, fervent and religious, with many quotations and allusions all expressed in a serious manner and usually far from the colloquial Hebrew.

Zakheim's style is informative, but even he goes beyond the informative instructive language at times and becomes somehow poetic when the opportunity presents itself. He attempts to be witty, possibly inspired by the eminence of his client whom he wants to impress.

Zakheim is a well-rounded man who enjoys showing off his knowledge; he is a smart professional who depends on capricious clients in order to make a living. It is surprising to see that he, too, (like Michael) carries social bitterness as a German Jew toward Russian Jews as he puts it in his emotional way: "Didn't you despise us and trample all over us, you the Frenchified Russian aristocracy of North Binyamina?" (p. 20 sees also p. 196).

In his letters Zakheim constantly uses English idioms and sometimes he translates to Hebrew or transliterates them. In the Hebrew text we find English interwoven with Hebrew: "And I shall be on my way right away," "go fuck yourself," "Just don't go mad, for God's sake," "just for the hell of it," "go right ahead, be my guest," "take it or leave it," "and that's all there is to it," "lo and behold." This style may be part of Zakheim's need to show his English off in a snobbish way, or it simply implies a need for an idiom without an exact Hebrew equivalent. Zakheim's partner, Roberto Dimodena, employs English even in his short communications, i.e. "no hard feelings" (p. 172). It seems that the implied author is a comparative languages game playing with the educated reader, implying that as rich as Hebrew is, it can still be enriched.

Zakheim can quote Shakespeare (i.e. p. 196), and he also can allude to biblical text. "They that shoot in tears shall bandage in joy?" he asks, alluding to the self-explanatory Biblical verses: "Thay that sow in tears shall rip in joy" (*Psalms* 126, 5). "As you have murdered, so shall you bind up?" he asks Alexander bitterly (p. 197), alluding to the Biblical verse "Hast you killed, and also taken possession?" (*First Kings* 21, 19).

Rahel's style is moderate, well balanced and without emotional outbursts.

These questions may explain why some critics (see Miron) found that the characters' styles in the novel are not persuasive and the human situations are not authentic.

The novel employs humor to tone down dramatic events. Boaz's misspelling problems create entertaining statements. Boaz is not aware of the humorous effects of his spelling errors, but the author and the reader are, and they share this humor.

Boaz erroneously exchanges certain Hebrew letters with others and this sometimes produces comic effects. In his letter to Michael, Boaz writes that he started to "put together" (p. 29) some equipment. By exchanging one letter, the Hebrew word for "putting together" ("markiv") becomes "to rot." In another instance, Boaz wants to write that he uses physical force only when he is completely right, but even in those situations he "just drop it" (p. 108). He misspelled the Hebrew word for "drop it" ("mevatter"), forgo, and as a result he describes himself as someone who cuts, dismembers.

Even the very serious Alexander is humorous at times. His humor is mostly sexual and at times vulgar. For example, Ilana asked him why he divorced her, and his first response is: "Rahab rides again — sleeps with three divisions then wonders why she's been divorced. Says: All I really wanted was to come out all right in the end" (p. 83). Rahab is the Biblical harlot from Jericho (Joshua 2). The word "rides" has a sexual connotation here and so does the Hebrew word "ligmor," which means "to finish," "to come" (it was translated as "to come out"). (See also pp. 43, 65, and 59).

Michael's sexual inexperience when he met Ilana also may evoke a smile on the reader's face. Ilana had numerous sexual experiences, and she reports to Alexander how Michael was during his first lovemaking to her: "...I still had quite a struggle before he showed signs of life...When I let out a little sigh, he was terrified and began to murmur: *Pardon*" (p. 83).

The bitterness of the religious Michael can make us smile even when he did not intend to achieve this affect. "Perhaps even in the world to come they need cooks and RPs, so that you may still see me saluting you at the barrier" (p. 217), he bitterly wrote to Alexander. In other cases, the reader may smile a smile of contempt at Michael. For example, Alexander arrogantly requested that Michael not bother him "with effusive expressions of gratitude in the Levantine style" (p. 13). Michael wondered: "Well, take note that it never even occurred to me to say thank you! Thank you for what? ...It seems to me that there is no limit to your impudence, sir..." (p. 54). The absurd human insensitivity can reach a preposterously entertaining level.

At times the reader may feel that the author is carried away when he puts long discourses that may raise questions into his characters' mouths. Would people in 1976, during a telecommunication age, write letters to each other even about emergent issues and under all circumstances? Alexander, during his last weeks of life, wrote a long confession letter (pp. 217-241) to Michael, and Alexander himself could not explain this action (p. 239). How did he become open enough to write his long confession to Michael, and how did he have the emotional and physical ability to do so? Why would Alexander portray with such a naturalistic detailed description of how Ilana will look when she ages in his letter to her (pp. 91-92)? Was it not merely the author's need to use a paragraph, which is beautifully written but structurally superfluous and not genuine? How do two serious efficient professionals such as Alexander and Zakheim get engaged in exchanging telegrams when some of them (for examples, pp. 26, 67-68) are silly and deteriorate to childish name-calling?

It is possible to find analogies between Ilana (Ilana — Israel and Palestine, Hebrew **Palestina**) and Israel. They both are treated with love and hatred; we find in them purity and sin. They both are torn between people who have different concepts and orientations, and they both have close people who left them and came back. Both Ilana and Israel are part of romantic dreams that became nightmares. Alexander struggled for both of them, loved both of them and deserted both. So, Ilana and Israel are left with Boaz-like Israeli-born. Alexander is attracted to both Israel and Ilana enough to want to die in Israel near Ilana even though he did not stay in Israel with Ilana.

Alexander can free himself of the conflicts with his country and only Ilana by death.

Michael wants both Israel and Ilana with their wholeness. He will not share either one of them with someone else, and he will not share Ilana with Alex and Israel with the Arabs.

Boaz reminds us that both Ilana and Israel are not well. Ilana and Israel are afflicted by their pasts and their hope is for help from overseas (Alexander for Ilana, and immigration and support for Israel). Boaz is inarticulate, however, his dedication to the estate is also dedication to Israel, and it helps Israel more than his father's sophisticated intellectual theories.

IMPLIED PREDICTION OF ISRAEL'S FUTURE

The novel presents serious concerns about Israel's doomed future. The view of Israel's future is pessimistic on both individual and national levels.

Gudonski had the ability to make money but, due to his mental condition, was committed to a mental institution. It is the money Gudonski made, not Alexander's money, that serves as a major tool to solve Alexander's problems, his son and his ex-wife. Yet money with all its power could not buy Gudonski or Boaz satisfying emotional lives and could not cure Gudonski, his son and grandson of their physical or mental illnesses. Money could not buy Boaz elementary knowledge of his mother's tongue. Alexander did not continue Gudonski's pioneering ventures; the new Zionist is Sommo; the ignorant and troubled Boaz is not the promise for prosperous future of Israel, and his future is unknown.

The encounter of national religious Jews with the Ashkenazi elite does not produce cooperation or amalgamation but perpetuation of a schism. The Ashkenazim, like Michael, are opportunists and are not above any of Michael's motives. When it comes to money, Zakheim does not miss an opportunity to have his son-in-law join a real-estate venture with Michael. Michael's patriotic ideology leads him to land acquisitions in order to expand Jewish territories, and Zakheim's monetary drive leads him to Michael. Zakheim makes the connection between his son-in-law and Michael for business reasons.

The son-in-law "is inclined to bet on a change of government within the next two years" (p. 106) — but he is only interested in using the economical implications of this change for his own gain. The name of the son-in-law is Zohar (Hebrew: glamour) Etgar (Hebrew: challenge) — his challenge and claim for glamour are not ideological, political, or intellectual, but merely materialistic, money is his main desire.

The Gudonskis will not play a major role in Israel's future. Alexander's father became inactive; he was committed to a mental institution. Alexander was committed to his intellectual reputation, not to Israel and to its future; he came to die in Israel on his father's estate and soon will die from cancer. The only emotional comfort he can give to his son Boaz is a short family reunion for few weeks. Boaz, the third generation, has a history of confusion and violence, and his way of finding balance is by being remote from interacting with daily life in Israel. When Alexander dies, the stage is opened for Michael's play. Michael is practical, active, vigor, energetic and committed to Israel and to his family. But Michael, like all of the other characters in the story, is also distraught. Israel will be a strange country with potentially destructive people.

Families such as those of Ilana-Alexander and Ilana-Michael do not promise a healthy national future. Gideon is willing to sell his land. Michael wants to buy it, but land is not a promise for an upright national future. Three generations of violence are described in the novel, and the violence did not solve any problem. Gudonski killed three Arabs with a sledgehammer. Alexander, "in a fit of rage, he picked up a chair and broke Monsieur's nose" (p. 238). When he became an adult, he beat his wife and son and inflicted emotional death on them and on him (pp. 65-66, 168); and Boaz hit his employer with a box. Gideon's research of violence does not guarantee his ability to clear the violence from his own private court. Physical violence was attributed in a stereotypic way to Sephardim, and Oz turned the tables on the stereotype.

Can the new Israeli-born generation save Israel? Does the generation born in Israel whose fathers were born in Israel have any glad tidings for Israel (see Ramraz Rauch)? Boaz does not have the intellect, perseverance, stability and strength to be a politically impactive man. He can, to a certain extent, restore his grandfather's estate, but he is limited and confused His acts, though, are constructive; they may imply that, before the Israelis occupy themselves so much with having more territories than they should, like Boaz, they rehabilitate when needed the territories they already have. Boaz's moderation and his acceptance of people are atypical of his people and are the key to his newly established success with people and to his leadership abilities.

Israel can be successful only by combining Michael's determination and dedication with Alexander's intellect and Boaz's physical strength and wisdom. But Alexander is a theoretician without a national commitment, and Michael's vision is not harmonious. The chasm between the Sephardi religious nationalist and the Ashkenazi secular "cosmopolitan" (or: pseudo-cosmopolitan) is too great to bridge and when there is no will there is no way. These two men, Alexander, the deserting biological father, and Michael, the other one who strives to be a kind of protective spiritual guide, did not provide role models for Boaz. The generation of these fathers failed to inspire the generation of the sons. It is the good earth that gives Boaz comfort and stability, not the fathers. Boaz is left to find his way in life without them and in spite of them. Boaz does not accept his father's emigration and Michael's willful impositions. Both Michael and Alexander are formally more articulate than Boaz, but Boaz's intentions, ideas and deeds are better than those of the fathers. Boaz's quest and his efforts to understand instead of accepting and copying without question are commendable. Boaz's problems generate communication between the characters that are in need of this communication but otherwise do not have the courage to initiate it. Once they started communicating, they have a chance to understand themselves and the other characters better.

Professional recognition and formal achievements in the novel end in premature death. One may have a professional record of excellence and be miserable. Loving family and devotion to national needs bring more satisfaction than detached intellectualism. This explains Alexander's death and Michael's vigor in 1976, and also the 1977 political transformation.

Oz does not view the novel as a comment on Israel, but as "an observation on the human condition, formulated on the Israeli scene" (See Charney).

THE MOVIE

Director: Yi'ud Lebanon. Producer: Gideon Coloring. Script: N'omi Sharon, Yi'ud Levanon (Literary adaptation. Based on the novel of Amos Oz). Photography: Avi Koren. Music: 'Adi Renart. Editor: Tali Halter-Shenkar. Cast: Bruria Albek, 'Ami Traub, Mati Seri, Amnon Maskin, Roni Ayalon, Sivan Alshekh, Keren Mor, Irit Gidron, Reuven Dayan, Renan Shor. 1993. Color. 95 minutes.

The British Channel 4 produced the movie *Black Box*. Perhaps this is the reason that we see London with its streets, architecture and sunshine in the movie instead of Chicago. The initiative to make *Black Box* into a film came after more than 100,000 copies of the book were sold in Israel. The novel was translated to English, French, German, Dutch, Swedish, Finnish, Norwegian, Danish, Spanish, Japanese and Hungarian. After the publication of this novel in France, Oz was honored with the French Prix Femina.

The director of the movie, Yi'ud Levanon, received "The Best Movie Award" in Israel at the end of the 1970s for his movie *Kesher ha-Haddevash* (*The Honey Connection*). He was one of the founders of a group (*Kayiz*) that opposed the Burekas movies (see introduction and the discussion of the movie *Three Days and a Child*). Yi'ud was an active and central person also in the initiative to establish *The Foundation for the Encouragement of Quality Movies*. As of today, the foundation supported 130 movies, only one of them succeeded in returning the foundation money.

Kronish thinks that the movie is "remarkably rich visually" (Kronish, p. 159), but Shnizer harshly argues that the "photography and illustrating are ugly" (Shnizer, p. 370). The photography at times surprises the viewer: for example, Jerusalem appears as a snow-covered city, a view that Jerusalem residents rarely see.

The movie, like the novel, does not follow a chronological order. It employs a large number of contrasts between situations and between characters. The song we hear at the first moments of the movie is an addition to the movie and provides a frame and a refrain to it, being that it is also the song that provides the closure for the movie. Ilana and Gideon are dancing to this song at the estate when they are young and happy. Everything is romantic and full of life and energy. The scene depicts happiness, youth, hope and togetherness.

Before we hear the song at the beginning of the movie, we see in a gothic scene the deserted castle with its wind and dust and emptiness and squeaking doors and spider webs at a late stage in Gideon's life. His happiness with Ilana is therefore countered with the deserted, ruined, ghostly estate that we see before the song. Then we see Gideon, alone during a flight, reading a letter from Ilana years after the divorce. At the end of the movie, the song is countered with Gideon's death, aging and Ilana's loneliness.

The dancing to the music of the song, like other romantic scenes in the movie, has a dream-like, dim golden lighting. The constant shifting between past and present is made easier by the distinguished yellow tinting scenes depicting the past.

The words of the song remind us that only in our imagination does time stop ticking. Only in our imagination our world has not been ruined and our home is still in its place with a white table set for our meal. Whatever was loved, passed, and there is no good reason to solve the unforgettable forgotten past and its losses. The two jolly dancers do not seem affected by the sadness of the song's words. They don't seem to acknowledge that the happiest moments are but an introduction for the distraction to come. Only life experience gets our attention to the words and makes us understand them.

There is a constant shift from what is calm and happy in life to what is troubled and destructive. The movie constantly illustrates that happiness is short-lived. For example, the sudden scenes of the troubled Boaz at the police station follow calm and happy scenes of the Sommo's family in a park or in their apartment. At the end of the movie, we see Sommo taking his little daughter away from her mother at the Gideon estate. This scene is accompanied by thunder and lightning, sadness and separation and is contrary to the wholeness of the happy scenes of Sommo's family — when Sommo plays, teaches and puts his daughter to sleep and loves his wife. Happy moments are an introduction again to the tribulation that awaits the characters.

Some of Ilana's most erotic memories of Gideon come to her mind when she lies in bed with her husband. Destruction and infidelity pierce the family life, which is calm only on the surface. Ilana's intimacy with her husband on the one hand and the longing for her ex-husband on the other are destructive elements.

Sommo's financial and status progress and the new image he builds accordingly also mark the destruction of his family life. Money and power corrupt.

On her way to the estate where Boaz lives, Ilana remembers how she and Boaz had to live at the estate after the divorce. The humiliating scene in which Zakheim stars is countered with her late return to the estate. This return could have happy moments but is colored gloomily by Gideon's impending death and the disintegration of her family.

The movie attenuates the last part of the novel due to its dramatic and touching aspects. In the movie, unlike the novel, it is only at the estate that Ilana understands that Gideon never intended to take custody of Boaz. The change of sequence makes the feeling of remorse even greater. When Gideon gets out of his car at his estate, Ilana is sweeping the yard with her back to him. The suspense is moving. The moment their eyes meet is chock-full.

Past is contrasted softly with the present again and again. When Zakheim tells Alex to go back home, he triggers a flashback in Gideon's mind a tender memory of home: He and Ilana are walking on his estate to a bench and are engaged in a long passionate kiss, birds sing and the flora is enchanting. Like other romantic scenes such as the first time Gideon and Ilana enter the estate after their wedding, this scene is bright and cheerful. In the next scene, we see Ilana alone looking through the fence at the deserted estate. The constant contrasts have grievous effects, sharpen the pain, make the situations clearer and keep reminding us that in one's happiness today is enfolded the misery of tomorrow.

Heroism is also short-lived. The sound of the scanning machine reminds Gideon of the war, machine guns and tanks and brings war memories to his mind. But now instead of the active hero warrior Gideon, we have the dying Gideon scanned by medical equipment, stretched helpless on his back without any possibility of taking control of his life and death.

Gideon's romance (an addition to the novel) with the young lady, who wants to have her own child with him, and not Boaz, is marked by pain. Her presence provides a vivid setting for depicting his memories. But the scene is marked with shallowness; nothing explains Gideon's marriage proposal or its very short life.

Gideon's personal face-to-face encounter with Sommo is another movie addition, while the dialogue is based on the characters' correspondence. The face-to-face encounters bring the correspondence to life. The two characters are so different in appearance, opinions and characteristics that letting them encounter each other and dragging their ideologies into their personal affairs certainly construct a theatrical episode. In the movie, this encounter naturally leads to some use of physical action with Gideon's cane and Sommo's hand.

Change of style is another cinematic device to get the movie close to the viewer. In the movie, when Gideon learns that the offer to buy his estate is made with Sommo's intervention, he uses colloquial language; he curses Zakheim and calls him "son of a bitch," "poor pimp," "fat pig," and "bold dog." The movie lowers Gideon's style to create a believable outburst. Similarly, Boaz uses a lower style in the police station. Boaz's spelling does not impact his verbal communication, which may make Boaz look in that sense better in the movie than in the novel.

Like in the movie Gideon seems too self-centered, somehow immature, ascetic, somehow depressed and full of himself, sure of his analytical intellect and full of theory that he deems original. At the same time, Sommo is practical with little theory and a lot of activity. Gideon talks and Sommo, his antithesis, acts. Gideon is rich and intellectual and famous and a hero and a super lover, and his life is an emotional failure followed by an early death. Ilana "is the link between two dynamic tendencies within society: the secular, cultured left wing and the insular, superstitious, religious right wing" summarizes Kronish (1996, p. 159). Kronish (p. 179) emphasizes the changes in Gideon: he matures and mellows with age, learns to cope with his emotions and responsibilities. "As the screen image of Israeli man moves from the macho to the vulnerable, from the heroic to the individualistic, and from the nationalistic to the private, often a more mature portrayal can be seen" observes Kronish (Ibid.).

The sexual scenes are brutal at times. Sexual scenes weigh in the movie more than the novel, on the account of the political, social and religious messages. The very sad scenes from Ilana and Gideon's marriage that we see through flashback are accompanied by monotonous, gloomy music that may remind us of death, destruction and loneliness. Ilana's voiceover is sensitive and not melodramatic. The voiceovers of Sommo and of Gideon well represent their characters. When one reads the letter of another character, we hear the voiceover of the letter's author to strengthen the author's presence. Whatever is not presented in voiceover is presented by showing the episodes that the characters wrote about.

"Ilana I love you," says Gideon to Ilana who is in his arms in bed. For a fraction of a second, her face expresses satisfaction and than her expression is dead. She does not answer. Is it because she does not believe him? Is it because of her strong feelings for Sommo? Is it because of her unfaithful nature? Is it because love is so close to death? Or is it because of all the years that could have been happy were wasted? When the characters finally mature and are able to appreciate happiness, fate fatally intervenes and makes it impossible.

———————

There were serious reservations in Israel about the movie; they will be presented to the viewer who will formulate his own view of the movie.

Hofman (1993) mentions the hardship of transplanting the epistolary-form novel to a visual medium. The scriptwriters used voiceovers from the letters; while the plot is "choppy and barely comprehensible...Too much happens too quickly. The various quick scenes are interrupted by flashbacks "washed in bilious bath of chemical lights." This critic thinks that Alexander's character suffers in particular from the changes from the book to the movie. He has been transferred from Chicago to London and seems less uptight than in the novel. While the novel blamed all parties for the failure of the marriage, the movie shifted the blame to Ilana alone. In the movie Ilana does not have the lively articulation she has in the novel. The acting of Albek as Ilana is of depression and non-presence, and it does not provide a reason for the Gideon of the movie to pay those checks or to write his passionate letters.

Amnon Lord (1993) did not read the novel; it is only "according to the reports the movie is faithful to the book," but this does not prevent him from concluding that "the movie is too faithful to the book" and that "apparently the book too is poor." "The fault lies in the first place with [the novel of] Oz. This reviewer thinks that the movie is grossly schematic in the description of the social-political clashes in Israel. Everything is stereotypic, shallow, inhuman and reflects a poor, shallow spiritual world, with some racism. Only Amnon Maskin acts well in his role as Zakheim.

Schwarz (1993) thinks that the movie remained too attached to the novel and that the feelings of the characters in the novel and the erotic and sensual elements were lost in the movie, while it has ample sex built on Ilana's (Bruria Albek) beautiful body. In both Ilana and Gideon's voiceovers ('Ami Traub), reading the letters one cannot sense love. Their faces do not express love, and love is not shown in the flashback of their memories. There is hardly any plot to the movie; the focus is on love-hate relationships, and the characters are stereotypical. The director selected rusty myths from the novel. The production is impressive, and the photography is spectacular, but the feelings of love and mercy were not communicated.

Kimhi (1993) differentiates between poetic movies that can express poetic literary compositions and conventional movies, in which the main goal is to entertain through the characters and the plot. A movie can be a good one even when it is a conventional movie made on the basis of a poetic novel. The movie *Black Box* is conventional while the novel is an allegorical canonical literary work. Every character in the novel is a personification of a philosophical or cultural idea, social class, or political ideology. It appears that Ilana is a personification of Israel — the big beautiful woman, who is torn between two lovers: Gideon, who conquers her and whom she admires for his intellectual and physical superiority, and Michael, the Sephardi immigrant, whom she likes. The novel ends by telling us that Gideon collapsed, and Sommo will inherit everything. The problem with the movie is that it is unreliable realistically and it does not have the support of the allegorical implications. While the allegorical implications support the absence of realistic foundations, the absence of the allegorical implications from the movie ruins it. This critic claims that various characters in the novel are symbolic literary entities, and therefore it is not critical that their acts are sometimes unreasonable and disbelieved. At the same time, in the movie, they are characters without any symbolic implications, and they have to be reasonable and believable, but they are not. The same is true about various sites in the novel, which are symbolic, while in the movie they are realistic. The Estate of Gideon is, for example, allegorical, representing European colonialism intruded by local flora that rejects the Zionist settlement; while in the movie it is portrayed as if it is a real place without allegorical implications, and it does not reflect any geographical reality.

The sophistication of these arguments should not make their weaknesses unseen. Why does this critic think that the novel is symbolic and the movie is not? Does it not belittle the novel to claim that its symbolic meaning makes up for its absence of realistic sites, reasonable conduct and characters? Would a symbolic meaning in a novel justify the absence of reasonable relations, characters and acts?

BIBLIOGRAPHY

Amoz , Dalia. "Petihat ha-Kufsa Ahrei ha-Nefila." *Proza*, July 1987.

Bahur, Yona. "Ha-Kesef Meshahrer." *Ha-Ir*, March 20, 1987.

Balaban, Avraham. "Ben Esh le-Efer." *"Yediot Aharonot*, 1987.

Boshes, Heda. "Ha-Shedim min ha-Bakbuk." Ha'arez , Feb. 19, 1987.

Carmel-Flumin, Nili. "Amos Oz Natan la-Mez i'ut le-Dabber." *Ma'ariv*, July 31, 1987.

Charney, Marc D. "Abasement Was Irresistible," *The New York times on the Web*.

Hasid, Eti. "Amos Oz and the *Black Box*." *Hadashot*, Nov. 11, 1986.

Hoffman, Adina. "An Empty Black Box." *The Jerusalem Post*, Nov. 12, 1993.

Kazir, Yehudit. "Roman Za'ir," *Kol Bo Haifa*, March 27, 1987.

Kimhi, Rami. "Kufsa Shehora: Ha-Roman ve-Hasseret." *Ma'ariv*, Dec. 12, 1993.

Kronish, Amy. *World Cinema: Israel*. Fairleigh University Press, 1996.

Lord, Amnon. "Shatuah, Dal ve-lo Enoshi." *Yerushalayim*, Nov. 26, 1993.

Lotan, Yael. "Mef'a'neyah Amos Oz." *'Al ha-Mishmar*, Jan. 23, 1987.

Meged, Aharon. "Mi-Saviv la-Kufsa'." *Ha'arez* , March 27, 1987.

Miron, Dan. "'Erev be-Opera." *Ha-'Olam ha-Zei*, Feb. 11, 1987.

Papirblat, Shlomo. "Kufsa Shehora, 'Akhshav ha-Seret." *Yediot aharonot*, August 22, 1989.

Paz, Miri. "Ve-ha-Anashim Hareveim Kemo Arzam." *Davar*, Jan. 23, 1987.

Rabbi, Y'acov. "Beno le-Venah—'al Derekh ha-Balshanut." *Al ha-Mishmar*, March 3, 1987.

Ramraz-Rauch, Gila."Hirhurim le-Mikra Kufsa Shehora le-Amos Oz." *Bizaron*, Winter-Spring, 1987.

Sarna, Yiga'al. "Ad Mavet." *Yediot Aharonot.*

Schnitzer, Meir. "Michael Shelli," In *Ha-Kolnoa' ha-Yisraeli*. Kinneret Publishing House, 1994, p. 283.

_____. *Kufsa Shehora*. In *Ha-Kolnoa' ha-Yisraeli*. Kinneret Publishing House, 1994, p. 370.

Schwarz , Oshra. "Hu' Bo'el ve-Hi' Gonahat." *Hadashot,* Nov. 14, 1993.

Weis, Hillel. "'Uru ha-Sefaradim." *Nekudda*, July 31, 1987.

Yeshua'a-Leght, 'Ofra. "Mishel Shelli: ha-Kufsa, ha-Ashpa ve-Hayyehudi." *Ma'ariv*, July 17, 1 987.

Zandbak, Shimon. "Ha-Mesapper Mul ha-'Olam." Ha'arez , July 24, 1987